SEBASTIAN FAULKS

Sebastian Faulks's books include the number one bestseller *A Week in December*, *Human Traces*, *On Green Dolphin Street*, *Charlotte Gray* and *Birdsong*, which has sold more than three million copies.

HOPE WOLF

Hope Wolf is a Lecturer in British Modernist Literature at the University of Sussex. Previously, she was a Research Fellow in English at Girton College, the University of Cambridge. She holds a PhD from King's College London, and her doctoral research focused on archives at the Imperial War Museum.

A BROKEN WORLD

Letters, Diaries and Memories of the Great War

EDITED BY
SEBASTIAN FAULKS
WITH HOPE WOLF

VINTAGE

1 3 5 7 9 10 8 6 4 2

Vintage
20 Vauxhall Bridge Road,
London SW1V 2SA

Vintage is part of the Penguin Random House group of companies
whose addresses can be found at global.penguinrandomhouse.com

Copyright © Sebastian Faulks and Hope Wolf 2014

Sebastian Faulks and Hope Wolf have asserted their right to be identified as
the authors of this Work in accordance with the Copyright, Designs and
Patents Act 1988

Every effort has been made to seek permission from the respective copyright
holders but if you consider yourself to hold publication rights for any
of the extracts included and have not already been contacted, the publishers
would be pleased to hear from you. Please see p. 297, which constitutes
an extension of this copyright page.

First published in Vintage in 2015
First published in hardback by Hutchinson in 2014

www.vintage-books.co.uk

A CIP catalogue record for this book is
available from the British Library

ISBN 9780099597797

Typeset by carrdesignstudio.com
Printed and bound by CPI Group (UK) Ltd, Croydon CR0 4YY

September. 1918

This afternoon was the colour of water falling through sunlight;
The trees glittered with the tumbling of leaves;
The sidewalks shone like alleys of dropped maple leaves,
And the houses ran along them laughing out of square, open
    windows.
Under a tree in the park,
Two little boys, lying flat on their faces,
Were carefully gathering red berries
To put in a pasteboard box.

Some day there will be no war,
Then I shall take out this afternoon
And turn it in my fingers,
And remark the sweet taste of it upon my palate,
And note the crisp variety of its flights of leaves.
To-day I can only gather it
And put it into my lunch-box,
For I have time for nothing
But the endeavour to balance myself
Upon a broken world.

Amy Lowell

CONTENTS

INTRODUCTION

A hundred years ago the world suffered a convulsion that not only took the lives of more than ten million men and brought down three empires but revised our idea of what kind of creatures human beings really are. A century later it is still hard to appreciate the scale of what happened or to make sense of it. This anthology cannot claim to offer any answers; what it hopes to show is how those who experienced such events responded to them. It was a world war, so we have included the witness of many nationalities. Women, as I hope these pages show, were much involved at home and at the front; children were also affected by the upheavals, and their perspective, also included here, is often poignant.

While a chronological order would have been natural for the testaments of soldiers only – recruitment, training, battle, leave and so on – the wider sample of writers here, including many who did not fight, persuaded us to organise the material in a different way – by place rather than by time. So the first section, 'Distant Hammers', includes reactions to the Armistice as well as to the start of the war; what links the pieces is that they are all written by people at some remove from the fighting. The second section, 'Mind and Matter', contains, by contrast, the responses and memories of those in the thick of it. The third part, 'Between Borders', records the effects of displacement on combatants, families, friends and dissidents; here we find refugees and prisoners alongside people whose sense of dislocation is more internal – soldiers whom the war alienated from their homes, from their countries or from themselves. The final section, 'White Spots', deals with the absences, both physical and mental, left by such a holocaust. And the search for what was lost continues to this day.

While a good deal of the writing here deals with the side-effects of war rather than the firing of guns, no anthology would be complete without the voices of the young men themselves, telling how they lived and fought and killed. Some of these are appalling or revolting; some are heroic, some wistful; some even have a note of exhilaration as men record the friendships and the invigorating sense of identity and purpose that the war could bring.

Our inclination has been towards unknown writers rather than to famous names, on the grounds that most people with an interest in the war will be familiar with the classic memoirs of the period. However, we have not hesitated to include such writers as Virginia Woolf, Ford Madox Ford, Helen Thomas and D. H. Lawrence when their gifts seem to have enabled them to say something essential. In fact, I think E. M. Forster's comment that 'The supreme evil of war is surely not death, but despair – the feeling that the incursion of the soul into matter has been a mistake, that we may just as well sit brooding among the ashes of happiness and beauty, that it is useless to work, useless to give help and even to receive it' is one of the most resonant in the book and could stand as its epigraph.

As for the unknowns and the unpublished, it has been a commonplace of commentary on the First World War to remark on the reticence of those who fought in it. Some men's reaction at twilight on the first day of the Somme, as they picked their way back through a carpet of corpses and over the groaning earth, was that they had witnessed the end of the world and were now present at the Day of Judgment. Naturally, it was difficult for them to write home to their mother or wife the next day and give them the news. No man in the history of the world had seen such things; and they didn't want their families to worry about them. Better, therefore, not to go into it.

Those on leave, meanwhile, found it difficult to convey either the texture or the enormity of what they had witnessed. The female world of home was a blessed change, but to many it was not the real thing any more. Some family or friends did not want to know what the war was like; others were curious or concerned, but hit a jarring note in their questions. Some men were actually glad to return to the Front and to the company of their fellow-soldiers, resigned to face whatever awaited them.

Then, after 1918, in a world forever changed, life had to continue; so what was the point in dwelling on the nightmare that was gone? Whatever the long-term political effects of the war in eroding distinctions between officers and 'other ranks', there was still in the 1920s a presumption in book publishing that only officer memoirs would have a claim on the reading public: lousy Tommy Atkins was not pursued by the gentlemen of Bloomsbury. Then, twenty years on, when the time was ripe to rethink our memory of 1914–18, another calamity intervened; and the Second World War was to be remembered immediately and more vigorously – in colourful books and motion pictures and Holocaust memorials.

So the idea of the silent Great War veteran, taking the unspeakable truth to his quiet grave, has some validity. And yet... I think the reticence may have been exaggerated. It's true that in the mid-twentieth century the arts of fiction, cinema and stage largely gave up on the First World War as workable subject matter, but when BBC Television undertook its twenty-six-part history of the war in 1963, it found no shortage of people willing to record their memories on camera. In March this year, BBC Two showed an hour-long edit of some of these previously unseen interviews under the title *I Was There: The Great War Interviews*. This was an extraordinary programme. Men spoke not only of the suffering but also of what fun it could be in France when there was not much going on. A German infantryman called Stefan Westmann (whose interview is quoted in part three of this book), recalled his horror at bayoneting a civilised man against whom he bore no grudge. One veteran spoke of the chivalry of aerial combat, where the machine not the pilot was the enemy; another of his lifelong regret at not having paused to give water to a dying man in his hurry to regain the safety of his trench. What they had in common was the modest courtesy of elderly men at that period and the haunted, exhausted look of those who had struggled for decades to reconcile what they had seen in those four years with what the rest of their lives had led them to expect.

The Imperial War Museum stored those tapes the BBC could not use. The documents collection at the museum, meanwhile, expanded in the 1970s and 1980s as the families of recently deceased veterans bequeathed their papers. These range from the sublime to the mundane, but while that great resource exists the texture of the war will never be lost. It was a privilege for this visiting reader in 1992 to be able to examine long card indexes ('SMITH J. L/cpl. Letters, diaries, misc items, some rain-damaged, concerning service in Ypres salient 1915–1917, with 4th Fusiliers. Details of trench repair work'), fill out a request form and find a buff folder held with a pink ribbon delivered twenty minutes later. One never knew what bathos or gold or tedium or heartbreak would tumble out on to the desk; but to touch and hold them was in many cases to be the first to do so since the day they were written. And here was reality.

We owe a debt to the Imperial War Museum, its trustees and its scholars, men such as the late Roderick Suddaby, whose knowledge of its document holdings may never be equalled. Max Arthur is one of several authors who have produced impressively edited selections in book form from the museum's daunting volume of material. Other determined individuals helped keep the means of memory alive. Dr Peter Liddle established his own document archive while teaching in the 1960s and this is now housed at the University of Leeds; Lyn Macdonald did invaluable work in tape-recording the memories of veterans while there was still time and using them in her bottom-up histories of the conflict. While the war had its share of academic historians, it is to those who did the unsung work in the years when no one seemed to care that our particular thanks are due. These include John Terraine, who was not attached to a university, and Martin Middlebrook, a Lincolnshire poultry farmer who was astonished on visiting the Somme battlefields in 1967 to discover that no history of 1 July 1916 existed – so wrote one himself.

My co-editor, Dr Hope Wolf, is responsible for the wide reach of this anthology and was tireless in her search for oblique angles and the international perspective. She brought an academic eye to the process and an enthusiasm for what had previously been overlooked. Any merit the anthology may have is the result of her labours. For her rapid response and helpful suggestions, I would also like to thank Emily Mayhew, author of *Wounded* (Bodley Head, 2014), which expertly uses documents to recreate the journey from battlefield to Blighty.

Now the centenary is finally upon us, there does seem to be a greater awareness and understanding of that conflict than there was thirty years ago. The books of Hew Strachan, Max Hastings, Christopher Clark and Margaret MacMillan, among others, have recently brought new light to bear on the period. Politicians and historians argue on television over whose fault it was; children in their thousands visit the battlefields of France and Flanders; the BBC is set to inform and entertain us for four long years. All this is encouraging in an educational sense, and this anthology hopes to add its tiny weight to the resources available to those curious for information.

The bigger questions, however, remain unanswered. To me the greatest of these is as follows. Did Europe's enthusiastic discovery of genocide in 1914–18 make a mockery of the preceding five hundred years, rendering such terms as 'the Renaissance' and 'the Enlightenment' simple self-delusion; and if this war showed the true nature of the human creature, its limitless capacity for killing once the means are in its hands, how are we to deal with our revised knowledge of what we are?

The last century has got us nowhere. The Great War seemed merely to license mass slaughter as a political process in Europe and Russia. We went collectively mad: it was as though the entire continent were shell-shocked. If the commemoration process of the next four years provides not only greater knowledge of what took place at the start of that benighted century but also some small progress towards answering the larger questions, then those young men who died in their needless millions may perhaps begin to sleep at last.

Sebastian Faulks, 25 March 2014

This is a postcard sent by H.J. Ewels to his wife from the Western Front in 1917. A collection of his postcards is currently archived at the Imperial War Museum, London. In each case the card has been censored: place names have been cut out.

DISTANT HAMMERS

Hearing and imagining from afar

D. H. LAWRENCE (1885–1930) was a writer and novelist. He was not in good enough health to enlist and was critical of the war. Along with his German wife Frieda, he was forced to leave his home in Cornwall in October 1917 as they were suspected of assisting the enemy. Lady Ottoline Morrell, to whom the following letter is addressed, was a literary patron, she and her husband Philip offered refuge to conscientious objectors during the war.

Greatham, Pulborough, Sussex.
March, 1915.

My Dear Lady Ottoline, –

I sent you the next batch of the MS. There will only be one more lot. I hope you will like it.

Monica has a motor-car every day to drive her out, so we go too. To-day we drove to Bognor. It was strange at Bognor – a white, vague, powerful sea, with long waves falling heavily, with a crash of frosty white out of the pearly whiteness of the day, of the wide sea. And the small boats that were out in the distance heaved, and seemed to glisten shadowily. Strange the sea was, so strong. I saw a soldier on the pier, with only one leg. He was young and handsome: and strangely self-conscious, and slightly ostentatious: but confused. As yet, he does not realise anything, he is still in the shock. And he is strangely roused by the women, who seem to have a craving for him. They look at him with eyes of longing, and they want to talk to him. So he is roused, like a roused male, yet there is more wistfulness and wonder than passion or desire. I could see him under chloroform having the leg amputated. It was still in his face. But he was brown and strong and handsome.

It seemed to me anything might come of that white, silent, opalescent sea; and the great icy shocks of foam were strange. I felt as if legions were marching in the mist. I cannot tell you why, but I am afraid. I am afraid of the ghosts of the dead. They seem to come marching home in legions over the white, silent sea, breaking in on us with a roar and a white iciness. Perhaps this is why I feel so afraid. I don't know. But the land beyond looked warm, with a warm, blue sky, very homely: and over the sea legions of white ghosts tramping. I was on the pier.

So they are making a Coalition government. I cannot tell you how icy cold my heart is with fear. It is as if we were all going to die. Did I not tell you my revolution would come? It will come, God help us. The ghosts will bring it. Why does one feel so coldly afraid? Why does even the coalition of the Government fill me with terror? Some say it is for peace negotiations. It may be, because we are all afraid. But it is most probably for conscription. The touch of death is very cold and horrible on us all.

D. H. LAWRENCE.

It is the whiteness of the ghost legions that is so awful.

—— • ——

NORMAN DEMUTH was a rifleman in the London Rifle Brigade. He was interviewed for the 1964 BBC *Great War* series. The following is taken from the Sound Archive of the Imperial War Museum, which was set up in 1972. It was edited by Max Arthur in association with the Imperial War Museum, and was published in *Forgotten Voices of the Great War* (2002).

As well as being given white feathers, there was another method of approach. You would see a girl come towards you with a delightful smile all over her face and you would think to yourself, 'My word this is somebody who knows me.' When she got to about five or six paces from you she would suddenly freeze up and walk past you with a look of utter contempt and scorn as if she could have spat. That was far more hurtful than a white feather – it made you curl up completely and there was no replying because she had walked on.

However, I was given a white feather when I was sixteen, just after I had left school. I was looking in a shop window and I suddenly felt somebody press something into my hand and I found it was a woman giving me a white feather. I was so astonished I did not know what to do about it. But I had been trying to persuade the doctors and recruiting officers that I was nineteen and I thought, well, this must give me some added bounce because I must look the part, and so I went round to the recruiting offices with renewed zeal.

—— • ——

SYLVIA PANKHURST (1882–1960) was a writer, artist and political activist, born in Manchester. She was the daughter of Emmeline Pankhurst and sister of Christabel. In 1903 Emmeline and Christabel set up the WSPU (Women's Social and Political Union), which campaigned for women's suffrage. Sylvia took a pacifist stance towards the war. The excerpt below, about a visit to Scarborough in 1914, is from her memoir, *The Home Front: A Mirror to Life in England during the World War* (1932).

In the brief Christmas days, when the slackening of propaganda gave me respite, I went with Smyth to see the havoc wrought by the Scarborough bombardment. Travelling by night we arrived in a cheerless dawn. The sky and sea were a leaden grey. The big amusement 'palaces' on the front were scarred and battered by shell-fire, iron columns twisted and broken, brickwork crumbling, windows gone. Yawning breaches disclosed the pictures and furnishings, riddled and rent by the firing, dimmed and discoloured by blustering winds and spray. The little steep streets, leading up from the foreshore, were barred by wire entanglements – the first I had ever seen – great stakes driven into the ground, with a mass of stout barbed wire threaded around and around them, and tangled about between. At many points were high barricades of sand-filled sacks, with a row of loopholes for the rifles.

We knocked at one of the sea-front boarding houses. The woman who opened to us was weary and dishevelled as though she had spent the night out in the storm. She gazed at us, startled and hostile, when we asked for a lodging. When we urged that we had come from London and understood she was accustomed to let, she hesitated suspiciously, then reluctantly explained that she had promised to hold herself in readiness to receive any shipwrecked seamen who might be saved from drowning. 'I've been up with them all night – some of 'em's gone, some of 'em's still here. We have to put 'em in hot blankets as soon as they're carried in.'

'But there won't be another wreck to-night!' we essayed, rather feebly, to rally her.

'There were three lots brought in here yesterday, and two the day before,' she answered mournfully, and pointed to the many craft out in the bay, telling us they were all minesweepers engaged in the perilous work of clearing away explosive mines laid by the German warships and daily causing the loss of many vessels.

This was an aspect of the German visit not recorded in the Press. In our ignorance of war, we heard her with shocked surprise.

She agreed at last that we should stay with her, on condition that we would leave at once if another party of shipwrecked mariners were brought in. Barely an hour had passed when her daughter flung open our door:

'Another boat's blown up! You'll have to go!'

Out we went to the blast. Groups of shawl-wrapped women were gazing seaward. 'They've landed some of them at that slip,' a woman told us, and pointed to a small dingy brown steamer with a cluster of people looking down at her from the quay. 'A motor-car's gone off with one of them – he was covered with a white sheet!' a shrill voice cried; and even as the words were uttered another car dashed away. A bent old crone ran by us wailing: 'He was a young man with black hair; with thick black hair; his head was all smashed in!'

Groups of people moved about us, awestruck, with a hand shading the eyes, gazing out to sea, or across to the little steamer at the end of the slip.

Someone advised us to enquire for lodgings at a near-by cottage, the front door of which opened directly on to the foreshore. A fisherman in his blue jersey was seated by the fire; his wife was too much troubled by the peril of the men out there in the bay, to consider whether or not she would give us a bed. She talked to us a long time before she could bring her mind to it. She spoke of the bombardment; it was terrible, the noise so loud, so fearfully loud, she thought she must go mad. Little children were killed; many people were injured. 'A lady who not five days before was singing in this Bethel' was helping a poor old woman down into her cellar, when she was struck dead by a piece of shell. No one knew when it might happen again; people could not settle down to ordinary life; all sense of security was destroyed. Her husband and the other fishermen were prohibited from following their calling because of the mines. Their means of support was stopped; yet he was best at home; yes, even if they should have to starve! She had a son in the Navy and a son-in-law on a mine-sweeper; that was enough!

[…]

On Christmas morning, climbing by winding ways above the town we saw the trenches recently dug by British soldiers along the cliffs; and higher still, great heaps of stone which fell from the old castle when its walls were shelled by the German ships.

Lodging among the cottages of the fisherfolk in these terraced streets of the old town seven years before, I had wandered often beneath those ancient walls, regarding them curiously as a relic of an age of barbarism long dead, confident in my faith in the sure advance of progress. To-day in face of the evidence of present barbarism, my thoughts were sad.

Vainly seeking my old landlady, for she had left the town, I was accosted by some neighbours of hers who remembered me. It was the anniversary of their wedding, and hospitably they would have us enter to celebrate it with tea and plum cake, in their warm kitchen. It was a Yorkshire custom, they said, to exchange visits of Christmas morning. The wife was a very pretty woman, turned forty, with the bluest of blue eyes, a little shy and diffident and pleased to let the rest of us talk. The husband was black-eyed and swarthy as a Spaniard, with great gold rings in his ears. He told us, as others in the town had done, that the German battleships came so close to the shore that the people (believing them British) feared they would run aground. He was at the window when the firing began, and he called to his wife: 'It's no good, lass, the Germans have come!'

Then he told her to go next door and help their neighbour to pacify her children. She was running to the back door, but he locked it and said: 'I'm an Englishman and a Yorkshireman, and they'll not make us go the back way!' He walked to the end of the terrace and stood facing the battleships. He was not hit, but he showed us a big bit of shell which had fallen beside him. Believing, like everyone else, that the Germans intended landing, he looked around for our soldiers. They were nowhere to be seen. After the bombardment ceased they got into their trenches and sang a hymn. 'They were no better than wooden soldiers!' he cried, indignant. His wife reproved him, with a timid glance at us: 'What use would it have been for our British soldiers to come out to be killed?'

[...]

Returning to our lodging we learnt that yet another boat had been blown up. It was bitterly cold; the wind howled fiercely. We huddled by the fire, saddened and chilled. A girl ran past the window sobbing and wailing. A few minutes later she passed again. As I heard her coming a third time I went out to her, and saw that she was about sixteen years of age, hatless and poorly dressed.

In abandonment of grief, she flung herself now against the wall, now leaned her head for a moment upon a window-sill, crying: 'Dad! Dad! Oh, Dad!' As I came up with her two women met her. They knew her and understood what she muttered between her sobs better than I. They told me that her father was on one of the mine-sweepers out in the bay. She shrank into trembling reserve and, faltering nervously that she must go to her mother, fled from us in the dusk.

Next morning we called on our first landlady to learn the news of the night. As we came in sixteen lately shipwrecked mariners, who had recovered in her house, were leaving the door. She told us six others had been drowned, and a third vessel since our arrival blown up. Another, another, and yet another vessel was sacrificed during the morning. Again we had notice to quit our lodging to make way for the sea-drenched men. Scarborough was too sad for me. 'Let us get away to-night,' I said to Smyth.

As we stood on the breakwater before leaving we saw the lifeboat set forth again to the rescue, over the cold grey waves in the gathering dusk.

—— • ——

W. F. TAPP was a child at the time of the First World War. This letter was an answer to a call for contributions by Professor Stanley Weintraub in 1979. Eyewitness accounts of the Armistice would be used to compile his book, A Stillness Heard Round the World: The End of the Great War, November 1918 (1985). Here W. F. Tapp details the moment when the Armistice was announced in Devonport, Plymouth.

Newton Abbot

12th October 1979

Dear Prof. Weintraub,

[…]

You ask for memories of Armistice Night at the end of World War I. I am 67 years old, having been born in August 1912, so I was only six years old at the time, but I am writing to you because there is one memory of that night which is still quite vivid in my mind.

I was born, and lived throughout that war, in the town of Devonport which was at that time a separate town but which was subsequently amalgamated with the City of Plymouth.

Devonport has for a couple of centuries been a very important depot for the Royal Navy, and throughout World War I an immense number of warships were built, repaired, fuelled, victualled and based in Devonport Dockyard.

At about 7 p.m. on Armistice Night I went to bed as usual, and soon fell asleep. A while later I was awakened by the most enormous racket I had ever heard. The news of the Armistice had been received by the navy in Devonport (the techniques of communication were pretty primitive then compared with those of today). And an instruction had obviously been signalled to every ship, of whatever size, to sound its siren in a staggering signal of victory and peace. Each warship had a very long siren which made a whooping sound, with a sudden rising note to a high-pitched peak, and each ship's siren had different characteristics from the others. The resulting din was almost enough to awaken the millions of dead from that war.

Being awakened by such noise, I was at first almost scared out of my wits, but older members of the family soon came rushing to my bedroom to tell me what it was all about. As a great treat, and to mark the occasion, I was allowed to go downstairs and drink a small glass of milk while the older ones had a drink of what I assume was something a bit stronger.

I expect you will get more accurate details about this victory celebration from older people, but I can vouch for its tremendous effect even on a young child.

Yours sincerely,

W. F. Tapp

———— • ————

HERMIA MILLS responded quite differently to Stanley Weintraub's request for memories. Her letter reports the possible suicide of a pilot on the day of the Armistice. She was sixteen years old at the time.

London

10.X.79

Dear Professor,

In reply to your letter in the 'Daily Telegraph' I enclose my recollections of Armistice Day 1918. The episode is a purely domestic one of which there must be many similar tragedies.

I was 16 years old at the time and with a school friend (we were both of St Paul's Girls School Hammersmith) was spending the half-term holiday with my friend's mother, Mrs Wildon Carr at her cottage at Houghton in Sussex. (Incidentally Mrs Carr's husband, Professor Wildon Carr, later became the Professor of Philosophy of the South California University at Los Angeles.)

Well I cannot recall which day of the week the Armistice was announced but we were all set to walk to Arundel to catch our London train. Just as we were leaving the cottage a telegraph boy arrived with a telegram stating the husband of an elder daughter of Mrs Carr had been killed falling from his aeroplane while waving the news of the Armistice to friends on the airfield below. It was later stated, and believed by his widow, that he was intending to commit suicide. He came of a well-known business family in the West Country and would have had no need to fear un-employment or post-war problems of that kind.

We walked into Arundel where all was jubilant. Flags were flying from every building, church bells were pealing, people dancing in the streets and troop trains passing through the station with soldiers either exultant or drunk.

Eventually we boarded our train and the poor mother wept quietly throughout the journey; while my friend and I, with adolescent gaucherie, knew not what to say or do.

Yours very truly
Hermia Mills

—— • ——

ALEX J. BOOTH also wrote to Professor Stanley Weintraub in 1979 in response to his call for memories of the Armistice (see also Tapp and Mills). This letter is from a file in the Weintraub collection entitled: 'Armistice in Remote Places and at Sea'.

Glasgow.

Dear Professor Weintraub,

Your letter a few days ago to the London *Daily Telegraph* prompts
me to send you my recollections of 11/11/1918, which are as clear
as if they happened yesterday.

With many others I had been brought down the Tigris River
from Baghdad to Basrah, in Mesopotamia (now Iraq of course).
The flat-bottomed hospital boat advanced about 500 miles on the
journey, which, as the crow flies is about 100 miles.

Active hostilities had ceased and most of us were suffering from
malaria and/or dysentry. The attendant discomforts of the latter
were epitomised by one man who remarked 'There are 23 patients
in this ward and 25 toilets, not nearly enough!'

On the fateful day we were in bed having had tea. The time there
was about 6p.m. A nursing sister appeared at the end of the ward
and stood silent. Then from the adjacent docks we could hear the
sound of ships' sirens, and suddenly it was as if an electric current
circulated through every man with the realisation that this was the
end of the war.

Patients, bed-ridden, seriously ill, some with temperatures up to
105°, lurched out of bed, donned their overcoats, scrambled to the
door, and went out into a heavy downpour and sea of warm mud,
about a foot deep. In the first two steps slippers were sucked off and
bare-foot we congregated at a central point. A military band of sorts
miraculously appeared and played all the popular well-loved tunes –
'It's a long way to Tipperary', 'Good-bye Piccadilly, farewell Leicester
Square', 'Keep the home fires burning', 'Dear Old Blighty', and then
finally 'God Save the King'. There we stood at attention as far as the

mud would allow with hearts very full, and visions of Homeland ahead; then trudged back to the ward and bed, apparently none the worse, ready to endure further injections and copious doses of quinine with its resulting deafness. Surely, if ever, a triumph of 'mind over matter'.

I was 22 years of age then, a gunner/driver in the artillery; now nearing 83, and grateful to the good Lord, for sparing me and giving me good health and unimpaired faculties to the present time.

I trust these reminiscences may be of interest to you in connection with your laudable project.

Yours sincerely
Alex J. Booth

——— • ———

MURIEL DAYRELL-BROWNING (1879–1935) worked during the war as a translator for the War Office. Her daughter Vivien married Graham Greene in 1927. The letter below, written to her mother, describes the destruction of a German airship SL11, brought down at Cuffley, Hertfordshire, on the night of 2–3 September 1916. It was the first enemy Zeppelin to fall on British soil.

Strathmore Hotel
15 Tavistock Square, W.C.
Sept 4. 16

Dearest Mums,

I will now tell you about The Raid last night – the Sight of my Life! It was the second night of London's lighting or rather no-lighting orders. At 2.30 I was wakened by a terrific explosion & was at the window in one bound when another deafening one shook the house. Nearly above us sailed a cigar of bright silver in the full glare of about 20 magnificent search lights. A few lights roamed round trying to pick up her companion. Our guns made a deafening row & shells burst all around her. For some extraordinary reason she was dropping no bombs. The night was absolutely still with a few splendid stars. It was a magnificent sight & the whole of London was looking on holding its breath. She was only a little way to the East of me & I had a topping view as there's a stone balcony outside my window. I yelled for field glasses to Captain Hermani but he was escorting the whole houseful to the cellars (cook was howling – she's Irish) so I sat on the window ledge in my dressing gown. The Zepp headed slowly north amid a rain of shells & crashing artillery fire from all quarters. She was pretty high up but was enormous, 600 ft long I shd say. Capt. H came up & joined me & we watched her for another 5 minutes when suddenly her nose dropped & I yelled 'Getroffen' ['hit' in German]. But she righted again & went into a cloud (wh – possibly she made herself!) then the search-lights scientifically examined that cloud to help the air men but she didn't appear & we thought the fun was over as the guns stopped. Then—from the direction of Barnet & very high a brilliant red light appeared (we thought it was an English fire balloon for a minute!) Then we saw it was the Zep diving head first. <u>That</u> was a sight. She dived slowly at first as only the foremost ballonet was on fire. Then the second burst & the flames tore up into the sky & then the third & cheers thundered all round us from every direction. The plane lit up all London & was rose red. Those deaths must be the most dramatic in the world[']s history. They fell – a cone of blazing wreckage thousands of feet – watched by 8 millions of their enemies.

It was magnificent, the most thrilling scene imaginable.

This afternoon I went out to Barnet (& so did 3/4 of London!) The wreck covers only 30 ft of ground & the dead are under a tarpaulin. The engineer was gripping the steering wheel & one man was headless. I hope they will be buried under full military honours. They were brave men. R.I.P! They say the air man who bombed them was only 18. His name won't be given as they will try for revenge as in the case of Warneford. The engine is at the W/O [War Office]. The Zepp fell close to Cuffley Church & telescoped when she hit the ground.

—— • ——

JOHN FREDERICK MACDONALD sought to strengthen understandings between French and English cultures in his writing. He died in 1915, and the volume from which the excerpt below has been taken, *Two Towns – One City; Paris – London* (1917), was published posthumously.

Lest this article should fall into the hands of the German Emperor – worse still, into the possession of Count Zeppelin – it is 'undesirable' to disclose the precise route taken by my friend into London's deepest darkness. Discreetly and vaguely, let me state that certain parts of Fulham, Hammersmith and Chelsea are plunged into almost total obscurity, whilst, here and there, stretch unimportant little streets enveloped – save for dim lights in the windows – in complete, silent blackness. Why should unimportant little side streets take 'precautions' against Zeppelins?

'Gasworks and waterworks all about here,' explains my friend, the authority on London's Darkness… Yes, for sheer, Silent Darkness, impossible to surpass certain corners of Fulham, Chelsea and Hammersmith… Round and about the gas and the water works, policemen, Territorials, or proud special constables.

The Embankment – an important bridge – and special constables and armed Territorials once again. Black, the river; extinguished, the blinking, lurid electrical advertisements of patent medicines and whiskies; invisible, the face of Big Ben. In Whitehall and the Haymarket more semi-darkness. The mixed life of Piccadilly Circus only half alive, Regent Street deserted, Portland Place funereal, Regent's Park enveloped in a pale, ghostly mist – all this chill and darkness depressing me, I persuade my friend to pull up at a small, vulgar coffee-stall.

Two lamps, anyhow. Two lamps of the kitchen description, and the eternal hard-boiled eggs, and slabs of bread and butter, and slices of sallow seed cake, and penny packets of Woodbine cigarettes, and the coffee-stall keeper himself absorbed in a tattered, greasy copy of the very latest 'extra special'.

No fewer than three eggs and two cups of coffee for my friend, the authority on Darkness. After that, a chilly sardine sandwich. 'À la guerre, comme à la guerre.' Which admirable French saying I translate into English for the benefit of the coffee-stall keeper.

'That's it, that's the proper spirit,' he cordially assents. 'If we was to start grumbling, wot would 'appen to the war, I should like to know! Business is rotten. On the top of that, prices gone up. Bar a couple of slices and cups of coffee, you're the only customers I've 'ad tonight. But am I down'earted?'

'N-o-oo,' respond my friend and myself, raising our cups of bitter coffee, in the mist, chill and darkness.

It was not until yesterday that Church Street and Bell Street – narrow, shabby little turnings off the Edgware Road – were 'hit' by the war. Up till then life and business had gone on as usual, and the air reeked with the fumes from the naphtha lamps that violently illuminated the various barrows of fruit, vegetables, skinned rabbits, millinery, crockery and fish. In fact, the favourite cheap shopping centre of the humble housewives of the neighbourhood – stout, garrulous ladies in seedy caps and shawls; whilst their children played about amongst barrows, and unshaven father, leaning against a lamp-post, clay pipe in mouth, lazily and indifferently surveyed the scene. However, war is war, and even the barrows off Edgware Road have now become involved in it. Not that they have been commandeered for service at the front. Nor yet that the dubious fish and ghastly rabbits have been impounded by the Officer of Health. What has happened is this: By order of the police, as a measure against Zeppelins, out and away with the flaming and flaring naphtha lamps.

Now, without naphtha, a street market not only loses its picturesqueness, but finds itself despoiled of its customers. At least, the customers are reluctant to buy goods in the semi-darkness. They want to examine them lengthily and exhaustively, under a strong light. When Mrs Briggs, of Church Street, goes shopping, it takes her at least five minutes to select a cucumber, then another five minutes about a cabbage, and a third over a cauliflower – and all three objects she closely holds up to the lamp, eyeing and sounding and pinching them all over. As for rabbits—

'Nothing doing, enuf to make yer cry,' a rabbit merchant informs me. 'Nice and 'ealthy they are, but you carn't get the old women to buy 'em. All becos they carn't 'ave a good look at 'em! Sick of it, I am. Why don't they turn the lights out altogether and bloomin' well 'ave done with it!'

Although dark and dejected, Church and Bell streets are by no means deserted. Nor is trade entirely at a standstill. Some of the barrows are dimly lighted by battered old bicycle lamps, and the lamps are being constantly removed from the nail on which they hang and swept across and pointed down upon the food-stuffs. Heavens, the lengthy inspection of this cabbage! In one hand a stout housewife holds a bicycle lamp, and with the other hand she pulls aside every leaf of the cabbage and peers down into the very depths of its heart. Another housewife overhauls at least twenty bananas before she finally selects three at the cost of a penny. And a third carries off a cauliflower for examination under the nearest gas-lamp, some twenty yards away.

'Don't forget to come back,' the costermonger cries after her. Then, turning to me: 'Four cabbages I never saw again last night, becos I let 'em be took as far as the gas-lamp.'

'And wot about me?' exclaims his neighbour, the rabbit merchant. 'Up comes an old woman, messes about with the rabbits, carn't make up 'er mind, so I lets 'er take two of the finest up to the gas-lamp and—'

'Done a guy, of course,' his colleague interrupts. 'That there gas-lamp wants watching by the perlice. A bit of Scotland Yard round it, that's wot it wants.' Then, most caustically to a passing constable: 'Any objection against me lighting a match for my pipe?'

I grieve to relate that, through the darkness, I dimly but positively behold little boys surreptitiously helping themselves to apples and nuts, and it furthermore pains me to announce that a small girl deftly and illegally obtains possession of a banana, which, however, she generously shares in a doorway with two friends. But, on the whole, the people of Church and Bell streets do not take excessive advantage of the darkness. Only a few rabbits and cabbages 'missing'; the majority of housewives who make the pilgrimage to the gas-lamp return in good time. On the other hand, it has incoherently got into the heads of these ladies that the lowering of London's lights should be accompanied by a corresponding reduction in prices. A rabbit in the darkness should be worth less than a rabbit in strong naphtha light.

'Becos,' one of the housewives confusedly informs me, 'becos rabbits, like everything else, is tricky and deceptive. You can't tell the time from the clock when it's dark: and the same applies to rabbits. So if I buys rabbits in the darkness, I takes a risk: and expects them to go down a penny a pound.'

—— • ——

MRS M. HALL was a munitions worker in London. The following extract, taken from the Sound Archive of the Imperial War Museum, is also reproduced in *Forgotten Voices of the Great War*.

I'd never been in a factory before, but the crisis made you think. I thought well, my brothers and my friends are in France, so a friend and I thought to ourselves, well, let's do something. So we wrote to London and asked for war work. And we were directed to a munitions factory at Perivale in London. We had to have a health examination because we had to be very physically fit – perfect eyesight and strong. We had to supply four references, and be British-born of British parents.

We worked ten hours a day, that's from eight in the morning till quarter to one – no break, an hour for dinner, back again until half-past six – no break. We single girls found it very difficult to eat as well as work because the shops were closed when we got home. We had to do our work and try to get food, which was difficult. I remember going into a shop after not having milk for seven days and they said, 'If you can produce a baby you can have the milk' – that was it! I went into a butcher's shop to get some meat because we were just beginning to be rationed and I said, 'That looks like cat.' And he said, 'It is.' I couldn't face that.

It was a perfect factory to work in: everybody seemed unaware of the powder around them, unaware of any danger. Once or twice we heard, 'Oh, so and so's gone.' Perhaps she'd made a mistake and her eye was out, but there wasn't any big explosion during the three years I was there. We worked at making these little pellets, very innocent-looking little pellets, but had there been the lightest grit in those pellets, it would have been 'Goodbye'.

We had to do a fortnight on and a fortnight off. It was terribly hard, terribly monotonous, but we had a purpose. There wasn't a drone in that factory and every girl worked and worked and worked.

I didn't hear one grumble and hardly ever heard of one that stayed home because she had her man in mind, we all had. I was working with sailors' wives from three ships that were torpedoed and sank, *Aboukir*, *Cressy* and *Hogue*, on the 22nd of September 1914. It was pitiful to see them, so we had to cheer them up as best we could, so we sang. It was beautiful to listen to.

After each day when we got home we had a lovely good wash. And believe me the water was blood-red and our skin was perfectly yellow, right down through the body, legs and toenails even, perfectly yellow. In some people it caused a rash and a very nasty rash all round the chin. It was a shame because we were a bevy of beauties, you know, and these girls objected very much to that. Yet amazingly even though they could do nothing about it, they still carried on and some of them with rashes about half an inch thick but it didn't seem to do them any inward harm, just the skin. The hair, if it was fair or brown it went beautiful gold, but if it was any grey, it went grass-green. It was quite a twelve-month after we left the factory that the whole of the yellow came from our bodies. Washing wouldn't do anything – it only made it worse.

—— • ——

THE STUDENTS OF GIRTON COLLEGE, CAMBRIDGE In 1916 and again in 1919, past and present students of Girton College, Cambridge (then an all-female college) were asked to supply information about their contributions to the war effort, by briefly listing their experiences on postcards. Invitations were sent to 1483, and 854 reponded to the request (Katherine Jex-Blake, 'War Work' in *The Girton Review*, 1920).

The cards below were received in 1919. Their contents have been transcribed exactly, although the addresses have been omitted.

Name A. F. E. Sanders
War work (a) Arranged for the Massage & Physical Treatment at Tunbridge Wells High School of wounded soldiers.
(b) the war work of the pupils of the above school 1914-1917 & of the Sydenham High School. 1917-18 i.e. prisoners' parcels – part furnishing of Belgian refugees houses – 1000s of bags for hospitals – collections of nuts – eggs – rags – foxglove leaves &c. Red Cross sales. Entertainments of Belgians & wounded soldiers – concerts at Hospitals – supplies to a military base hospital &c &c.

(This is not personal work. Perhaps I should not send it?)

Name Mrs Howard Priestman (L. D. Pearson Mods Tripos 1905)
War work
The circular accompanying this postcard seemed to imply that a reply was asked for even if 'war work' has been an impossibility, owing to a young family, a shortness of maids & too little assistance in a large garden. I am sorry I have done no 'war work' – at all.

Yours sincerely. L. D Priestman

Name Helen E. Macklin
War work Ill health has prevented my doing any real work. I have belonged to the Bedford County Folk Visitation Society, for visiting wounded soldiers in hospital; and have acted as marraine to some Belgian soldiers, and done similar things. But I feel none of them can be called work or be worth recording.

Name Muriel E. Jackson

War work I have been Gardening since August 1917 at North Cray Place, Sidcup, Kent. It is a small Boarding School for girls & I am one of several Lady Gardeners who keep the school provided with vegetables. We do not grow flowers. I don't know whether you consider this 'War Work'. The Head Gardener had been called up.

Name May S. Gratton

War work

Analytical chemist, at Calico Print Works, Dinking Nr Manchester. From June 1918 to Jan 31st 1919.

This post was vacant owing to predecessor being called up. They had never had a lady chemist before. My predecessor was demobilised, & took up the work again when I left, so I consider it 'War Work'.

Name Gertrude Exton

War work

<u>One month</u> 'on the land' at the Flanders nurseries.

<u>Four months</u> as Technical Assistant in the Department of Aircraft Production in the Ministry of Munitions.

(This is hardly worth sending but I was teaching for very nearly four years.)

Name Joan Denny

War work – nothing, I fear – beyond helping in the big work Bath High School undertook from our Prisoners of War in Germany. We packed parcels ourselves as long as we were allowed, & then raised about £120 a year to send food etc to the men through their

Committees. I fear this is nothing to count, but it is all I can boast of.
J.Denny

Name F. E. Ashwell Cooke. Mrs
War work
The work I have done for the war has been of a very ordinary kind –
for the Red Cross, alien English women – & the Belgians. It is not
worth chronicling.
April 5th 1919

Name L. E. Blyth
War work
1) Visitor for Soldiers' & Sailors' Families Assoc.

2) Sewing for soldiers – joined 2 local centres.

3) Private parcels for Prisoners of War & allied soldiers, known to be
needy – through relations at front.

4) Household work – only keeping one maid instead of two. Taking
up poultry-keeping etc. seriously.

Name M. R. G. Bell
War work
Have done nothing official. Merely knitted socks, mittens, mufflers
etc & made respirators sandbags, splints & bandages.

Name Janet Case
War work None
Aug-Dec 1914 I worked with the women's coop. guild in their
campaign for Maternity centres, who I shd probably not have done

except for the war But the programme was drawn up prior to the war and we defended it.

Dec 1914-1919 prevented by illness from doing any outside work, but as a pacifist I shd not in any case have undertaken anything of the nature of actual war work.

J. E. C.

Name Mrs Ayrton

War work Invented a fan to drive back poisonous gases & clear them out of trenches, dug-outs &c both after a gas attack & during shell bombardments. Hundreds of thousands of these fans were sent to the French Front – & the demand was still greater than the supply quite towards the close of the war. I presented the invention [to] the ~~the~~ nation for the period of the war.

Name Edith Helen Pratt

War work

1) Staff Inspector of National Filling Factories, Ministry of Munitions.
Aug. 1915 – March. 1917

(First Woman Inspector appointed at the Ministry)

2) Deputy Chief Controller. W.A.A.C (Overseas)
March 1917 – March 1918

3) Deputy Commandant. Womens' Royal Air Force
March 1918 – July 1918

Created O.B.E. ~~Sept~~ 1917

Name Lucy Rose Stephen

~~War work~~

I have just received information that the above my daughter a former student at Girton died on the 8 April 1918 at Calgary Alberta Canada.

J H Stephen

——— • ———

THE SURVIVORS OF THE SINKING OF THE *LUSITANIA* On 1 May 1915 the British Cunard liner, the RMS *Lusitania*, embarked upon its journey from New York to Liverpool. As the ship approached the Irish Coast on 7 May, she was sunk by a torpedo from a German U-boat. Of 1,962 on board, only 764 survived. Rescue ships brought the dead and the living into Queenstown Harbour; relatives were permitted to identify the missing in temporary morgues. Richard Preston Prichard was aboard the liner; he was returning to Britain having been training in medicine at McGill University in Canada. His mother, living in Ramsgate, received no news about him. Mrs Prichard and her son Mostyn wrote to survivors asking if they had seen Richard.

Ramsgate

June 18th 1915

Dear Sir –

I have heard from one of the survivors that you may be able to tell me something of my son whose photo with description I enclose. His cabin was D. 90. Do you think if he were in his cabin he would have had time to get on Deck – or did the ship list to such an extent as to prevent his getting up the stairs – I believe you were saved on a raft. I suppose amongst the other men with you on it – my son was not amongst them –

Do you remember whether the majority of the men jumped at the last & did most of them have life belts – I should be most grateful to you if you will kindly tell me all you can remember – as I long so to hear something about my dear son – & what he went through at the last…

Were there many injured by the falling wreckage etc. & did the men seem to realise their danger –

My son was a medical student.

> Believe me –
> Yrs faithfully –
> M. Prichard –

If you know the names of other survivors I should be most grateful if you would kindly send me their address that I may write to them –

My son had a <u>very</u> <u>deep</u> dimple in his chin.

> Bayswater
> Nov. 26th 1915

Dear Mrs Pritchard [sic]

I received your two letters safely. Am extremely sorry not to have answered before, but I have not yet recovered from the fearful shock and tragedy of that awful affair 'the sinking of the Lusitania' and writing about it is still very painful to me. No doubt you have heard of my terrible experience and how when the ship went down it carried my darling baby girl and self with it and how I held her in my arms under the water until I became unconscious and then she was dragged away from me and I have never seen her since. Twice I went under the water and the second time on coming to the surface I held on to a piece of wreckage and drifted around amongst the dead for some considerable time. I cannot say just how long I was in the water it seemed to me an eternity, but when I was rescued I was not taken straight into a life boat, but three men who were sitting on an over-turned boat pulled me out of the water when I happened to drift their way, and it was some time afterwards that a boat load of people came along and took me on to their boat. When I got on board my life was almost gone and I do not remember who was in charge of the boat, but I can say that while I was there I did not see any man who passed away. Two or three were in a state of exhaustion but I think after a time they recovered somewhat. I do not know what happened to them afterwards because a fishing smack the Flying Fish I think by name came along and took us on to her. I wish I could tell you something to comfort you in your great distress but unfortunately I cannot. I do not even remember seeing your dear son and if I did I fear I should not have recognised him. It all happened so swiftly and everybody was more or less insane, but there is one thing I feel you can rest assured about and that is if your son did pass away on a boat his body would not have been left there, but would have been brought into Queenstown with the others.

I feel I cannot write any more just now, it distresses me too much. My darling babe who I have lost was my only child and all the world to me. Since she has been taken from me in such a cruel way my whole life seems different. I loved her so much and at times I feel I cannot go on living without her. I know too what you must be suffering and my heart goes out in sympathy for you. I have written this letter as bereaved Mother to bereaved Mother and am sure you will understand.

Must now close, my deepest sympathy to you and yours

believe me to remain

Your sincerely

Lilian Pye

Renton

10.9.15

Dear Mrs Pritchard [sic]

Received your letter this morning and on opening the leaflet I recognised your son in a moment.

Many times I have thought of him and wondered if he had been saved. He sat directly opposite me at the table and I noticed the dimple you refer to in your description of him. I can see his face so clearly in my mind so sunburned and full of life and ambition. He kept us in good spirits relating different experiences he had during his travels and was very nice to everybody. I appreciated his efforts as I was very sick during the whole journey and [he] was especially nice to me. Well the eventful Friday arrived and in the course of conversation Mr Pritchard remarked that I had a double on board and that he had spoken to this girl mistaking her for me. One or two of the other men at the table it seems did the same thing. So Mr Pritchard volunteered to point her out to me after lunch. I agreed and went down for my hat and coat. We went up on deck and was looking around when the awful crash came. The ship listed so much that we all scrambled down the deck and for a moment everything was confusion. When I came to myself again I glanced around but could find no trace of Mr Pritchard. He seemed to have disappeared. I ran around the deck looking for a life belt but could not get one. I then ran along to the first class deck to try the life boats there when the second torpedo struck her. I felt all hope was gone as far as the boats were concerned she was sinking so rapidly so ran back to my place where I was standing when she was first struck took off my heavy coat and climbed over the rail and jumped into the water with the hope of catching hold of a piece of wreckage[.] The suction pulled me down and I felt that I was going to my death but fortune came my way and I rose to the surface this time caught a small piece of wood and floated with it until I was picked up by a collapsible life boat and eight hours after was landed, at Queenstown. On Saturday morning I made inquiries regarding Mr Pritchard from one or two persons that knew him but could not gain any news of him at all.

I had the hope that perhaps he had been saved and brought to some other place. Several times I have mentioned in my home about Mr Pritchard taking me to see my double and how sadly it all ended. You have my heartfelt sympathy in your sorrow. People have forgotten about it but only those who had loved ones on board the Lusitania will never forget it. Time alone will efface the horror of the cruel deed.

Trusting these few lines will be of some use to you coming from one who probably was the last to speak to your son on the Lusitania.

Yours Sincerely

Grace Hope French

P.S. There was another girl at our table who was also saved I don't remember her name but I asked her at Queenstown if she saw anything of your son but she did not. Also one other man a Mr Bilborough he is in the Canadian [word unclear] now. I don't think he knew anything of him either.

There was another Canadian a very dyspeptic sort of fellow who sat next to Mr Pritchard. If I remember rightly I asked him too but he didn't know anything either. A Mrs Middlemast was also in our company she sat several seats down from us. She came all the way to Liverpool with the party I was with. She was with Mr Bilborough when the disaster happened so do not think she will know anything.

I hope you will gain some little satisfaction out of this rather badly written letter. I should also like to have the leaflet if you have one to spare in memory of Mr Pritchard.

Grace H. French

11th Sept 1915

Dear Mrs Prichard,

I am very pleased to be able to tell you a little about your son.

I remembered his face as soon as I saw his photograph. I saw him many times on deck, but only spoke to him once & that was only for a few minutes. A party of us used to have a game of skipping everyday. One of the boys tried to lasso me, the day before we were torpedoed, but did not manage to do it very well so this young gentleman, your son, had been watching us, came forward & said, I will show you how to do it. He seemed to be an expert at lassoing & caught quite a few in the rope, when he handed me the rope back he remarked that he had lassoed before. I never saw him again after this.

I was having lunch when the torpedo hit us. 70 D. deck was I think on the same floor, we had time to get onto the boat deck, even though the boat was tilted at such an angle, by pulling ourselves up the banisters, having to go up 6 flights of stairs. If your son <u>were</u> in his cabin he would have time to get on deck. I was taken out of the water & put onto an upturned boat, & afterwards taken out to a collapsible boat. I was not in Mr Parry's nor Mr Morton's boat & did not see anyone with a life belt on like you mention.

Sorry I can't tell you anything more about your son. My heart goes out to you, in your great loss. Oh it is just terrible to think about!!!

I will enclose address of some of our rescued party – Hoping you will hear more of your loved one.

Yours very sincerely
Olive North.

———— • ————

SERGEANT E. COOPER, VC was in the 12th Battalion, King's Royal Rifle Corps. This extract was taken from documents and recordings made by the historian Lyn Macdonald and reproduced in 1914–1918: *Voices and Images of the Great War* (1988).

I'd never been home for 16 months and my leave came through and it was usual for the men to go back with the Transport Sergeant when he delivered the rations and the mail. Well, I knew the ground fairly well, so I said to the Sergeant, 'I'm not going to wait for you, I'm going cross-country.' Well, in the meantime, in that very mail he was taking up, there was a notification that I had been awarded the Victoria Cross. It was to appear in Battalion Orders the next morning.

I sent a telegram to my parents to tell them I'm in England and would be home this evening. Outside King's Cross station, there was a YMCA hut so I went in there, had my bun and a cup of tea. I knocked a newspaper on to the floor. As it fell, it opened out. I stooped down to pick it up and I saw the big heading, *Eleven new VCs*. I was in this list!

The first thing that flashed through my mind was, 'What a surprise I'll give my mother when I get home tonight and tell her I've won the VC.'

Of course, in the meantime, my parents *had* got to know that I'd won the Victoria Cross, so, of course, when they knew I was in England, they told Mrs Smith next door and Mrs Jones further up the street and before long everyone in Stockton knew that I was home and they put it on the screen in the pictures that I was coming on the train that evening and when I got home, of course, everybody knew.

At Darlington, I had to change, I had to dash for the train to Stockton, haring along the platform, and somebody threw their arms around me. It was my father! I said, 'Come on, Dad, let's get the train.' It was packed with troops of course. I was sat in one corner and my father in the other and he said, 'Why didn't you tell us?' I said, 'Tell you what, Father?' He said, 'You know.' I said, 'I don't know what you're talking about.' He couldn't contain himself any longer. He said, in front of all the others, 'This is my son and he's won the VC.' The papers in London had told the local press in Stockton that there was a VC in *The London Gazette* and, of course, they'd looked up all the Coopers. They found the address and knocked and my mother answered the door. They said, 'You have a son, Sergeant Cooper?' 'Yes.' 'King's Royal Rifles?' 'Yes.' And, of course, she began to worry then, thinking it was bad news, and she let out a little cry. My sister went to the door and wondered what they were doing, upsetting my mother, and they said, 'We've got good news for you Mrs Cooper and you've got nothing to worry about. Your son's got the VC.' She didn't know what the VC was! When my father came home for his midday meal, they told him what had happened and he didn't go back to work that day. I think it was the first day he'd ever missed half a day's work in his life. So he'd set off to meet me at Darlington.

When we got to Stockton station, I was first out of that train and dashed down the subway and there was a Superintendent of Police racing after me. 'Stop!'

I said, 'What's the matter?'

He said, 'The Borough Corporation are here to give you an address of welcome.'

I said, 'I don't want it. I want to get home to my mother.'

They threw the station doors open and of course all the crowd came in and they picked me up and carried me away and that was my homecoming. I was 21. I'd only seen my mother once since I went to France.

[...]

People said, 'Now you must wear a ribbon.' There was a sports shop that sold sporting guns etc. and I said to the lady behind the counter 'Have you any medal ribbons?' 'Oh, yes. What did you require?' I said, 'The Victoria Cross.' After recovering, she said, 'Well we haven't any of that ribbon in, but I can get it for you.'

Sure enough, on the Wednesday, it was there. The lady said, 'Let me be the first to put it on your breast.' Well, I just stood in front of her and she put it on the right-hand side! Further down the High Street, there was a little photographer. He was stood on the doorstep of his shop and he persuaded me to go in and have my photo taken and so I've got a photo with the VC ribbon on the wrong side!

———— • ————

HELEN THOMAS (1877–1967) was born in Lancashire, and is perhaps best known for the autobiographical accounts of her relationship with the poet Edward Thomas, whom she married in 1899. Edward was killed at Arras on 9 April 1917. In the 1931 edition of *World Without End* from which the excerpt below is taken, some names are changed and Edward is referred to as David.

Christmas had come and gone. The snow still lay deep under the forest trees, which, tortured by the merciless wind, moaned and swayed as if in exhausted agony. The sky, day after day, was grey with snow that fell often enough to keep the surface white, and to cover again and again the bits of twigs, and sometimes large branches that broke from the heavily laden trees. We wearied for some colour, some warmth, some sound, but desolation and despair seemed to have taken up her dwelling place on the earth, as in our hearts she had entered, do what we would to keep her out. I longed with a passionate longing for some sign of life, of hope, of spring, but none came, and I knew at last none would come.

The last two days of David's leave had come. Two days and two nights more we were to be together, and I prayed in my heart, 'Oh, let the snow melt and the sky be blue again!' so that the dread which was spoiling these precious hours would lift.

The first days had been busy with friends coming to say good-bye, all bringing presents for David to take out to the front – warm lined gloves, a fountain pen, a box of favourite sweets, books.

This was not a time when words of affection were bearable; so they heaped things that they thought he might need or would like. Everyone who came was full of fun and joking about his being an officer after having had, as it were, to go to school again and learn mathematics, which were so uncongenial to him, but which he had stuck to and mastered with that strange pertinacity that had made him stick to all sorts of unlikely and uncongenial things in his life. They joked about his short hair, and the little moustache he had grown, and about the way he had perfected the Guards' salute. We got large jugs of beer from the inn near by to drink his health in, and an end to the War. The hateful cottage became homely and comfortable under the influence of these friends, all so kind and cheerful.

Then in the evenings, when just outside the door the silence of the forest was like a pall covering too heavily the myriads of birds and little beasts that the frost had killed, we would sit by the fire with the children and read aloud to them, and they would sing songs that they had known since their baby-hood, and David sang new ones he had learnt in the army – jolly songs with good choruses in which I, too, joined as I busied about getting the supper. Then, when the baby had gone to bed, Elizabeth would sit on his lap, content just to be there, while he and Philip worked out problems or studied maps. It was lovely to see those two so united over this common interest.

But he and I were separated by our dread, and we could not look each other in the eyes, nor dared we be left alone together.

The days had passed in restless energy for us both. He had sawn up a big tree that had been blown down at our very door, and chopped the branches into logs, the children all helping. The children loved being with him, for though he was stern in making them build up the logs properly, and use the tools in the right way, they were not resentful of this, but tried to win his rare praise and imitate his skill. Indoors he packed his kit and polished his accoutrements. He loved a good piece of leather, and his Sam Browne and high trench boots shone with a deep clear lustre. The brass, too, reminded him of the brass ornaments we had often admired when years ago we had lived on a farm and knew every detail of a plough team's harness. We all helped with the buttons and buckles and badges to turn him out the smart officer it was his pride to be. For he entered into this soldiering which he hated in just the same spirit of thoroughness of which I have spoken before. We talked, as we polished, of those past days: 'Do you remember when Jingo, the grey leader of the team, had colic, and Turner the ploughman led her about Blooming Meadow for hours, his eyes streaming with tears because he thought she was going to die? And how she would only eat the hay from the Blooming Meadow, and not the coarse hay that was grown in Sixteen Acre Meadow for the cows? And do you remember Turner's whip which he carried over his shoulder when he led Darling and Chestnut and Jingo out to the plough? It had fourteen brass bands on the handle, one for every year of his service on the farm.' So we talked of old times that the children could remember.

And the days went by till only two were left. David had been going through drawers full of letters, tearing up dozens and keeping just one here and there, and arranging manuscripts and note-books and newspaper cuttings all neatly in his desk – his face pale and suffering while he whistled. The children helped and collected stamps from the envelopes, and from the drawers all sorts of useless odds and ends that children love. Philip knew what it all meant, and looked anxiously and dumbly from his father's face to mine.

And I knew David's agony and he knew mine, and all we could do was to speak sharply to each other. 'Now do, for goodness' sake, remember, Jenny, that these are the important manuscripts, and that I'm putting them here, and this key is for the box that holds all important papers like our marriage certificate and the children's birth certificates, and my life insurance policy. You may want them at some time; so don't go leaving the key about.' And I, after a while, 'Can't you leave all this unnecessary tidying business, and put up that shelf you promised me? I hate this room, but a few books on a shelf might make it look a bit more human.' 'Nothing will improve this room; so you had better resign yourself to it. Besides, the wall is too rotten for a shelf.' 'Oh, but you promised.' 'Well, it won't be the first time I've broken a promise to you, will it? Nor the last, perhaps.'

Oh, God! melt the snow and let the sky be blue.

The last evening comes. The children have taken down the holly and mistletoe and ivy, and chopped up the little Christmas-tree to burn. And for a treat Elizabeth and Polly are to have their bath in front of the blazing fire. The big zinc bath is dragged in, and the children undress in high glee, and skip about naked in the warm room, which is soon filled with the sweet smell of the burning greenery. The berries pop, and the fir-tree makes fairy lace, and the holly crackles and roars. The two children get into the bath together, and David scrubs them in turn – they laughing, making the fire hiss with their splashing. The drawn curtains shut out the snow and the starless sky, and the deathly silence out there in the biting cold is forgotten in the noise and warmth of our little room. After the bath David reads to them. First of all he reads Shelley's *The Question* and *Chevy Chase*, and then for Polly a favourite Norse tale. They sit in their nightgowns listening gravely, and then, just before they kiss him good-night, while I stand by with the candle in my hand, he says: 'Remember while I am away to be kind. Be kind, first of all, to Mummy, and after that be kind to everyone and everything.' And they all assent together, and joyfully hug and kiss him, and he carries the two girls up, and drops each into her bed.

And we are left alone, unable to hide our agony, afraid to show it. Over supper, we talk of the probable front he'll arrive at, of his fellow-officers, and of the unfinished portrait-etching that one of them has done of him and given to me. And we speak of the garden, and where this year he wants the potatoes to be, and he reminds me to put in the beans directly the snow disappears. 'If I'm not back in time, you'd better get someone to help you with the digging,' he says. He reads me some of the poems he has written that I have not heard – the last one of all called *Out in the Dark*. And I venture to question one line, and he says, 'Oh, no, it's right, Jenny, I'm sure it's right.' And I nod because I can't speak, and I try to smile at his assurance.

I sit and stare stupidly at his luggage by the wall, and his roll of bedding, kit-bag, and suit-case. He takes out his prismatic compass and explains it to me, but I cannot see, and when a tear drops on to it he just shuts it up and puts it away. Then he says, as he takes a book out of his pocket, 'You see, your Shakespeare's *Sonnets* is already where it will always be. Shall I read you some?' He reads one or two to me. His face is grey and his mouth trembles, but his voice is quiet and steady. And soon I slip to the floor and sit between his knees, and while he reads his hand falls over my shoulder and I hold it with mine.

'Shall I undress you by this lovely fire and carry you upstairs in my khaki over-coat?' So he undoes my things, and I slip out of them; then he takes the pins out of my hair, and we laugh at ourselves for behaving as we so often do, like young lovers. 'We have never become a proper Darby and Joan, have we?'

'I'll read to you till the fire burns low, and then we'll go to bed.' Holding the book in one hand, and bending over me to get the light of the fire on the book, he puts his other hand over my breast, and I cover his hand with mine, and he reads from *Antony and Cleopatra*. He cannot see my face, nor I his, but his low, tender voice trembles as he speaks the words so full for us of poignant meaning. That tremor is my undoing. 'Don't read any more. I can't bear it.' All my strength gives way. I hide my face on his knee, and all my tears so long kept back come convulsively. He raises my head and wipes my eyes and kisses them, and wrapping his greatcoat round me carries me to our bed in the great, bare ice-cold room. Soon he is with me, and we lie speechless and trembling in each other's arms. I cannot stop crying. My body is torn with terrible sobs. I am engulfed in this despair like a drowning man by the sea. My mind is incapable of thought. Only now and again, as they say drowning people do, I have visions of things that have been – the room where my son was born; a day, years after, when we were together walking before breakfast by a stream with hands full of bluebells; and in the kitchen of our honeymoon cottage, and I happy in his pride of me. David did not speak except now and then to say some tender word or name, and hold me tightly to him. 'I've always been able to warm you, haven't I?' 'Yes, your lovely body never feels as cold as mine does. How is it that I am so cold when my heart is so full of passion?' 'You must have Elizabeth to sleep with you while I am away. But you must not make my heart cold with your sadness, but keep it warm, for no one else but you has ever found my heart, and for you it was a poor thing after all.' 'No, no, no, your heart's love is all my life. I was nothing before you came, and would be nothing without your love.'

So we lay, all night, sometimes talking of our love and all that had been, and of the children, and what had been amiss and what right. We knew the best was that there had never been untruth between us. We knew all of each other, and it was right. So talking and crying and loving in each other's arms we fell asleep as the cold reflected light of the snow crept through the frost-covered windows.

David got up and made the fire and brought me some tea, and then got back into bed, and the children clambered in, too, and we sat in a row sipping our tea. I was not afraid of crying any more. My tears had been shed, my heart was empty, stricken with something that tears would not express or comfort. The gulf had been bridged. Each bore the other's suffering. We concealed nothing, for all was known between us. After breakfast, while he showed me where his account books were and what each was for, I listened calmly, and unbelievingly he kissed me when I said I, too, would keep accounts. 'And here are my poems. I've copied them all out in this book for you, and the last of all is for you. I wrote it last night, but don't read it now… It's still freezing. The ground is like iron, and more snow has fallen. The children will come to the station with me; and now I must be off.'

We were alone in my room. He took me in his arms, holding me tightly to him, his face white, his eyes full of a fear I had never seen before. My arms were around his neck. 'Beloved, I love you,' was all I could say. 'Jenny, Jenny, Jenny,' he said, 'remember that, whatever happens, all is well between us for ever and ever.' And hand in hand we went downstairs and out to the children, who were playing in the snow.

A thick mist hung everywhere, and there was no sound except, far away in the valley, a train shunting. I stood at the gate watching him go; he turned back to wave until the mist and the hill hid him. I heard his old call coming up to me: 'Coo-ee!' he called. 'Coo-ee!' I answered, keeping my voice strong to call again. Again through the muffled air came his 'Coo-ee'. And again went my answer like an echo. 'Coo-ee' came fainter next time with the hill between us, but my 'Coo-ee' went out of my lungs strong to pierce to him as he strode away from me. 'Coo-ee!' So faint now, it might be only my own call flung back from the thick air and muffling snow. I put my hands up to my mouth to make a trumpet, but no sound came. Panic seized me, and I ran through the mist and the snow to the top of the hill, and stood there a moment dumbly, with straining eyes and ears. There was nothing but the mist and the snow and the silence of death.

Then with leaden feet which stumbled in a sudden darkness that overwhelmed me I groped my way back to the empty house.

———— • ————

VERA BRITTAIN (1893–1970) was born in Staffordshire and studied at Oxford. She begins her memoir *Testament of Youth* (1933) saying, 'When the Great War broke out, it came to me not as a superlative tragedy, but as an interruption of the most exasperating kind to my personal plans.' Her fiancé Roland Leighton was killed in France in December 1915; her brother Edward in Italy in June 1918. Brittain worked as a nurse during the war, and joined the VAD (Voluntary Aid Detachment). This work took her to London, Malta and France.

In Sussex, by the end of January, the season was already on its upward grade; catkins hung bronze from the bare, black branches, and in the damp lanes between Hassocks and Keymer the birds sang loudly. How I hated them as I walked back to the station one late afternoon, when a red sunset turned the puddles on the road into gleaming pools of blood, and a new horror of mud and death darkened my mind with its dreadful obsession. Roland, I reflected bitterly, was now part of the corrupt clay into which war had transformed the fertile soil of France; he would never again know the smell of a wet evening in early spring.

I had arrived at the cottage that morning to find his mother and sister standing in helpless distress in the midst of his returned kit, which was lying, just opened, all over the floor. The garments sent back included the outfit that he had been wearing when he was hit. I wondered, and I wonder still, why it was thought necessary to return such relics – the tunic torn back and front by the bullet, a khaki vest dark and stiff with blood, and a pair of blood-stained breeches slit open at the top by someone obviously in a violent hurry. Those gruesome rags made me realise, as I had never realised before, all that France really meant. Eighteen months afterwards the smell of Étaples village, though fainter and more diffused, brought back to me the memory of those poor remnants of patriotism.

'Everything,' I wrote later to Edward, 'was damp and worn and simply caked with mud. And I was glad that neither you nor Victor nor anyone who may some day go to the front was there to see. If you had been, you would have been overwhelmed by the horror of war without its glory. For though he had only worn the things when living, the smell of those clothes was the smell of graveyards and the Dead. The mud of France which covered them was not ordinary mud; it had not the usual clean pure smell of earth, but it was as though it were saturated with dead bodies – dead that had been dead a long, long time… There was his cap, bent in and shapeless out of recognition – the soft cap he wore rakishly on the back of his head – with the badge thickly coated with mud. He must have fallen on top of it, or perhaps one of the people who fetched him in trampled on it.'

Edward wrote gently and humbly in reply, characteristically emphasising the simple, less perturbing things that I had mentioned in another part of my letter.

'I expect he had only just received the box of cigarettes and the collars and braces I gave him for Christmas and I feel glad that he did get them because he must have thought of me then.'

So oppressively at length did the charnel-house smell pervade the small sitting-room, that Roland's mother turned desperately to her husband:

'Robert, take those clothes away into the kitchen and don't let me see them again: I must either burn or bury them. They smell of death; they are not Roland; they even seem to detract from his memory and spoil his glamour. I won't have any more to do with them!'

What actually happened to the clothes I never knew, but, incongruously enough, it was amid this heap of horror and decay that we found, surrounded by torn bills and letters, the black manuscript note-book containing his poems. On the fly-leaf he had copied a few lines written by John Masefield on the subject of patriotism:

'It is not a song in the street and a wreath on a column and a flag flying from a window and a pro-Boer under a pump. It is a thing very holy and very terrible, like life itself. It is a burden to be borne, a thing to labour for and to suffer for and to die for, a thing which gives no happiness and no pleasantness – but a hard life, an unknown grave, and the respect and bowed heads of those who follow.'

The poems were few, for he had always been infinitely dissatisfied with his own work, but 'Nachklang' was there, and 'In the Rose Garden', as well as the roundel 'I Walk Alone', and the villanelle 'Violets', which he had given me during his leave. The final entry represented what must have been the last, and was certainly the most strangely prophetic, of all his writings. It evidently belonged to the period of our quarrel, when he was away from his regiment with the Somerset Light Infantry, for it was headed by the words:

HÉDAUVILLE. November 1915:

The sunshine on the long white road
That ribboned down the hill,
The velvet clematis that clung
Around your window-sill,
Are waiting for you still.

Again the shadowed pool shall break
In dimples round your feet,
And when the thrush sings in your wood,
Unknowing you may meet
Another stranger, Sweet.

And if he is not quite so old
As the boy you used to know,
And less proud, too, and worthier,
You may not let him go—
(And daisies are truer than passion-flowers)
It will be better so.

What did he mean, I wondered, as I read and re-read the poem, puzzled and tormented. What could he have meant?

Five years afterwards, as I motored from Amiens through the still disfigured battlefields to visit Roland's grave at Louvencourt, I passed, with a sudden shock, a white board inscribed briefly: 'HÉDAUVILLE'.

The place was then much as it must have looked after a year or two's fighting, with only the stumpy ruins of farmhouses crumbling into the tortured fields to show where once a village had been. But over the brow of a hill the shell-torn remnants of a road turned a corner and curved steeply downwards. As the car lurched drunkenly between the yawning shell-holes I looked back, and it seemed to me that perhaps in November 1915, this half-obliterated track had still retained enough character and dignity to remind Roland of the moorland road near Buxton where we had walked one spring evening before the war.

———— • ————

VIRGINIA WOOLF (1882–1941) was a British novelist, essayist and diarist. The First World War echoes through some of her major works of fiction: from the shellshocked veteran Septimus Warren Smith in *Mrs Dalloway* (1925) to the death of Andrew Ramsay in *To the Lighthouse* (1927). The following is an extract from an essay published in *The Times* on 15 August 1916 (signed 'from a correspondent'). Woolf and her family had spent most of the previous month on the edge of the Downs near Lewes, Sussex.

Two well-known writers were describing the sound of the guns in France, as they heard it from the top of the South Downs. One likened it to 'the hammer stroke of Fate'; the other heard in it 'the pulse of Destiny'.

More prosaically, it sounds like the beating of gigantic carpets by gigantic women, at a distance. You may almost see them holding the carpets in their strong arms by the four corners, tossing them into the air, and bringing them down with a thud while the dust rises in a cloud about their heads. All walks on the Downs this summer are accompanied by this sinister sound of far-off beating, which is sometimes as faint as the ghost of an echo, and sometimes rises almost from the next fold of grey land. At all times strange volumes of sound roll across the bare uplands, and reverberate in those hollows in the Downside which seem to await the spectators of some Titanic drama. Often walking alone, with neither man nor animal in sight, you turn sharply to see who it is that gallops behind you. But there is no one. The phantom horseman dashes by with a thunder of hoofs, and suddenly his ride is over and the sound lapses, and you only hear the grasshoppers and the larks in the sky.

Such tricks of sound may easily be accounted for by the curious planes of curve and smoothness into which these Downs have been shaped, but for hundreds of years they must have peopled the villages and the solitary farmhouses in the folds with stories of ghostly riders and unhappy ladies forever seeking their lost treasure. These ghosts have rambled about for so many centuries that they are now old inhabitants with family histories attached to them; but at the present moment one may find many phantoms hovering on the borderland of belief and scepticism – not yet believed in, but not properly accounted for. Human vanity, it may be, embodies them in the first place. The desire to be somehow impossibly, and therefore all the more mysteriously, concerned in secret affairs of national importance is very strong at the present moment. It is none of our business to supply reasons; only to notice queer signs, draw conclusions, and shake our heads. Each village has its wiseacre, who knows already more than he will say; and in a year or two who shall limit the circumstantial narratives which will be current in the neighbourhood, and possibly masquerade in solemn histories for the instruction of the future!

The pencil inscription reads: 'This hole caused by sh[ell] which killed Harry Brown 21st October 1918 in France'. Private Harry Brown was serving in the 9th Battalion of the Cameronian (Scottish Rifles) Labour Corps. The postcard was sent by Vincent Brown, Harry's brother, and father of 'Little Raymond', who is pictured on the front (opposite).

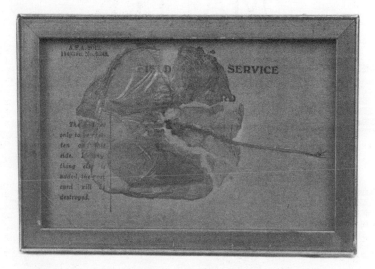

The writing on the left of the Field Service Postcard onto which the pressed poppy is mounted reads: 'The address only to be written on this side. If anything else is added, the postcard will be destroyed.'
The postcard did, however, reach Rosemary (Biddy) Shaddick, wife of Joseph Shaddick, who picked the poppy from a Flanders field and sent it home during his war service. It is currently held at the Imperial War Museum.

MIND AND MATTER

Experience at
close quarters

RUDOLF BINDING (1867–1938) was born in Basel, Switzerland, and studied in Germany. He was a writer and a poet. He served on the Western Front and was in command of a cavalry squadron. *A Fatalist at War*, which included diary entries and excerpts from letters written during the war, was published in 1927 and translated in 1929.

Easter Letter [1915]
West Flanders

I have not written to you for a long time, but I have thought of you all the more as a silent creditor. But when one owes letters one suffers from them, so to speak, at the same time. It is, indeed, not so simple a matter to write from the War, really from the War; and what you read as Field Post letters in the papers usually have their origin in the lack of understanding that does not allow a man to get hold of the War, to breathe it in although he is living in the midst of it. Certainly it is a strange element for everyone; but I probably find it even stranger, and feel more like a fish out of water than many who write about it – because I try to understand it. The further I penetrate its true inwardness the more I see the hopelessness of making it comprehensible for those who only understand life in terms of peace-time, and apply these same ideas to war in spite of themselves. They only think that they understand it. It is as if fishes living in the water could have a clear conception of what living in the air is like. When one is hauled out on to dry land and dies in the air, then he will know something about it.

So it is with War. Feeling deeply about it, one becomes less able to talk about it every day. Not because one understands it less each day, but because one grasps it better. But it is a silent teacher, and he who learns becomes silent too.

The stagnation that this siege warfare has brought about gives a superficial observer the illusion of peace. One regulates inter-course with the local population as well as one can, one tries to arrange for the tillage of the land, one trains men as well as possible in mud and filth, one visits the officers of neighbouring units, one spends hours in discussion. The War is ignored; for not everyone has the capacity or the habit to notice it in everything and everyone. Yet it is behind everything and everyone; that is the strange part of it! The starlings that winter hereabouts in hordes whistle like rifle-bullets; and as the bullets cannot have learnt to whistle from the starlings one may safely presume the opposite. And everything whistles its tune of the War – the houses, the fields, men, beasts, rivers, and even the sky. The very milk turns sour under the thunder of shell-fire.

You will think I am romancing. But I am not. Only … the others do not notice this. They do not listen to the starlings; they hardly look at the fields; mankind has not changed since yesterday; and the milk has got sour through standing.

What exactly do they experience of the War? They know that the dug-outs in the line are comfortably fitted up, that they have brought up a mirror and a clock, that they have barbed wire in front of them, that the gunners hide their shells carefully, that troops are flung here and there, that the Field Post functions, that there are brave men who have been rewarded with the Iron Cross.

Then again, they notice effects. They see the wounded, hear of the dead, hear of towns that have been taken, of positions lost or won. But that is not the melody of war. It is as if one were to describe and understand the being and the melody of the wind by saying that it chases dead leaves, that the weathercock creaks, and that the washing on the line dries. All that is not its melody; as the fitting out of a trench, the Iron Cross, and even the dead are only infinitesimal outward and recognisable signs of an unknown and hidden mystery, be it sublime or cruel.

Perhaps some poet has already seen this majesty unveiled – heard this melody, which may be nothing but a bellow, so that it can be reproduced. As for myself, the sounds increase, but the melody and rhythm remain obscure.

And if I could summon all the poets of past times to sing the War they might all remain silent – unless one should answer who has been through hell.

So you may appreciate how hard it is to write about the War. Its Being is veiled; and where the greatness is recognisable human speech has no expression to cope with it. What do you make of it when I tell you that I live in a house with no architectural style, windows that do not shut properly, and high rooms; that I have a bed; that two little old women wait on me and do my cooking; and that I curse the eternal rain that the sky of Flanders pours down upon us? All this seems to me so immeasurably dull compared with the War; just as one can only bear the insignificant things of life by not talking about them. I use the same soap in peacetime; I have time to brush my teeth in the morning; I have a brown coffee-pot and a stove that does not heat well. Why should I tell you about them? The piping of the starlings, the aspect of the sickly fields, the thunderous air and the sour milk will tell you much more.

But in the midst of the monstrous event stands Man; the thousands and the hundreds of thousands, the combatants and the non-combatants; who all have one wish and one goal: to cast aside the War; to render its effect invisible so far as they can be understood; to let a well-earned Peace grow its grass over the victims and to carry on as before, broadly speaking. The times may be as big as they will; man remains small. Transformation and cleansing have nothing to do with him.

They say, they know, that we will win; what a wonderful thing it is to know this and to say it. But we shall not conquer ourselves. We will carry on as before and think what wonderful new things we have set up in place of the old. For many things that ought to be scrapped; and many that are as yet undiscovered are worth bringing to life.

That sounds very hard, doesn't it? But it should at least be allowed to him who feels the hardness of the times to speak out his hard words. You will ask what I would put in the place of that which is past or what new things there are to be discovered.

I believe that it could be expressed thus – a religion of defensive power – for all peoples. There should be a belief in the right to be in a state of defence, to defend oneself; this and nothing more. This would give to us and to the world, which would adopt our religion, such immense strength – for religions outlast history, peoples and empires, civilisation and philosophy, discoveries and the progress of man – so that no nation or concourse of nations would stand up to us. Defensive power would stand sanctified, with the weapons of defence in her hand, as with the products of toil in her arms; unattackable, uniting through the strength of the idea, resting on a joyous security of belief, inspiring piety because of man's belief in her. I would not challenge this time to bring forth a religion did I not know how great it is. It bears the child; we are but clumsy helpers in her heavy hour; and who shall deny either the immensity of the event or the helplessness of mankind – even for our people alone – to turn it into good?

An enormous longing arises in the world, not longing for strange countries, not for seas, fortresses, riches, and power – but for a gift of grace from these times that are worthy alike of themselves and of us.

———— • ————

BERT BAILEY was a rifleman in the 11th Battalion of the Rifle Brigade. The passage below is from a letter included in *1914–1918: Voices and Images of the Great War* by Lyn Macdonald. He was killed a few hours after it was written.

Wednesday, 27 October [1915]

My Darling Wife,

Another night has passed and another morning come and I am still in trenches and in good health. Although all day and night on Monday it rained steadily yet Tuesday (yesterday) morning broke fair and fine and we had a nice day except that underneath everything was mud and slosh. We were employed all morning and afternoon in putting down boards along the trenches and have greatly improved it for walking. As I stopped to rest awhile I could not help being struck by the exceptional beauty of the moon as the clouds kept flitting past. The moon was nearly full, partially obscured by the thin fleecy clouds but these soon passed by and after a spell of clear shining dimly through a great rift in the clouds, then the whole closed up. The sky at that spot was absolutely black, but there was no rain, and although the great black ugly side was turned to me I knew the other side must be shimmering with the pure white light. Let us hope that this time of our lives is like that, a great dark cloud which passes away, so that afterwards the light is brighter than before. It has been raining in fitful showers all this morning up till now (ten o'clock) and we have not had to fall in for working yet.

Just a few words now about your last parcel. I don't often mention everything, but I do appreciate the rag you sent me, it is so very useful. The piece this week is lovely and I make a very shrewd guess that, when I am using it as a tablecloth, it was not always used for that purpose but once formed part of my lady's – 'Oh dear, oh dear, what am I saying?' – nevertheless it is grand to wrap my bread in and keep my food clean and nice. *Cigarettes – capital* but don't send any more until I ask you to. *Toffee, condensed milk, candles, rice and potted meat*: the toffee, milk, rice and one candle have all gone. Potted meat for tea today, candle tonight if necessary. The Oxo cubes will be very nice to augment my soup with no doubt. Don't send me any more Oxo or Bovril until I ask you to, Darling, will you. The little pat of butter is always welcome, and the bread dodge I think is an improvement on buying expensive cakes. Of course a little home-made cake is nice, but I was never a lover of cake. Good substitutes for things I have asked you not to send would be sardines, pickles, or a bit of cheese. Please discontinue sending tea, sugar and salt for a bit, Darling, as I have plenty. Don't think I am trying to economise and stint myself because it is not that, and it all helps us, dear, doesn't it? And you never know I may want something ever so expensive one of these times, eh, what!

Now my little Darling you must be patient with me won't you and don't get cross because I have been having a lot to say about the parcels. You are a pet to send them and you know you asked me to guide you as to what I most required, didn't you?

The pastry of your own make was absolutely A1, and a perfect success – and she's the little girl who said, 'Oh, I can only cook a plain dinner.' One great thing is off my mind and that is that I need never fear for my life in the future when you send me or make me pastry!

The weather has remained fine all the afternoon and let's hope it will be fine tonight. A cold night's bad, but a wet cold night is worse. You must not worry about me, Darling, because I am just as able to look after myself as the other chaps. So, dearest little one, just keep cheerful and enjoy yourself all you can, and wrap up now the cold is here. If you require new clothes in the way of overcoat or mac or gloves or anything in fact for the winter, don't let yourself go short will you? Just take it from the cash and note it in the book as I told you, so that we can see how the cash is made up for the sake of keeping proper accounts. Now, love, I will answer the other letters later. I'm afraid I twaddle a lot but never mind.

I remain

ever your own devoted

      Bert.

—— • ——

FRANK COCKER served as a private and a lieutenant fighting in France and Belgium. The excerpts below detail his friendship with Lance Corporal Charlie Wood. Both had girlfriends at home. The letters were written by Cocker, and were sent to his girlfriend Evelyn and to his 'homefolks'.

The Front,

France.

June 12/15

My own sweet lassie,

[…] During the time we were at the 'redoubt' of which I wrote a few weeks ago, I met a young fellow there, a stretcher-bearer and first-aid man he is, and a lance corpl.

It is a curious thing, but you will understand what I mean when I tell you that wherever I go I am always interested in people's faces, and I scrutinize them a good deal, – why? I asked myself the question the other day as we passed another battalion on the march and I found myself searching every face that passed as though looking for some one I knew. Then I realized that it was my soul searching for a kindred spirit in tune with my own. And though I searched every face that passed not one was there which really pleased me. When I first met Alfred whom we now know so well, I had that pleased feeling which told me that here was a soul which would harmonise with my own, and the friendship since developed, has meant many hours of pleasure to me. So when I met Lce. Cpl. Charlie Wood, we looked at each other and mutually agreed that we liked each other straight off, though neither of us has said so in so many words, but both have since shown it. I first met him at 4 o'clock one morning just as the sun was rising. It was the first morning after our arrival at the 'redoubt'. We had all come the previous night in the dark. I had noticed that the ground behind the 'dug-outs' was rather too high to be quite safe, and as I felt rather chilly, I picked up a spade and set to work to lower a portion of it, in fact to make a shallow trench right along. I had been engaged on this occupation for about half an hour and was just resting my spade and looking far away over the channel (you know where), when I became aware of someone crawling out of one of the 'dug-outs', first two hands, then a head wearing a knitted cap and then the rest of the figure, crawling on hands and knees. I was watching him, not particularly interested, but when he stood up and I saw his face I was interested at once. We looked at each other for about ten seconds and then he smiled and said 'Good morning corporal'. I said 'Good morning', and then 'You're busy early, – not a bad job either for a cold morning, ugh!' – he shrugged his shoulders and seized a pick and began to make the muck fly while I sort of observed him and weighed him up.

[…]

Somewhere in Belgium
July 1/1915

My dear dear Evelyn,

Your sumptuous parcel reached me yesterday morning after a long march the night before, and as we had another long march to face at sunset, the contents of the parcel were subjected to a rather extravagant consumption. The tin of peaches and most of the maltwheat loaf disappeared at dinnertime, with the aid of a few willing friends. Charlie was not to be found then, the reason being, it turned out, that he had not arrived, for about the middle of the afternoon a timber waggon [sic] drove up into the field in which we were, and a cheery voice which I at once recognised, shouted 'Gentlemen, we have arrived', and I looked round and saw Charlie's lithe figure springing off the wagon and unloading his belongings. I was just starting on an errand so did not get to speak to him just them [sic]. He spied me though and called out his usual 'Hello Frank me lad, how are we?' 'Oh, in the pink, – see you later!' 'Right O!'

I saw him at tea time and after opening the tin of pineapples and cutting the nice ginger cake, I put some out on a tin plate, with two pieces of the cake and walked across to him and presented to him, – you should have seen his eyes open wide, – I said, – 'With the gracious compliments of a girl somewhere in England.' He jumped to his feet and made a most elaborate bow, and while his left hand accepted the dish, his right hand threw kisses to the invisible donor, 'Aha! monsieur, merci beaucoup, give the dear young lady my grateful thanks and kind regards.' There were a lot of fellows sat round and he amused himself by making them green with envy, by taking a spoonful of the fruit and inviting them to look at it, and then slowly moving it to his mouth and taking it in and making goo-goo eyes to express his enjoyment, finishing each spoonful with a smack of the lips, until they got exasperated and threatened to throw lumps of bread at him.

[…]

Tuesday August 17th

[Following the description of an attack]

Poor Charlie returned and I had some hot tea for him. He looked fagged out but revived somewhat afterwards. On Sunday however the inevitable reaction set in and by evening he was in the blues properly. I tried my best to console him and I realized that a great love had sprung up between us. We suddenly caught each other's glance and both his eyes and mine were wet with tears. He tried his best to smile but it was a very sickly attempt. He said, 'I'm afraid I am making but a poor companion Frank, but it's no use, I'm done and I must go down and see the doctor.' I urged him to do so and so he went, and the doctor sent him to hospital for a rest.

The Trenches
Belgium
August 26/1915

My dear sweet lassie,

You will no doubt have heard the bad news by now [Frank's brother, Private John F. Cocker, known amongst friends as 'Jack', had been killed by a German sniper]. My heart is so stunned I don't know whether it is broken or not. I cannot realize that I shall never see him again. The fellows have been very kind to me and shown every consideration and sympathy. I was asleep in a dug-out in the reserve trench when I was awakened by a corporal who handed me a letter addressed to Jack from Eddie, and at the same time said, 'They say your Jack's been hit'. I jumped up immediately, never dreaming the truth. 'Where is he,' I asked. 'They'll tell you on yonder,' he said. Something about his face however, made me anxious, and I had not gone far before I was informed of the truth. I then sought out Charlie and found him asleep in his dug-out. I woke him gently and when he opened his eyes and saw me, such a look of tender love and sympathy came into his face and he drew me into his arms as a mother might have done, and there I shed a flood of tears which relieved somewhat the stunning ache in my heart.

[...]

Written at 'HOUTKIRKE'
Somewhere in France
(Belgian Frontier)
Jan 6/16

Dear old homefolks,

It is the hour of 8 pm. and I am writing by the light of a candle in an old barn somewhere in Northern France. This particular barn is built on the fresh-air principle, or rather I should think it has developed the fresh-air principle with age, for the breeze which wafts round nearly blows the candles out. Still, we manage to keep fairly warm at night, and the place is no worse for its ample venti-lation, will it Eddie? Fortunately the weather has been very mild for this time of year.

Today I have received Minnie's letter of Jan. 2; also the parcel, a letter from Evelyn, 'Public Opinion', and some papers from Eddie. Thanks Minnie dear for such a nice letter.

I'm glad you like Charlie. I thought you would be fascinated by his face. I have watched Charlie's face intently under all manner of circumstances, but I think I never thought his expression so beautiful as one occasion in the front line when a heavy bombardment was in progress. There he sat on the firing step, while the shells whizzed and banged and crashed all over the place, with his medical case beside him, and his face looked like the face of an angel, serene with a faraway look in his eyes, as though he were sitting in a peaceful garden with beauty all around. I gazed at him and loved him. Suddenly the call came 'Stretcher-bearers'! His expression changed immediately to one of energetic purpose. He was up, bags in hand, 'Come on kid', (to a junior S.B. next to him) and he was off like a 'whizz-bang' to his case. Yes, Monie, you are right, his heart is as tender as a true woman's, and with all the strength of a true man besides. You are right too, in your psychological diagnosis of his humerous [sic] qualities. I have seen Charlie dance and caper around and keep a roomful of fellows entertained and I have seen him turn the tables on a man who was trying to pull his leg with such a mouthful of withering satire as you never heard. You would notice his stalwart physique, the result of twelve years' Boys Brigade gymnasium instruction. I can understand full well the consolation it is to you that Charlie's hands tended our laddie, though he could do nothing but reverently cross his hands on his breast and leave him until dark.

I am eagerly looking for his return tomorrow.

[...]

Somewhere in France.

Jan 12/16

My own dear lassie,

It is the hour of 6pm. and I am sitting in our barn-billet as I write this. The sweet mellow tones of Charlie's clarinet float over the partition which divides the barn into two parts. He came back the other day, a day a day [sic] after your letter with its description of your meeting. He gave me the knife, an exact replica of the one I had lost, and also 4/6 in silver from you. Thank you <u>very</u> <u>very</u> much, lassie darling. He also gave me a flashlamp from Arthur. It gives a splendid light and will be very useful. Then he remembered a letter he had for me in his pocket. It contained Arthur's £1 note and a 10/- note for Charlie. I read Arthur's short letter and then handed it to Charlie. He was much touched and declared that he didn't deserve it, and all that sort of rot, and then he laughed and confessed that he had only threepence left in his pocket. He was very pleased I could see plainly. Later we went out for a walk and he told me all the story of his leave, especially of his visit to Brighouse. He congratulated me warmly on my <u>girl</u>. It seemed strange to hear him talking about you and Arthur, and Mother and Father, as one who knew you all personally and tangibly. When we got back to the billet it was dark and I was shining my light to see the way. As we arrived at the barn-door he said, 'Just a minute, Frank, before we go in I've something else to give you – put that light out.' I put the lamp out and into my pocket, wondering what was coming. Then I felt an arm round my neck, and the dear lad kissed me once – 'that's from Evelyn' he said; then he kissed me again and said, 'that's from your Mother'. I returned his tender salute and said, 'that's from me'. There we were, two men, like a couple of girls – but then, there was no one about, and the matter was a sacred one between us, <u>and</u> <u>you</u>.

Well sweetheart, it has made me long to see you again, but I'm afraid it will be a while yet before my next leave, and as to the commission, that's a slow business too, and the war doesn't seem to present any striking signs of finishing, so there's nothing else for it but to lay in a new stock of patience.

—— • ——

JACK DORGAN was a sergeant in the 7th Battalion of the Northumberland Fusiliers. The following is taken from the Sound Archive of the Imperial War Museum, also reproduced in *Forgotten Voices of the Great War*.

During the attack on St Julien on the 26th of April a shell dropped right in amongst us, and when I pulled myself together I found myself lying in a shell-hole. There was one other soldier who, like me, was unhurt, but two more were heavily wounded, so we shouted for stretch-bearers.

Then the other uninjured chap said to me, 'We're not all here, Jack,' so I climbed out of the shell-hole and found two more of our comrades lying just a few yards from the shell-hole.

They had had their legs blown off. All I could see when I got up to them was their thigh bones. I will always remember their white thigh bones, the rest of their legs were gone. Private Jackie Oliver was one of them, and he was unconscious. I shouted back to the fellows behind me, 'Tell Reedy Oliver his brother's been wounded.' So Reedy came along and stood looking at his brother, lying there with no legs, and a few minutes later he watched him die. But the other fellow, Private Bob Young, was conscious right to the last. I lay alongside of him and said, 'Can I do anything for you, Bob?' He said, 'Straighten my legs, Jack,' but he had no legs. I touched the bones and that satisfied him. Then he said, 'Get my wife's photograph out of my breast pocket.' I took the photograph out and put it in his hands. He couldn't move, he couldn't lift a hand, he couldn't lift a finger, but somehow he held his wife's photograph on his chest. And that's how Bob Young died.

IVOR GURNEY (1890–1937) writes 'I might be a good soldier could I forget music and books', at the end of the second letter below. It was sent to Marion Scott, a musicologist and a close friend of Gurney's from their first meeting in 1912 (he was then at the Royal College of Music). Gurney was a poet and composer, born in Gloucester. He enlisted as a private in 1915, and was injured by a bullet and gas in 1917. He suffered from mental illness (showing symptoms before the war, although his experiences may have intensified them) and died in the City of London Mental Hospital in 1937.

To Catherine Abercrombie

Somewhere in France

June 1916

[...]

Once we were standing outside our dugout cleaning mess tins, when a cuckoo sounded its call from the shattered wood at the back. What could I think of but Framilode, Minsterworth, Cranham, and the old haunts of home.

This Welshman turned to me passionately. 'Listen to that damned bird,' he said. 'All through that bombardment in the pauses I could hear that infernal silly "Cuckoo, Cuckoo" sounding while Owen was lying in my arms covered with blood. How shall I ever listen again...'! He broke off, and I became aware of shame at the unholy joy that had filled my artist's mind. And what a thin keen face he had, and what a voice – for speaking I mean. Gibson may have had this same thought as he listened to the cuckoo this spring. Shakespeare also maybe –

O word of fear

Unpleasing to a soldier's ear.

But I can hardly write a coherent letter as you may guess. Never did I have such material, and never, O never was writing paper so dear; 1 franc 50 for this. A veritable horror of war!

[...]

To Marion Scott
21? June 1916

Ideal Parcel would contain matches.

Dear Miss Scott

Thank you for the amount of general interest in your letter, your pretty verses and the news about my songs, which has given me great pleasure. Of course you can use them. The Piano accompaniment is quite adequate, but as to the sacrilege of ever having a piano instead of a harp – well, I think it would be an admirable substitute. I never thought at all about the harp quality save in one or two places, but merely the getting of a background for tunes or counterpoint. Well...

I like your grey Mayday altogether – save only 'invisible like Fate', which is out of the picture. And people under counterpanes do not naturally enough suggest the labour of climbing the sky at all. Apparently he dived under the bed clothes and started work – an unusual proceeding. But I like this sonnett.

As for the other
Line 3 Verse one seems to me awkward. Why not 'on' for across? (*On* and *run* I suppose.)
Line 3 Verse 2 don't suit me at all.

But do let's have some more. (Have just received letter thank you.)

There is a gentleman in Mark Twain, who used poetry, statistics, pathos, bathos, blasphemy etc to prove his case; and won it. Write letters of this sort – anyhow letters. Run wild letters. Cockeyed and topsy turvy letters. Anything but the ordinary polite correspondence. For which I have no polite uses.

I hope this poetic outburst means that you are on the mend, and likely to be able to do more according to your desires before long. This has been a vile washout of a Spring, whateffer, look you! Today has been fine, but the sunset is closing with stormy looking clouds and cold breezes. High up in the air like harmless gnats British aeroplanes are sailing – but No Germans – and ever and again as they come round in their circles lovely little balls of white fleece, or dark fleece or occasionally ruddy, gather in their track and up above and below. But they take about as much notice as of so many peas. They go round and come back to the accompaniment of thumps like a soft tap on the bass drum when distant, or a loud tap on timpani when near.

Being in first line trenches in a soft part of the line is easily the best thing that falls to our lot out here. But lately, I have had a very soft time, being newly made (6 weeks?) a signaller, and being on an out of the way Post with two others. 'Cushy' is le mot juste. It is like Heaven to be away from our sergeant major, who, I am glad to note is not quite such a Prussian in the trenches. Give me signalling, first last and all the time. Had I but known before, O the drudgery I should have escaped!

What Ho, for the Russians! Surely that means the war is highly likely to finish soon, even quite soon? It is the Great Test, and Mr Garvin is tying himself into knots to swallow all his pessimism in time to be there first. Hey for Hilaire, who has Faith and doesn't emit noisome darkness like a squid – 'but in the first does always see the last.'

Stap me, but it's cold!

The naval news is great. I could wish no more. We had to force them into action somehow, and did it by sacrificing the cat squadron. Bien! There are men like them – proud of them – ready to do the same. Only Fritz will find some difficulty even in coming out for a bolt back.

The books I mean to lend you will arrive someday.

Songs of Joy (if it can be found)

Nature Poems

Farewell to Poesy

and

Foliage

All very good Davies, especially the first. There are some more too, if I can remember them. Yeats' later plays. Masefield's book on Shakespeare. One or two more also.

Madam, I distinctly remember that months ago you offered to send me a parcel, if the need arose. Well it – well *has* arisen. They give us quarter of a loaf in the trenches, where men may stay (1st line and reserve) a fortnight. This deserves pity – for there is no means of getting any but by taking it up, and they do not, if they can help it, allow us to carry extras. (Some day you shall hear my candid opinion of the British Officer.)

To speak very personally now –

My feelings about my being connected with the whole affair are

(1) It is a weird queer war – this, against unseen enemies.

(2) That I have really no part in it. I wake up with a start from my

dreams of books and music and home, and find I am – here, in this!

(3) That I have as little fear as anyone I have seen around me. Partly because I am more or less fatalistic; partly because my training in self-control not yet finished, has been hard enough. Partly because I possess an ingrained sense of humour. (A whizzbang missed me by inches over my head and exploded ten yards from me – and the impression it gave and gives me now is chiefly of the comic.)

(4) The conviction that prayer is no use to me.

(5) The fineness of the men. (The officers *may* develop.)

(6) My increasing love of music.

(7) An absolute belief (not so very old) that once out of the Army I can make myself fit. (Trench mortar starts.) (But does not stop the Cuckoo, which cannot be far from the battery.)

and so on.

(Queer! it is a deuced queer thing.)

(8) The conviction, also, that in hand to hand fight I shall be damned dangerous to tackle. A useful one to have; but I hope to God that He has a nice blighty ready for me and that there will be no need of such vulgar brawling – greatly against my taste as it is.

And now here's the end of my letter (Bang! Bang! – Phutt! Phutt!) and here's to the end of the war – now I must believe not very far off. (Shell goes down the chromatic scale from]

Good bye,
Yours very sincerely,
Ivor Gurney.

Letter 2

Your book – my book has just arrived, and it is finished. Only to increasing certainty that Davies was once an exquisite poet – of which time he has now but occasional memories, and that he knows himself to be failing in power and is bitter at the knowledge. I happen to know it is true, from private information, but anyone who knows his earlier work must feel sad. He is now – merely a 'boom' 'Tramp-poet'. And yet – 'April's Charms', 'The White Cascade', 'The One Singer', 'Come Thou sweet Wonder'... These are bon, but alas, after *Foliage* he is practically Na pooh. Thank you very much for so charming a present.

Thank you also for sending the *Times Literary Supplement*, but I have one sent already. However both are passed on, and read with enthusiasm by one and another.

Tonight an aeroplane has been sailing high up in the blue – right over the German lines, and occasionally leaving at his back a flock of tiny white clouds; looking so innocent as they unfold, that unless one has caught the tiny flash of the explosion it is perfectly impossible to think that these are anything but the tiny clouds of Summer W H D loves to sing of. I might be a good soldier could I forget music and books. Indeed I try to fill my still-sick mind with thoughts of these. Which makes a strange combination, as you may imagine.

A sense of beauty is every hindrance to a soldier; yet there would be no soldiers – or none such soldier had not men dead and living cherished and handed on the sacred fire.

I. B. G.

[*P.S.*] If you will send me a parcel, will you please send it when you receive a PC with 'telegram' untouched, a sign that we are either going or have gone out to trenches?

——— • ———

ERNEST SWINTON (1868–1951) was commissioned into the Royal Engineers in 1888 and served in the Boer War. He was appointed official war correspondent in the First World War by Lord Kitchener. His alarm at loss of life in the infantry made him one of the principal proponents of the tank, a prototype of which came into service in late 1916. Swinton was knighted in 1923 and was Professor of Military History at Oxford University from 1925 to 1939. The following is taken from *Twenty Years After* (1938).

It was one of the many last evenings before going again up the line. The sergeant-major came to say that a piano had been found and that for a small fee the owner was willing to let us take it to the orchard for the evening provided we kept a tarpaulin over it to keep out the damp. Would the officer come and would the adjutant play the piano? We assembled in the orchard in the dusk, 150 men lying about on the trodden grass, talking and smoking. A thin haze of tobacco smoke hung as pale blue shadow against the darkening sky, and two candles in the piano sconces gave a round blur of yellow light. The air was still and in the distance the rumble of far-off shellfire served as an echo to the thunder of the limber wagons passing along the road. We sang a chorus or two somewhat untidily to weld us into a unity of mood. Some forms had been lashed together to make a precarious platform and on this the sergeant-major, by virtue of his office the president, stood to announce that Corporal Jackson would oblige with a song. Jackson walked across to the piano. 'Music?' asked the adjutant with a smile. 'No, sir, got no music.' 'What are you going to sing?' 'Don't stop me, sir.' 'I won't, but what's the tune?' Jackson bent down and hummed into the adjutant's ear. 'Right you are, Corporal. Carry on.' Jackson walked to the centre of the stage and gave an expert shuffle with his feet to test its stability. 'Mind them boots, Corporal. The quarter's looking,' shouted someone. The words and the tune were old even in those days. 'Don't stop me. Don't stop me. I've got a job to do. T'was advertised in ninety-eight. If I'm not there I'll be too late.' Then Private Walton hunched his shoulders and adjusted the weight of his body carefully from one leg to the other until he found a position of equilibrium. From his pocket he pulled out a mouth-organ, wiped it carefully on the underside of his sleeve, shook it, knocked it gently against his palm to remove any crumbs or tobacco or biscuit then suddenly burst into harmony. He blew and tapped his foot and swayed until he made his audience sing to his tune. And then another tune forced itself onto the surface of his mind, breaking through the years and silence to remind me that Signaller Downes also stood up to sing. It was the long-drawn-out sequence of Gertie Gitana's 'Nev-vah-mind', a song which declined in speed as it grew in sentiment. The moon rose in the blue sky, grey now, mellowing the darkness and deepening the shadows under the trees. Over the subdued chatter of many voices and the noise of the occasional lighting of a match came the silvery splay of notes from the piano. The adjutant was playing quietly to himself, meditating in music. The talk ceased and men turned away from their comrades to listen until there was dead silence under the trees to make a background for the ripple of the piano. The silence broke in upon the player and he removed his hands from the keyboard for an instant. The world plunged into a deep pool of stillness, rising again to hear a supple cascade of showering notes as he played one of Debussy's arabesques. When he had finished, there was a pause for a second or two before the applause began – enough of a gap to show that the listeners had been travelling with him into a foreign land.

—— • ——

EDWARD THOMAS (1878–1917) was a poet born in London to Welsh parents and married to the writer, Helen Thomas. His *Collected Poems* were published in 1920. In July 1915 he joined the Artists' Rifles and was killed by a shell at the Battle of Arras on 9 April two years later. The following are extracts from the Faber edition of his war diary.

23 [February 1917]. Chaffinch sang once. Another dull cold day. Inspected stables, checked inventory of new billet for men in Rue Jeanne d'Arc, went with Colonel round 244, 141 and 234 positions and O.P. in Achicourt. Afternoon maps. Partridges twanging in fields. Flooded fields by stream between the 2 sides of Achicourt. Ruined churches, churchyard and railway. Sordid ruin of Estaminet with carpenter's shop over it in Rue de Jeanne d'Arc – wet, mortar, litter, almanacs, bottles, broken glass, damp beds, dirty paper, knife, crucifix, statuette, old chairs. Our cat moves with the Group wherever it goes, but inspects new house inside and out, windows, fireplace etc. Paid the Pool gunners (scrapings from several batteries doing odd jobs here). 2 owls in the garden at 6. The shelling must

have slaughtered many jackdaws but has made home for many more. Finished Frost's 'Mountain Interval'. Wrote to Frost. A quiet still evening. Rubin brought over letters from Helen and Oscar.

[…]

14 [March 1917]. Ronville O.P. Looking out towards No Man's Land what I thought first was a piece of burnt paper or something turned out to be a bat shaken at last by shells from one of the last sheds in Ronville. A dull cold morning, with some shelling of Arras and St. Sauveur and just 3 for us. Talking to Birt and Randall about Glostershire [sic] and Wiltshire, particularly Painswick and Marlborough. A still evening – blackbirds singing far off – a spatter of our machine guns – the spit of one enemy bullet – a little rain – no wind – only far-off artillery.

[…]

8 [April 1917]. A bright warm Easter day but Achicourt shelled at 12.39 and then at 2.15 so that we all retired to cellar. I had to go over to battery at 3 for a practice barrage, skirting the danger zone, but we were twice interrupted. A 5.9 fell 2 yards from me as I stood by the f/c post. One burst down the back of the office and a piece of dust scratched my neck. No firing from 2-4. Rubin left for a course.

On the last pages of the diary are these notes:

The light of the new moon and every star

And no more singing for the bird…

I never understood quite what was meant by God.

The morning chill and clear hurts my skin while it delights my mind.

Neuville in early morning with its flat straight crest with trees and houses – the beauty of this silent empty scene of no inhabitants and hid troops, but don't know why I could have cried and didn't.

Loose inside the diary, strangely creased by shell-blast like the diary, is a photograph of Helen and an army pass to Loughton/Lydd dated 3.12.16. Also a slip of paper with the addresses of S. N. Jones of Newport, H. K. Vernon of Oxford, J. N. Benson of Upper Tooting, Lewis John of Upminster, his brother Julian Thomas in Tooting. On the reverse of this in pencil is written:

Where any turn may lead to Heaven
Or any corner may hide Hell
Roads shining like river up hill after rain.

——— • ———

PAUL KLEE (1879–1940), one of the greatest Modernist painters, was born in Switzerland to a Swiss mother and a German father. He studied painting in Munich and was called up for military service in 1916. The following are excerpts from his diary.

[1916]

1021. 11.10. Guard duty on Sunday, beginning at noon; I shall have to be back at 9 a.m. Today, had to help clean up the wrecked airplane in which two flyers lost their lives day before yesterday. Badly damaged motor, etc.; really inspiring work. I told Poschenrieder that

I am often called on to help Section Two. He promises to stand by me. At least I shall have had the experience of the crashed plane.

[…]

1026. 11.17. Slept magnificently at the hotel, after having led a dirty gypsy's life since last Saturday. Cologne is sensational, polished to a smoothness, and large. Particularly impressed by it last night! The affluence in the main streets, those people in uniform! The mad railroad station. Right in front of it, that more-than-lifesize museum piece, the cathedral. The Hohenzollern bridge, totally dark and heavily guarded. The river. The sharp beams of four wily search-lights. Far above the towers of the cathedral, the bright little bar of a Zeppelin, manoeuvring gracefully, speared by one of the beams. I have never seen any city put on such a nocturnal spectacle, truly a solemn festival of evil.

Stroll over the bridges. Had coffee for breakfast. Museum: Bosch, Breughel, 'Crucifixion' by the Master of the 'Life of Mary'. Cathedral. Lunched at the Red Cross by the main railroad station, then went to the Artists' Association, then to the Deutsche Ring, as a courtesy to Wildermann, and had a look at his sculptures on the children's playground. Strolled along the Rhine, pastry shop, dinner again at the station, left for Frankfurt at 8 p.m.

[…]

1917

1089. 10.22. Arrived safely here, was glad I took the next to last train. Found much work waiting for me. Paymaster away on a trip. 'It must be done and shall be done. We'll manage it.'

10.24. Just enough work. The doctor went on leave yesterday, amid much fussing and protracted preparations. I hurry so as to have some free time, since the office is now very peaceful and makes a good studio in the evening.

10.26. I again work more in black and white than in colour. Colour seems to be a little exhausted just now; new reserves have to accumulate. If it weren't for the duties, this might be a good time to push my plastic experiments further. This is probably the only damage inflicted on me by the war. For whether I'll catch up on it later is questionable; perhaps I shall then stand at a point outside of this domain.

1090. 10.27. No miracle occurred. As the only one present, I had to be on duty and shall have to be on duty again tomorrow morning, since there will be flying. Otherwise I might at least lock the office. Perhaps the weather will be favourable in the afternoon and I'll be able to pay a last visit to the meadows along the Lech, which have become so dear to me, before the end of autumn. I worked yesterday and today as if I were at home; the only difference being that I work in my drawer, which protects me against surprises.

It was a black day for the flying school; in the morning one cadet crashed and broke a number of bones; in the afternoon a lieutenant crashed to his death from a considerable height. *Guten Appetit* for tomorrow's Sunday flying. To be sure, I sit here safe and warm and feel no war within me. The battle of Isonzo, which is becoming a disaster for the Italians, is, moreover, only being fought there so we can return home a bit sooner.

Tagore is not very heavy reading. I prefer to read the excellent futuristic lansquenet's song about the battle of Pavia or some other good work about this area. I wonder whether civilians can still travel unhampered or whether they need a pass? This is also very important.

[…]

1918

1106. 2.21. This week we had three fatal casualties; one man was smashed by the propeller, the other two crashed from the air! Yesterday, a fourth came ploughing with a loud bang into the roof of the workshop. Had been flying too low, caught on a telephone pole, bounced on the roof of the factory, turned a somersault, and collapsed upside down in a heap of wreckage. People came running from all sides; in a second the roof was black with mechanics in working clothes. Stretchers, ladders. The photographer. A human being pulled out of the debris and carried away unconscious. Loud cursing at the by-standers. First-rate movie effect. This is how a royal regiment celebrated a golden wedding. In addition, three smashed airplanes are lying about in the vicinity today. It was a fine show.

1107. 2.25. Another Sunday in camp! Paymaster suddenly forced to go on leave. I worked a lot, at least. Painted and drew and ended by forgetting completely where I was. In amazement, I caught sight of the horrible warrior's boots on my feet.

—— • ——

HORACE PIPPIN (1888–1946) was an African-American painter, born in Pennsylvania to a domestic worker. He fought in France as a corporal in the U.S. Army in 1917 and was shot in his painting arm. He was sent home in 1919. No changes have been made to the following letter, written around 1943.

my Dear friends

my life story of art. that is my art. and no one else, I will not go in to detail of all of my life. But I will hit on some of the hilights. for instant when I were a Boy I loved to make Pictures, no one paide me aney minde. But the sunday school gave a fistival this is in Goshen n.y. the A M. E [African Methodist Episcopal] — Churtch. for the sunday school members were to Give somtheing to sell. so I went to a stor and got a yard of muslin and cut it into 6 pieces and fringed them, then I drew Pictures on them such as Jesus ascending in to Heaven and so on, they were sold that night, to some one, a weeke after a old lady called me and said, did you — make them 6 doilies. I tole her I did and she said to me look at this and showed me one of the doilies. and said I washed them this is all that I have of them. and I seen a cleen pice of matieral in her hand. she did not realier that they were made with crayon; so time went on. on tell the war of 1917. I went over seas with the old 15th n.y. inf. fighting no 369 inf; this Brought out all of all the art in me. I made some seens of france, something like a hundred of them yet at last i hatto to given them up, But I can never forget suffering, and I will never forget sunset. that is when you could see it, so I came home with all of it in my mind, and I Paint from it to Day, I no nothing this is my – feature art – it came the hard way with me; I thank you,

> Horace Pippin
> 327 W. Jay st
> West Chester
> P.A.

———— • ————

STEPHEN GRAHAM (1884–1975) was a writer born in Edinburgh. He fought in the Scots Guards as a private during the war, and wrote about his experiences in *A Private in the Guards* (1919). He also published works of travel writing, detailing his journeys around Russia, Jerusalem and the Rockies. The passage below is from another work of travel writing, *The Challenge of the Dead* (1921). In this book he visits the battlefields of the Western Front after the war.

But no rhyme in any language ever expressed that lurid splash on the night-sky when a bomber was destroyed, that effusion of crimson which caused men's eyes to dilate looking up at it, that sense of dreadfulness and awe and satisfaction, that banishment of pity through fear's reaction which steeped men's minds, as if on the floor of their souls an answering red glow appeared. It was tragical to be bombed, but how much more so to see the bomber die. They died most dreadful deaths, those Zeppelin crews and aero-bus teams, and yet of course they merely died. They met the common soldier's destiny— Nevertheless you could not lessen the sensation of watching an airman's death by reasonableness. In the lurid spectacle in the heavens men saw not death but a hieroglyphic – a sign.

Men did not liken them to Lucifer cast from heaven, but their fall was like the rebel angels' fall –

With hideous ruin and combustion, down

To bottomless perdition.

Day-flying was different and affected the mind in an entirely different way. Even the stricken night-bomber, when his charred remains were seen by daylight, became in enemies' eyes nothing but honourable. The triumph over him was forgotten in a sort of triumph in him. There was a naturally chivalrous attitude towards dead airmen. That chivalry was sometimes spoiled by human jackals – but the majority nevertheless instinctively preserved it.

Many of the graves of our airmen were marked by crosses which are adorned with carven wings, and in this speaks not only a military but a human pride. Foot-soldiers did not see in the aeroplane a mere mechanical contrivance but a new human victory over matter. The feats of airmen flattered pedestrian souls, who knew thereby that they could fly if they would, flattered us all. Because men had to enter some section of the fighting services thousands chose to fly and fight who otherwise would not have been tempted off the firmer elements of land and sea. They conquered the first nausea of fear, and learned to live with danger as with a wife. They tumbled above us and we marvelled, not taking anywise into account the war-sting which started them, bidding neither sit nor stand but go. One is not sorry that the guns speak no more. One is not sorry that the night-bombers and Zeppelins have ceased to menace us. But the emptiness of the heavens by day has its sadness now in France, its human wanness and melancholy. One realises that the war brought out the flier – as it were before his time, and we must wait long ere we see in peace the state of air society which he prefigured.

Down below the airmen trudged heavy-footed men. The airmen were literally supermen; those below were a sort of undermen. In heavily weighted boots, with backs bent and not straightened by war's routine, with clumsily encumbered bodies, trudged under-humanity, through mud, along gullies, into holes and pits, down into subterranean chambers. The underman enjoyed no human exaltation except occasionally at the prospect of getting free; he had no mercurial lightness on his heels, no rapid quicksilver of mounting imagination; instead, he was gripped downward and held till he died or there was peace. It used to be a common saying that from the moment you stepped off at Havre you were a slave. You walked in the chains of the war. Men's hearts hardened. They told themselves they wanted nothing and cared nothing. Their minds fell victims to a dull passivity or false boisterousness. They banished the bright ego and took up with a Cerberus, yowled the dog-language of the army, and got selfishly irate over biscuits and slops and bully-beef. They grew more and more dirty and came out in boils. Coarse hair grew apace, brows grew lower, hands that had any cunning in them grew to mere claws and clutches, eyes dulled, and the ear-gate stood ajar for the sound of animal noises and animal confessions. The war was a Bacchanalia for the animal in man.

—— • ——

MARTIN HIEBER (1891–1917) was a student of law at Tübingen and flew fighter planes over the Western Front in the war. He was born on 18 June 1891 at Tuttlingen, Germany, and was killed on 6 July 1917, near Brimont (Rheims).

December 4th, 1916.

... I have always disliked hearing people talk of the aviator as the 'Conqueror of the Air'; of his pride in having fulfilled the dream, the longing of humanity; of the sublime sensation of being able to accomplish so much more than the feeble little beings crawling about down there on the earth, down there among the trees, roads and meadows. So much in the descriptions of those who had once 'been up' seemed to me exaggerated, or like the bragging of a scorching 'road-hog'. The flying-man who really flies does not talk about his feelings, for when one knows that everything depends on such small details, then the super-man attitude vanishes. One has a roaring engine in front of one which effectually prevents any sensation of 'boundless space and solitude'. Only gradually does one get, in addition to the consciousness of forming part of a branch of war-service where the individual man does still count for something, a real appreciation of the beauties which are continually revealed during a flight. And another feeling may be bound up with this – that of having a pull over the rest of mankind, who can't see all these things, just as the Alpine climber prides himself on being superior to people who can't reach such heights as himself.

The sensation of conquest is also, I think, only acquired by degrees. The Pilot is haunted at first by the stories of Daedalus and

Icarus; but later, when he gains in self-confidence, he is certainly more to be envied than the Observer, who after all, during a flight, occupies more the position of looker-on. My heart swells when I look down on the sunlit earth and see the mountain ranges stretched below me and the streams finding their way through the marvellous colour-scheme of green woods and meadows, dark blue sea, violet mist on the vanishing horizon, and pink cloud. The almost flat landscape here on the Somme is exceptionally beautiful from above. The broad valley with its shimmering marshes; the villages with their lush meadows; the yellowish-gold of cornfields; the roads pencilling delicate lines through this mosaic; the intervening shadows of hills: all this constitutes such a wealth of colour and form that one can hardly take in all the details at once.

But beyond the Somme and farther north – the raging battle; the churned-up earth; the blazing and smoking ruins; the never-ceasing flashes and explosions of shells; the suddenly rising columns of smoke; the constant roar of drum-fire which smothers everything in dirt and smoke: this is a gruesomely beautiful spectacle.

One only receives these impressions by degrees; the war-picture, especially, only develops quite slowly because it takes time and leisure to grasp it all, and both these conditions are only possible on the Somme during 'lucid intervals'. For here the feeling of 'boundless solitude' does not exist. About fifty aeroplanes are always whizzing about in the air. From one side a squadron of five machines is approaching; and there flies one of our Leader-Planes; there are so many observations to be made, and one must not lose touch with the rest of the Flight. Moreover it is all at the rate of 250 miles an hour. Over on the enemy's side Caudrons and

Farmans, Nieuports and B.E.'s are flying round. One can hardly distinguish friend from foe. A one-seater fighting plane goes up – one is on the alert to see if he drops – an anti-aircraft shell bursts close to one and one has to bank – four Nieuports are rising skyward, so one must get the machine-gun into position and signal to the Leader – a Nieuport is attacking a German plane – away to help him – a Halberstadt is swooping down on a Frenchman – one must have one's eyes everywhere at once. And while a fight is going on in the air – when one hears the rattle of bullets – when a Nieuport is right on top of one – or (what has only happened once so far) when he is hit and hurtles to the ground – Hurrah! – one has not much time for enjoying the 'boundless space and solitude'!

—— • ——

SIDNEY ROGERSON (1894–1968) published his First World War memoir, *Twelve Days*, in 1933. The memoir focuses on a brief period of what B. H. Liddell Hart, in the foreword, described as the 'fag-end' of the Battle of the Somme (1916).

For two reasons it is difficult to convey a satisfactory impression of that camp's surroundings. First, one had lost the habit of looking afield. This was due to the cramping effect of trench life, where a man was a member of a very small community from which, sleeping or waking, he was never separated, and was confined for days at a stretch within the narrow limits of a trench. 'Keep your head down' was a piece of advice which became second nature, with the result that, metaphorically speaking, he slunk about from hole to hole, from one piece of cover to the next, his head down, not daring, or else forgetting, to look about him. His vision changed, he began to lose the wider view, and instead to see falconwise the minutest details around, details which will ever survive in his memory. How many men who fought and lived around Ypres or Arras for months carry any mental picture of the general aspect of the countryside? But ask them to describe the Kirchner pictures pinned to the walls of their dug-out, the particular brand of bully-beef tin which hung on the wire, and they will find little difficulty.

Secondly, we had grown accustomed to living in a region where almost every natural landmark had been obliterated. Country that had once been the twin sister of the Sussex Downs, with little comfortable villages nestling round their churches in the folds of the hills, had been battered into a vast monotony of drab. Churches, houses, woods, and hedgerows had all disappeared. Our landmarks were provided for us in the shape of military noticeboards in the back areas, or by such débris as wrecked aeroplanes, derelict tanks, dead horses, and even dead men nearer the front line.

Suffice it, therefore, to say that the camp was situated on an open space of what had once been grassland between the mangled remains of Trones and Bernafay Woods. The distance was shrouded by rain and mist, from out of which the boom of gunfire came distant and muffled.

'Camp 34' itself was a camp in name only – a few forlorn grounds of rude tarpaulin-sheet shelters huddled together, as though they shrank from the surrounding desolation. One or two bell-tents there were, it is true, here and there, but even they looked as unhappy as if they knew themselves to be but insecurely at anchor in the rising sea of mud. Though even these few tarpaulin-sheets and bell-tents might have been sufficient shelter for the pitiful remnant of the Scottish regiment, they were entirely inadequate for a Battalion more or less up to strength. Since no shelter had been prepared for us, necessity forced us to take steps to procure it for ourselves. In other words, we were reduced to looting, or in the more picturesque language of the ranks, 'scrounging' additional cover. With the grim determination of the British soldier, bedraggled men set off with the hearty approval, if not the verbal permission, of their officers to see what they could find. I am not ashamed to confess that, unofficially, I strongly encouraged the more experienced soldiers – who were therefore less likely to be caught! – to scour the dripping countryside for anything likely to improve the company's accommodation, and even gave them permission to leave the camp 'to visit the canteen, sir.' Needless to say, that canteen was never discovered, but other valuable things were.

So far as I was concerned, the first incident was the arrival of the Colonel, imperturbable as always, though inwardly raging at the lack of organisation which subjected men going in to battle to such experiences. Behind him, looking indescribably sheepish, stood my young servant, Briggs.

'I congratulate you on your servant,' the Colonel said casually. 'Why, sir?' I queried. 'Well, as I walked into the very commodious trench shelter reserved for Battalion Headquarters, I saw your man walking out at the other end with the stove. And you hadn't been in camp five minutes! A good boy, that. But I'm sorry I could not spare the stove!' The Colonel smiled, and moved on.

Every minute saw an addition to 'camp stores,' the greatest triumph being the purloining, by Privates Purkiss and Kiddell, from under the very noses of the rightful owners, of a huge balloon tarpaulin which proved big enough of itself to house more than half the company! In less than a couple of hours I was satisfied that reasonably dry and warm quarters had been contrived for every man, of B Company at least. Meanwhile, a hot meal had been issued from the cookers and – the rain stopped. Spirits began to mount again, and as a setting sun was wanly mirrored in the water-logged shell-holes, snatches of song began to rise with the smoke of braziers from the improvised shelters.

Not least remarkable was the transformation of the bell-tent allotted for Company Headquarters. On arrival this had flapped lugubriously on its sagging ropes over a patch of mud, but within the hour it had been pitched afresh, taut and confident in appearance; a neighbouring R.E. dump had provided enough new trench boards for a complete floor, and a brazier had been lit.

The enlargement of that camp in so short a time is worthy to rank among the minor miracles of war.

The day closed with an issue of rum. The first stage of the relief was over.

———— • ————

A SIKH IN PALESTINE The letter below was sent by a Sikh in Palestine to his uncle. It is part of a book of translated, transcribed and censored letters from Indian soldiers serving in Palestine and Egypt during final operations against the Turks. The book was compiled in 1918 by D. C. Phillott, lieutenant colonel and chief censor at the Indian Base, Port Said. The writer is unnamed (in other letters names were cut or deliberately changed) but he was probably with a cavalry regiment on the coast of Jaffa.

After greetings, let it be known to you that by the Grace of God I am well & flourishing & even praying to God for your health & well being. I pray God that your dutiful servant may soon get a sight of you & obtain the privilege of kissing your feet. I am a traveller, & in a strange country, & have scanty leisure; these are the reasons for my not writing before. Hence you must continue to inform me of your welfare without waiting for a letter from me. Two or three days ago the Indian mail came in, but there was no letter by it from Uncle — nor from you. I did get one from my mother's brother Diyāl Singh, which said that my maternal grandmother had taken up her abode in Heaven. I grieve for her loss. Such was God's will. Strange are the ways of Providence. What dangers and vicissitudes are written in my Fate. At one time, the sufferings of heat; at another, the pains of cold. At one moment I perish from thirst; at another I have a surfeit of water. At times I roost on a rock, at times I repose on soft sand. At one time not a morsel of food; at another an abundance of grapes & melons. In short mysterious are the ways of the Immortal God. From passing through innumerable changes of life & in surroundings, the very structure of my body has undergone change. At one time from residing in a cold climate my complexion was as fair as a British soldier's; at another, from exposure to heat & sun, it was as black as a negro's. As to the hairs of my head & beard, what can I say of them? They too, poor things, have seen all sorts of changes; at one time brown, at another white, at another black. At times glossy with perfumed oils; at times begrimed with dust & dirt & so on & so on.

Now listen to a description of my present surroundings. We are camped on the sea-shore & the breeze is cool. Near my tent, that is in about one-hundred-and-fifty yards from the sea, a net is erected from it to within fifty yards of me: this net is decreed as a death-by-the-stake for poor helpless tired-out quails.

When the cold sets in, the quails migrate from cold countries to save their lives & fly to a warmer climate. After a long journey over the 'Greek Sea' (a lake) they arrive weary & worn, hungry & thirsty. When not at sea & high up in the air they view the distant land & drop joyfully to alight in it. There they are snared in the miles of nets erected by tormentors & become suspended, heads up & legs down. If by any chance any bird escapes the nets, the poor thing lies on the ground helpless from exhaustion. These are gathered by hand by the fowlers, to become delicate morsels for rich & poor.

I pray to Almighty God to guard in safety all my relatives, intimates & friends, & to hasten the day of my return to them.

—— • ——

GUY CHAPMAN (1889–1972) served with the Royal Fusiliers in France and Belgium winning the MC and twice being mentioned in despatches. After the war, he worked in publishing and married the writer Storm Jameson in 1926. He also served in the Second World War, after which he became Professor of Modern History at Leeds University. The following extract is from A Passionate Prodigality: Fragments of Autobiography (1933).

Next day we were marching. It was the 18th October and the smell of autumn lay heavy on the air; a chill colourless morning, but the sun broke through as we passed a lonely sentry before a lonely handsome château near Ranchicourt, an army or corps headquarters; at least, something too august for our acquaintance. Our trench-camped limbs were already growing aware of their novel freedom. We stepped lighter and with a rhythmical swing. That night we came to Magnicourt-en-Comté, and there we lay two days.

When we moved out, there was a nip in the air. The first frosts had come. Beeches showered us with copper and yellow coin. Briars shaken by our tread flung us the crystals from their sprays. The way was lined with brave colours; streamers of travellers' joy waved in the faint breeze and hawberries shook their crimson heads at the tramp of our boots. As we passed under a tunnel of dark trees, the band broke into its thunderous jollity. Blow, fife; rattle, drum. On this morning the clatter of *Brian Boru* is better than all Beethoven's nine symphonies. Even the immortal Ninth pales before the chorus: *And we'll buy a pair of laces orfer pore–old–Mike.* The battalion is moving as one man; very strong, very steady, with a sway in the shoulders and a lilt in the feet. We have regained our youth; we have recovered the innocence with which we came to France, an innocence not now of ignorance but of knowledge. We have forgotten whither we are marching: we do not greatly care what billets we find tonight. We are content to live in the moment, to feel the warm sun, to enjoy the strength of our bodies, and to be lulled by the rhythmical momentum with which we march. We are no longer individuals but a united body. The morning, the sun, the keen air, and the rhythm of our feet compound a draught more heady than the doctored *vin blanc,* than the forgotten kisses of the girl in the billet. Few had forebodings of their destiny. At the halts they lay in the long wet grass and gossiped, enormously at ease. The whistle blew. They jumped for their equipment. The little grey figure of the colonel far ahead waved its stick. Hump your pack and get a move on. The next hour, man, will bring you three miles nearer to your death. Your life and your death are nothing to these fields – nothing, no more than it is to the man planning the next attack at G.H.Q. You are not even a pawn. Your death will not prevent future wars, will not make the world safe for your children. Your death means no more than if you had died in your bed, full of years and respectability, having begotten a tribe of young. Yet by your courage in tribulation, by your cheerfulness before the dirty devices of this world, you have won the love of those who have watched you. All we remember is your living face, and that we loved you for being of our clay and our spirit.

—— • ——

STUART CLOETE (1897–1976) was a South African novelist and essayist. He was born in Paris to a Scottish mother and South African father. He was educated at Lancing College in Sussex and was commissioned second lieutenant at the beginning of the First World War in 1914, at the age of seventeen, in the Ninth King's Own Yorkshire Light Infantry. The passage below is from his memoir A *Victorian Son* (1972) and refers to his experiences on the Somme, when, at the age of nineteen, he was an acting captain in charge of a company.

The sun swelled up the dead with gas and often turned them blue, almost navy blue. Then, when the gas escaped from their bodies, they dried up like mummies and were frozen in their death positions. There was even a man bandaging himself who had been killed by a shell fragment as he unrolled the bandage. There were sitting bodies, kneeling bodies, bodies in almost every position, though naturally most of them lay on their bellies or on their backs. The crows had pecked out the eyes of some and rats lived on bodies that lay in the abandoned dugouts or half-buried in the crumbled trenches. These rats were very large and many of them piebald, blotched with pink, where they had lost great patches of their hair. They were quite fearless, their familiarity with the dead having made them contemptuous of the living. One night one fell on my face in a dugout and bit me. It must have been running along a beam above me and the vibration of a shell exploding nearby had knocked it off.

Burial was impossible. In ordinary warfare the bodies went down with the limbers that brought up the rations. Now there were hundreds, thousands, not merely ours but German as well. And where we fought several times over the same ground bodies became incorporated in the material of the trenches themselves. In one place we had to dig through corpses of Frenchmen who had been killed and buried in 1915. These bodies were putrid, of the consistency of Camembert cheese. I once fell and put my hand right through the belly of a man. It was days before I got the smell out of my nails. I remember wondering if I could get blood poisoning and thinking it would be ironic to have survived so much and then be killed by a long-dead Frenchman.

The only previous experience I had had of rotting bodies had been at Serre, where, as a battalion, we dealt with the best part of a thousand dead who came to pieces in our hands. As you lifted a body by its arms and legs they detached themselves from the torso, and this was not the worst thing. Each body was covered inches deep with a black fur of flies which flew up into your face, into your mouth, eyes and nostrils, as you approached. The bodies crawled with maggots. There had been a disaster here. An attack by green, badly led troops who had had too big a rum ration — some of them had not even fixed their bayonets — against a strong position where the wire was still uncut. They hung like washing on the barbs. Like scarecrows which scared no crows since they were edible. The birds disputed the bodies with us. This was a job for all ranks. No one could expect the men to handle these bodies unless the officers did their share. We worked with sandbags on our hands, stopping every now and then to puke.

[…]

This period was extraordinary. A terrible nightmare of fear, hardship, exhaustion and unbelievable loneliness. I had lived with two gods – Mr Luck and Mr Death. I was not particularly afraid of being killed. I think what most of us feared was being crippled, blinded or hit in the genitals. There seems to be a natural instinct when fighting to lean forward, bending to protect them. Freud's castration complex is a reality in action.

[…]

The Somme Battle was a period of fantastic contrasts. One day while the battalion was being rested and fattened up with food and new drafts of men I could be galloping Rajah over untouched fields, riding down partridges – if you marked them, they generally made three flights, you could catch them if you could find them – and the next we were back in it. It was a period of summer hayfields, singing birds and flowers on the one hand, and of mud, blood and the stink of dead bodies on the other, with nothing to separate these two worlds, the summer idyll and the inferno, but a few hours of marching time.

[...]

I was out of it in the best possible way [Cloete was wounded in August 1916] for a while. But thinking it over I was amazed at the courage I had seen. I had not had time to think of it before. Of all the men I had seen hit. Of the badly wounded men lying on stretchers by the aid posts and casualty clearing stations. I had hardly heard one cry out. When they were hit they would gasp and say, 'I'm hit', and someone would shout for stretcher bearers. Word would be passed on, echoing down the line. I have heard boys on their stretchers crying with weakness, but all they ever asked for was water or a cigarette. The exception was a man hit through the palm of the hand. This I believe to be the most painful wound there is, as the sinews of the arm contract, tearing as if on a rack. Men with stomach wounds moaned. Otherwise there was silence.

—— • ——

JOE MURRAY was an ordinary seaman in the Hood Battalion, Royal Naval Division. This is a transcription of a recording made by the BBC in 1964 that is preserved in the Imperial War Museum Sound Archive and was printed in *Forgotten Voices of the Great War*.

Dysentery was a truly awful disease that could rob a man of the last vestiges of human dignity before it killed him. A couple of weeks before getting it my old pal was as smart and upright as a guardsman. Yet after about ten days it was dreadful to see him crawling about, his trousers round his feet, his backside hanging out, his shirt all soiled – everything was soiled. He couldn't even walk.

So I took him by one arm and another pal got hold of him by the other, and we dragged him to the latrine. It was degrading, when you remember how he was just a little while ago. Neither my other pal nor I were very good – but we weren't like that. Anyway, we lowered him down next to the latrine. We tried to keep the flies off him and to turn him round – put his backside towards the trench. But he simply rolled into his foot-wide trench, half-sideways, head first in the slime. We couldn't pull him out, we didn't have enough strength, and he couldn't help himself at all. We did eventually get him out but he was dead, he'd drowned in his own excrement.

———— • ————

S. W. BROWN was part of the Ambulance Service Corps and won a Military Medal for his service. This short letter, sent to the BBC on 2 August 1963, tells a single anecdote of a curious mistake made whilst in Neuve Chapelle in France. Brown was responding to the BBC's 1963 call for 'vivid' memories of the war. The aim was to produce a 26-part documentary series for the half-centenary. *The Great War* series was first broadcast in 1964, and featured eyewitnesses reminiscing against black-and-white film footage. Only a small number of veterans who responded to the initial call were interviewed; the majority of veterans' letters were unanswered. Many of the responses in this book have been reproduced here for the first time.

2. 8. 63

Dear Sirs,

I served with the A.S.C. in 1915 attached to the 11th India Field Ambulance, Lahore Div with horse ambulance. One night I had to go up to get some wounded from dressing station in the Neuve Chappel district. Among those we got was one who had a boot lace with what we thought were figs but when we looked again we found they were ears.

Yours,

S. W. Brown M. M.

Fleet

———— • ————

A. F. HIBBERT was a gunner in the Royal East Kent Mounted Rifles, serving in Gallipoli. The following is the text of his 1963 letter to the BBC.

GALLIPOLI

Banstead

Surrey

12. 7. 1963.

Referring to Radio Times July 6th-12th. The Great War 1914-18. I herewith send you anecdote which happened to me during the first 18 months of the 1914-18 War.

(1.)

In July 1915 at Cape Helles Gallipoli my comrade and myself erected a small bivouac a few yards from the trenches and we both noticed a very nasty smell during the night and removing a small quantity of sand in the morning we found we had been lying on a dead Turk as he had been partly buried there.

(2.)

Another incident at Gallipoli December 1915. After coming out of the trenches at night my comrade and myself went to the cookhouse and enjoyed a feed of which we thought was rice and currants, the next morning we were told by the cook it was plain rice & the lid had been left off the dixie the feed, therefore, was rice and flies.

Gunner A.F. HIBBERT

Royal East Kent Mounted RIFLES 1914

CAPTAIN. MACHINE GUN CORP. 1918.

—— • ——

E. W. J. EDGLEY was a lieutenant in the Loyal North Lancashires who saw action in the major battlefields of the Western Front. This letter was another response to the call for memories for the BBC's *Great War* series.

THE SCHOOL OF INFANTRY,

SUPPORT WEAPONS WING,

NETHERAVON, WILTS.

17th September 1963

THE GREAT WAR.

I served in France and Flanders during the whole of 1917 and the first half of 1918.

I was then a Lieutenant in the 2/4th Batt. The Loyal North Lancashire Regt, (now The Loyal Regiment) of 170 Brigade in 57 Division, but served during this period in the 170th Light Trench Mortar Battery, which usually co-operated with my Battalion.

My strongest recollections are: –

(1) Mud.

(2) The difficulty of movement in the mud and the hopelessness of the attacks at Passchendaele.

(3) The size of the rats in the ramparts at Ypres.

and in retrospect, the patience and endurance of the soldiers.

E. W. J. Edgley

(Major E. W. J. Edgley TD Retired)

—— • ——

TOM ADLAM, VC was an officer in the 7th Battalion, Beds and Herts Regiment. The following passage is from the Imperial War Museum Sound Archive and was reprinted in *Forgotten Voices of the Great War.*

We'd been in the reserve when our battalion was called in to try and straighten out the line. Then just before we went up, my CO was called away so I was put in charge of the company. I was briefed at headquarters and it was impressed upon me that we had to do this at night, because they'd already tried several times in daylight and been held up by various strongpoints. So we had to get into the trench at night, then try and bomb our way to these strongpoints.

Luckily, just before we started the attack my CO came back and took over. But by then it had taken us so long to get into position it was almost daylight. I knew we weren't supposed to do this in daylight but the CO said, 'We'll get over.' The section of trench my platoon faced was only about a hundred yards away, so we did get quite a long way before the machine-guns started up.

We dived into shell-holes and I thought, 'We've got to get into this trench somehow or other.' So I went crawling along from shell-hole to shell-hole till I came to the officer in charge of the next platoon. I said, 'What do you think, Father?' (We all called him Father, it was his nick-name.) He said, 'I'm going to wait till it gets dark then crawl back. We can't go forward.' I said, 'Well, I think we can. Where I am, I'm not more than fifty yards from the trench.'

He shook hands with me solemnly and said, 'Goodbye, old man.' I said, 'Don't be such a damn fool. I'll be back all right.' I got back to my platoon and said to them, 'Get a bomb in your hand, pull out the pin and hold it tight. As soon as I yell "charge", stand up, run two or three yards and throw it. And I think we'll get into that trench, there's practically no wire in front of it.'

And they did. They all got up and ran, and we got into our bit of trench. In it, we found bags of German bombs that looked like condensed milk cans on the top of sticks. On them was written '5 secs', so I experimented with one. I pulled the string and said, 'I'm going to count one, two, three, before I throw it.' My servant was beside me looking over the top of the trench and he said, 'Bloody good shot, sir, hit the bugger in the chest.' I think when the Germans found their own bombs coming back at them it rather put the wind up them.

So the men brought armfuls of these bombs along, and I just went gaily along, throwing these bombs and shouting, 'one, two, three' each time. It was most effective. Then we got close to where the machine-gun was, and got a whole lot of bombs ready. I started throwing as fast as I could until my servant said, 'They're going, sir, they're going.' So I yelled, 'Come on, chaps, run in,' and we charged up the trench. We never caught the Germans, but we drove them out.

Eventually we got to a certain point and the CO saw two trenches leading up towards Schwaben Redoubt. And he said, 'It would be a good idea to get an advance post up there.' So they started off and a man got killed straight away. I said, 'Oh, damn it. Let me go, I can do it.' So I went on with some men and we bombed up the trench. We took more prisoners in dugouts and got our advance point out towards the enemy.

Then we went back for the night. Some grub came up and we sat down and had a meal. Then another company came up and took over from us, and we moved a quarter of a mile back. We were able to rest, then lined up again next morning. The attack on Schwaben Redoubt was going to be at one o'clock, and as our company had done most of the fighting the day before they put us in the last line of the attack, with three other companies in front. We got in position at twelve, and chatted away to keep our spirits up. Told dirty stories and made crude remarks. There was a nasty smell about and of course we all suggested somebody had had an accident. But it wasn't that, it was a dead body I think.

Then the shelling started and we went forward. You wouldn't think anything could have lived through the bombing that went on at Schwaben Redoubt. By the time we got close to it there was a huge mine crater there about fifty feet across. It was lined with Germans popping away at us. So I got hold of the old bombs again and started bombing them out. After a bit we got them out and started charging the trench, all my men coming on behind very gallantly. We'd got right to within striking distance of Schwaben Redoubt itself when I got a bang in my right arm and found I was bleeding. But having been a bombing officer who could throw with both arms I was able to use my left one for a time. I found I could bomb pretty well with it.

We went on for some time, holding this position and working our way up the trenches as far as we could. Then my CO came up and said, 'You're hurt, Tom.' I said, 'Only a snick in the arm.' He said, 'Let's have a look at it,' and he put a field dressing on it. He said, 'You go back, you've done enough.' So I sat down for a time, and the fighting went on.

It was a surprise when I got the VC for my actions, because I just did a job out there, I'd never realised there was anything unusual about it.

———— • ————

FORD MADOX FORD, formerly Ford Hermann Hueffer (1873–1939), was born in Surrey to a German father and an English mother. He was a writer, a novelist, and one of the most important contributors to literary Modernism. His best-known pre-war novel is *The Good Soldier* (1915). He enlisted in 1915 and served as an officer on the Western Front, where he suffered concussion and consequent memory loss. His tetralogy *Parade's End* drew on many of his experiences, including one of the incidents described below in a letter to the writer Joseph Conrad.

9/Welch

19th Div., B. E. F.

6. 9. 16

My dear,

I will continue, 'for yr information and necessary action, please,' my notes upon sounds.

In woody country heavy artillery makes *most* noise, because of the echoes – and most prolonged in a *diluted* way.

On marshland – like the Romney Marsh – the *sound* seems alarmingly close: I have seldom heard the *Hun* artillery in the middle of a strafe except on marshy land. The *sound*, not the diluted sound, is also at its longest in the air. [An arrow is drawn from the 'e' in the following paragraph to the 'e' in this paragraph.]

On dry down land the sound is much *sharper*; it hits *you* & shakes *you*. On clay land it shakes the ground & shakes you thro' the ground. A big naval (let us say) gun, fired, unsuspected by us out of what resembled (let us say) a dead mule produced the 'e' that I have marked with an arrow.

In hot, dry weather, sounds give me a headache – over the brows & across the skull, inside, like migraine. In wet weather one minds them less, tho' dampness of the air makes them seem nearer.

Shells falling on a church: these make a huge '*corump*' sound, followed by a noise like crockery falling off a tray – as the roof tiles fall off. If the roof is not tiled you can hear the stained glass, sifting mechanically until the next shell. (Heard in a church square, on each occasion, about 90 yds away.) Screams of women penetrate all these sounds – but I do not find that they agitate me as they have done at home. (Women in cellars round the square. Oneself running thro' fast.)

Emotions again: I saw two men and three mules (the first time I saw a casualty) killed by one shell. A piece the size of a pair of corsets went clear thro' one man, the other just fell – the mules hardly any visible mark. These things gave me no *emotion* at all – they seemed *obvious*; rather as it wd. be. A great many patients on stretchers – a thousand or so in a long stream is very depressing – but, I fancy, mostly because one thinks one will be going back into it.

When I was in hospital a man three beds from me died *very* hard, blood passing thro' bandages and he himself crying perpetually, 'Faith! Faith! Faith!' It was very disagreeable as long as he had a chance of life – but one lost all interest and forgot him when one heard he had none.

Fear;

This of course is the devil – & worst because it is so very capricious. Yesterday I was buying – or rather not buying – flypapers in a shop under a heap of rubbish. The woman was laughing & saying that all the flies came from England. A shell landed in the chateau into whose wall the shop was built. One Tommie said, 'Crump!' Another: 'Bugger the flies' & slapped himself. The woman – about thirty, quick, & rather jewish – went on laughing. I said, 'Mais je vous assure, Madame, qu'il n'y a plus comme ça de mouches chez nous.' No interruption, emotion, vexed at getting no flypapers. Subconscious emotion, 'thank God the damn thing's burst.'

Yet today, passing the place, I wanted to gallop past it & positively trembled on my horse. Of course I cdnt. gallop because there were Tommies in the street.

Yrs,

——— • ———

RONALD SKIRTH (1897–1977) was born in Chelmsford and grew up in Bexhill-on-Sea. He volunteered for service and was a bombardier in the Royal Garrison Artillery. He became disillusioned with the war and with his commanding officer. After the Battle of Passchendaele, in which he suffered concussion and shell-shock, he was moved to the Italian Front. Here he made deliberate miscalculations in setting British guns so that the enemy should have a chance to evacuate an area. He left a notoriously contrary set of papers to the Imperial War Museum, some contemporaneous, some written later. A selection was edited by Duncan Barrett and published in book form under the title *The Reluctant Tommy* (2010).

Just then the Old Man [Skirth's commanding officer, Major Snow] appeared from behind his partition. He almost froze me with a frown. But again the silence was broken by a roaring low overhead and before he could speak a salvo of shells all burst together. The combined crashes were followed by a series of rapid crumps and muffled explosions and then one vast crack that made the pill-Box quiver.

'My God!' I called to Jock. 'That's our ammo gone up, Harry's there with—' I didn't finish for I was watching Snow's face. Shelling or not, the showdown was coming. Jock was depending on me.

More shells burst close outside, making the Pill Box floor tremble. Fritz was making up for lost time now.

Our Commander had been taken aback by the suddenness of the outburst. Now he stepped towards me, glowering. I must let him make the first move. Desperation, or near-madness, dispelled all my fear of the madman I was facing. I felt no anger now, only a chilly contempt for this monster who for eight months had intimidated and humiliated me. I steeled myself, determined to make the stand I knew was necessary. I turned myself into a sort of spectator, watching and listening to <u>another</u> nineteen-year-old youth defy his Commanding Officer.

'Bombardier, why did you leave your post without permission?'

'I thought it necessary, sir.'

'That is an insolent remark.'

More shells were flying over. They were falling and bursting nearer.

'Sorry sir, I can't hear with that damn noise going on. I wish to make a report.'

'This is insolence. If I want a report from you I'll ask for it. Get up, Gunner Shiels, the bombardier will take over.'

'Do as the O.C. orders, Jock.'

Jock left the table and moved towards our sleeping area.

'Sit down.'

From sheer force of habit I obeyed, removing my helmet and placing it on my end of the table. Then, suddenly realising I was faltering in my intentions, I pushed the chair back and stood up defiantly.

'I said <u>sit down</u>! That is an order.'

(Standing) '<u>I</u> said I wish to report to you that—'

'Damn it, man. This is insubordination! Have you taken leave of your senses?'

'Perhaps, sir.'

'<u>That is</u> insolence!'

Snow thrust himself into the chair, picked up the dead telephone to No. 1 Gun and buzzed. No reply, of course. I remained standing. Snow, now fuming, turned to Jock and shouted, 'This line is cut. Get outside, trace the fault and repair it.'

'Better obey orders, Jock.' (He picked up his box of repair gear.) 'Wait for me, I'm coming too, in a moment.'

'You will not leave your post, Bombardier. I am giving you an order: SIT DOWN.'

(Still standing.) 'Gunner Shiels will <u>not</u> repair the dead line, sir. It is unnecessary. There are no men at No. 1 Gun. Repeat. <u>NO MEN</u>. <u>That</u> is what I am reporting.'

'I am placing you under arrest.'

'No sir. You can't, sir. There are not enough men present for you to arrest anybody.'

Outside there came more roaring and more deafening crashes. I was amazed at my temerity. I still felt like an onlooker, not a participant.

Snow rose from his chair, his face paler than I had ever seen it. I lifted my helmet from the table and put it on. Jock reappeared. He had been listening between the gas curtains. Over the din we could hear Snow raving – 'Disobeying orders ... death penalty' etc., – none of which threats meant anything to me then. My eyes were following the movement of his hand towards the holster at his hip. This was a development I hadn't foreseen. So we'd not only got a lunatic but a homicidal one. Jock had seen the danger, pulled the candle out of the nearest bottle and grasped it by its neck. (I remembered a demonstration of unarmed combat we had seen at Aldershot; I knew exactly where to put the boot in if Snow drew his pistol.) Jock and I backed to the doorway. His tinhat and respirator were on, the bottle ready for hurling. I gestured to him to get out. Then I stepped back.

At the gas curtain I shouted; 'My pal and I have had enough of you, and your bloody war. We're getting out of it. Understand? We're getting out.'

I don't think he was able to grasp the full significance of the words he heard or the evidence of his eyes. I am certain it was the first time in his military career he had encountered open defiance from his men.

My final words to him were, 'Call it desertion, if you like. Call it cowardice if you like. Call it any bloody thing. Jock and I are off.'

Jock's final message to him was, 'And go to bloody hell!'

Snow's hand was still on the holster when we left.

———— • ————

FREDERICK WALTER NOYES was in the Fifth Canadian Field Ambulance. This is an excerpt from his book *Stretcher Bearers...at the Double!* (1937).

[July 1916]

'We Summer at Boeschepe'

Boeschepe is a French town of 2,500 souls. It lies about one mile from the Belgian frontier and approximately the same distance northeast of Mont des Cats. Here the men had a real home and it remained our headquarters until late in August.

The Fifth's job was to run a rest camp, consisting of a marquee and about a dozen bell tents and a 'self-inflicted hospital' in the local school house, where those men who had deliberately wounded themselves received treatment.

Opposite the schoolhouse was a orderly room where courts-martial were held and we regretfully record that some of the scenes therein enacted left us stunned with horror and sickened with disgust. It seemed to us that many of the poor lads who came before their military judges in this place received very unsympathetic hearings from the officers appointed to try them. We wondered whether any consideration ever was given to the fact that a prisoner was a volunteer soldier, had borne himself bravely in many battles and was no longer in control of his mental and physical reactions – that he was merely a physical and mental wreck because of many terrible months of exhausting trench life. We used to wonder (and still do!) what some of those well-fed, comfortably-billeted, all-powerful trail officers would have done had they been through the same tragic circumstances their prisoner had experienced – had been obliged to eat the same food; undergo the laborious work of digging trenches, dugouts, etc; carry the same weight on long marches and in the Line; depend on the occasional issue of rum, instead of having the ever-available bottle of Scotch from the Officers' Supplies Stores, and go through in general all the innumerable dispiriting ordeals reserved for the common soldier only.

All too often were the medical officers called upon to officiate at the post-mortem of some young lad who had been shot for 'desertion' – some mother's son who had enlisted with the ideal to uphold all that was good and noble and righteous, and had carried on until his brain and body had reached the breaking point. Surely there must have been some other way out, than by having him shot down in cold blood by his own comrades. 'Shot for desertion' was the way the court records closed such a case, but we wonder if the correct entry should not have read 'MURDERED, *by the Prussianism in our own army!'*

We have in mind one young infantryman, under twenty, who was shot for desertion. A Field Ambulance lad who was waiting to bring the boy's body away, became sick to his stomach and attempted to avoid witnessing the actual execution. The officer in charge of the shooting party forced him, under threat of severe punishment, to remain and watch the poor victim's frightful death. The padre who was with the infantryman during his final few hours was hysterical for many hours afterwards. A brother of the executed lad was a member of the same unit. His reaction to the trial and execution of his unfortunate brother must have been terrible.

It might be said that these officer judges were, themselves, victims of the military machine. To a great extent they were – but their very rank implied a certain amount of willingness to act as trial officers and acquiesce in the verdicts of courts-martial.

Humphrey Cobb has stated that a soldier always looks through lenses made of the insignia of his own rank. We are trying to present the case for the victims of such courts as seen through our lenses – even though those lenses showed us a distorted picture. Surely similar injustices should not be permitted to take place in any future war!

[...]

Do you remember how one of our Horse Transport men served first field punishment at this place, being tied to a wheel and undergoing all the other indignities of this manifestation of so-called army justice? Were you there the day Solley showed his rations to Captain Silcox, complaining that there was not sufficient for a man to live on – and the Captain remarked, 'I would consider that ample ration for myself.'? Solley looked his disgust. 'There might be enough for you, sir, but not for a man!' Solley, of course, meant that there wasn't sufficient for one who had to work as hard as he was working just then.

Were you there that dark night at Zillebeke when our bearers were busy collecting wounded from the Maple Copse area? Happy Carlisle was stumbling about in the inky blackness when an infantryman told him to stop walking on the bodies of the dead! 'What do you mean?' retorted Happy, stepping gingerly off what he took to be some bundles of sandbags. 'Why, that's our corporal in one sack and our sergeant in the other,' complained the infantryman 'and you've been walking all over them!'.

—— • ——

ELLEN N. LA MOTTE (1873–1961) was born in Kentucky, and trained as a nurse at John Hopkins Hospital. She worked in a field hospital in Belgium from 1915 onwards. *The Backwash of War: The Human Wreckage of the Battlefield as Witnessed by an American Hospital Nurse* was first published in 1916. Below is the introduction and first section, 'Heroes'.

This war has been described as 'Months of boredom, punctuated by moments of intense fright.' The writer of these sketches has experienced many 'months of boredom,' in a French military field hospital, situated ten kilometres behind the lines, in Belgium. During these months, the lines have not moved, either forward or backward, but have remained dead-locked, in one position. Undoubtedly, up and down the long-reaching kilometres of 'Front' there has been action, and 'moments of intense fright' have produced glorious deeds of valour, courage, devotion, and nobility. But when there is little or no action, there is a stagnant place, and in a stagnant place there is much ugliness. Much ugliness is churned up in the wake of mighty, moving forces. We are witnessing a phase in the evolution of humanity, a phase called War – and the slow, onward progress stirs up the slime in the shallows, and this is the Backwash of War. It is very ugly. There are many little lives foaming up in the backwash. They are loosened by the sweeping current, and float to the surface, detached from their environment, and one glimpses them, weak, hideous, repellent. After the war, they will consolidate again into the condition called Peace.

After this war, there will be many other wars, and in the intervals there will be peace. So it will alternate for many generations. By examining the things cast up in the backwash, we can gauge the progress of humanity. When clean little lives, when clean little souls boil up in the backwash, they will consolidate, after the final war, into a peace that shall endure. But not till then.

Heroes

When he could stand it no longer, he fired a revolver up through the roof of his mouth, but he made a mess of it. The ball tore out his left eye, and then lodged somewhere under his skull, so they bundled him into an ambulance and carried him, cursing and screaming, to the nearest field hospital. The journey was made in double-quick time, over rough Belgian roads. To save his life, he must reach the hospital without delay, and if he was bounced to death jolting along at breakneck speed, it did not matter. That was understood. He was a deserter, and discipline must be maintained. Since he had failed in the job, his life must be saved, he must be nursed back to health, until he was well enough to be stood up against a wall and shot. This is War. Things like this also happen in peace time, but not so obviously.

At the hospital, he behaved abominably. The ambulance men declared that he had tried to throw himself out of the back of the ambulance, that he had yelled and hurled himself about, and spat blood all over the floor and blankets – in short, he was very disagreeable. Upon the operating table, he was no more reasonable. He shouted and screamed and threw himself from side to side, and it took a dozen leather straps and four or five orderlies to hold him in position, so that the surgeon could examine him. During this commotion, his left eye rolled about loosely upon his cheek, and from his bleeding mouth he shot great clots of stagnant blood, caring not where they fell. One fell upon the immaculate white uniform of the Directrice, and stained her, from breast to shoes. It was disgusting. They told him it was *La Directrice*, and that he must be careful. For an instant he stopped his raving, and regarded her fixedly with his remaining eye, then took aim afresh, and again covered her with his coward blood. Truly it was disgusting.

To the *Médecin Major* it was incomprehensible, and he said so. To attempt to kill oneself, when, in these days, it was so easy to die with honour upon the battlefield, was something he could not understand. So the *Médecin Major* stood patiently aside, his arms crossed, his supple fingers pulling the long black hairs on his bare arms, waiting. He had long to wait, for it was difficult to get the man under the anaesthetic. Many cans of ether were used, which went to prove that the patient was a drinking man. Whether he had acquired the habit of hard drink before or since the war could not be ascertained; the war had lasted a year now, and in that time many habits may be formed. As the *Médecin Major* stood there, patiently fingering the hairs on his hairy arms, he calculated the amount of ether that was expended – five cans of ether, at so many francs a can – however, the ether was a donation from America, so it did not matter. Even so, it was wasteful.

At last they said he was ready. He was quiet. During his struggles, they had broken out two big teeth with the mouth gag, and that added a little more blood to the blood already choking him. Then the *Médecin Major* did a very skilled operation. He trephined the skull, extracted the bullet that had lodged beneath it, and bound back in place that erratic eye. After which the man was sent over to the ward, while the surgeon returned hungrily to his dinner, long overdue.

In the ward, the man was a bad patient. He insisted upon tearing off his bandages, although they told him that this meant bleeding to death. His mind seemed fixed on death. He seemed to want to die, and was thoroughly unreasonable, although quite conscious. All of which meant that he required constant watching and was a perfect nuisance. He was so different from the other patients, who wanted to live. It was a joy to nurse them. This was the *Salle* of the *Grands Blessés*, those most seriously wounded. By expert surgery, by expert nursing, some of these were to be returned to their homes again, *réformés,* mutilated for life, a burden to themselves and to society; others were to be nursed back to health, to the point at which they could again shoulder eighty pounds of marching kit, and be torn to pieces again on the firing line. It was a pleasure to nurse such as these. It called forth all one's skill, all one's humanity. But to nurse back to health a man who was to be court-martialled and shot, truly that seemed a dead-end occupation.

They dressed his wounds every day. Very many yards of gauze were required, with gauze at so many francs a bolt. Very much ether, very much iodoform, very many bandages – it was an expensive business, considering. All this waste for a man who was to be shot, as soon as he was well enough. How much better to expend this upon the hopeless cripples, or those who were to face death again in the trenches.

The night nurse was given to reflection. One night, about midnight, she took her candle and went down the ward, reflecting. Ten beds on the right hand side, ten beds on the left hand side, all full. How pitiful they were, these little soldiers, asleep. How irritating they were, these little soldiers, awake. Yet how sternly they contrasted with the man who had attempted suicide. Yet did they contrast, after all? Were they finer, nobler, than he? The night nurse, given to reflection, continued her rounds.

In bed number two, on the right, lay Alexandre, asleep. He had received the *Médaille Militaire* for bravery. He was better now, and that day had asked the *Médecin Major* for permission to smoke. The *Médecin Major* had refused, saying that it would disturb the other patients. Yet after the doctor had gone, Alexandre had produced a cigarette and lighted it, defying them all from behind his *Médaille Militaire*. The patient in the next bed had become violently nauseated in consequence, yet Alexandre had smoked on, secure in his *Médaille Militaire*. How much honour lay in that?

Here lay Félix, asleep. Poor, querulous, feeble-minded Félix, with a foul fistula, which filled the whole ward with its odour. In one sleeping hand lay his little round mirror, in the other, he clutched his comb. With daylight, he would trim and comb his moustache, his poor, little drooping moustache, and twirl the ends of it.

Beyond lay Alphonse, drugged with morphia, after an intolerable day. That morning he had received a package from home, a dozen pears. He had eaten them all, one after the other, though his companions in the beds adjacent looked on with hungry, longing eyes. He offered not one, to either side of him. After his gorge, he had become violently ill, and demanded the basin in which to unload his surcharged stomach.

Here lay Hippolyte, who for eight months had jerked on the bar of a captive balloon, until appendicitis had sent him into hospital. He was not ill, and his dirty jokes filled the ward, provoking laughter, even from dying Marius. How filthy had been his jokes – how they had been matched and beaten by the jokes of others. How filthy they all were, when they talked with each other, shouting down the length of the ward.

Wherein lay the difference? Was it not all a dead-end occupation, nursing back to health men to be patched up and returned to the trenches, or a man to be patched up, court-martialled and shot? The difference lay in the Ideal.

One had no ideals. The others had ideals, and fought for them. Yet had they? Poor selfish Alexandre, poor vain Félix, poor gluttonous Alphonse, poor filthy Hippolyte – was it possible that each cherished ideals, hidden beneath? Courageous dreams of freedom and patriotism? Yet if so, how could such beliefs fail to influence their daily lives? Could one cherish standards so noble, yet be himself so ignoble, so petty, so commonplace?

At this point her candle burned out, so the night nurse took another one, and passed from bed to bed. It was very incomprehensible. Poor, whining Félix, poor whining Alphonse, poor whining Hippolyte, poor whining Alexandre – all fighting for *La Patrie*. And against them the man who had tried to desert *La Patrie*.

So the night nurse continued her rounds, up and down the ward, reflecting. And suddenly she saw that these ideals were imposed from without – that they were compulsory. That left to themselves, Félix, and Hippolyte, and Alexandre, and Alphonse would have had no ideals. Somewhere, higher up, a handful of men had been able to impose upon Alphonse, and Hippolyte, and Félix, and Alexandre, and thousands like them, a state of mind which was not in them, of themselves. Base metal, gilded. And they were all harnessed to a great car, a Juggernaut, ponderous and crushing, upon which was enthroned Mammon, or the Goddess of Liberty, or Reason, as you like. Nothing further was demanded of them than their collective physical strength – just to tug the car forward, to cut a wide swath, to leave behind a broad path along which could follow, at some later date, the hordes of Progress and Civilisation. Individual nobility was superfluous. All the Idealists demanded was physical endurance from the mass.

Dawn filtered in through the little square windows of the ward. Two of the patients rolled on their sides, that they might talk to one another. In the silence of early morning their voices rang clear.

'Dost thou know, *mon ami*, that when we captured that German battery a few days ago, we found the gunners chained to their guns?'

PARIS
18 December, 1915

——— • ———

SARAH MACNAUGHTAN (1864–1916) was a volunteer nurse and writer. Her diaries, which detailed her work at home in Belgium, in Russia and on the Persian Front were published after her death in a collection entitled *My War Experiences in Two Continents* (1919).

[September 1914]
We arrived at Antwerp on the 22nd, twenty-four hours late. The British Consul sent carriages etc to meet us. Drove to the large Philharmonic Hall, which has been given to us as a hospital. Immediately after breakfast we began to unpack beds, etc., and our

enormous store of medical things; all feeling remarkably empty and queer, but put on heroic smiles and worked like mad

[…]

27 *September* – Yesterday, when we were in the town, a German airship flew overhead and dropped bombs. A lot of guns fired at it, but it was too high up to hit. The incident caused some excitement in the streets.

Last night we heard that more wounded were coming in from the fighting-line near Ghent. We got sixty more beds ready, and sat up late, boiling water, sterilising instruments, preparing operating-tables and beds, etc etc. As it got later all the lights in the huge ward were put out, and we went about with little torches amongst the sleeping men, putting things in order and moving on tip-toe in the dark. Later we heard that the wounded might not get in till Monday.

The work of this place goes on unceasingly. We all get on well, but I have not got the communal spirit, and the fact of being a unit of women is not the side of it that I find most interesting. The communal food is my despair. I cannot *not* eat it. All the same, this is a fine experience, and I hope we'll come well out of it. There is boundless opportunity, and we are in luck to have a chance of doing our darndest.

28th *September* – Last night I and two orderlies slept over at the hospital as more wounded were expected. At 11pm word came that 'les blessés' were at the gate. Men were on duty with stretchers, and we went out to the tram-way in which the wounded are brought in from the station, twelve patients in each. The transit is as little painful as possible, and the stretchers are placed in iron brackets, and are simply unhooked when the men arrive. Each stretcher was brought in and laid on a bed in the ward and the nurses and doctors undressed the men. We orderlies took their names, their 'matricule' or regimental number, and the number of their bed. Then we gathered up their clothes and put corresponding numbers on labels attached to them – first turning out the pockets, which are filled with all manner of things, from tins of sardines to loaded revolvers. They are all very pockety, but have to be turned out before the clothes are sent to be baked.

We arranged everything, and then got Oxo for the men, many of whom had had nothing to eat for two days. They are a nice-looking lot of men and boys, with rather handsome faces and clear eyes. Their absolute exhaustion is the most pathetic thing about them. They fall asleep even when their wounds are being dressed. When all was made straight and comfortable for them, the nurses turned the lights low again, and stepped softly about the ward with their little torches.

A hundred beds all filled with men in pain give one plenty to think about and it is during sleep that their attitudes of suffering strike one most. Some of them bury their heads in their pillows as shot partridges seek to bury theirs among autumn leaves. Others lie very stiff and straight, and all look very thin and haggard. I was struck by the contrast between the pillared concert-hall where they lie with its platform of white paint and decorations and the tragedy of suffering which now fills it.

At 2am more soldiers were brought in from the battlefield, all caked in dirt and we began to work again. These last blinked oddly at the concert-hall and nurses and doctors, but I think they do not question anything much. They only want to go to sleep.

— • —

LESLIE HOLDEN wrote a 27-page letter from a hospital bed in France on 6 December 1916. Although it is signed 'From Leslie' it has no addressee. Instead it begins with a title – *A Little Graffic Experience of A Coolgardie Boy* – marking out the manuscript as part memoir and part letter. This extract, retaining the spelling and grammar of the original, is taken from the end of the letter. The corrective note at the foot of the page is written in a different hand.

Well at Boniville about forty of our lads left us there, in Motor Busses for Beacourt Wood on Fatigues. After a few days stay at Boniville we were on the move again, and when we arrived at Rebumpre we had another forty lads, leaving us there for detonating Bombs etc at Gordon's Dump and also at Alberts, all of the[m] out of our platoon but Gil. W. Boulter, A Perratt and myself. We we [sic] moved up to Alberts the following day bivuacing in a field, where we stayed for about three days, there was then only about a dozen of our Coy with us. Then on the Saturday afternoon we were off again, passing through 'La Bosielle', about four miles from Alberts, and on up to Chalk Pit; we were on fatigues up to the front line, about 2 miles away. Taking up bombs, ammunition, Water etc.

Well we made our first trip when we arrived there. Sunday three time[s] and once at night then two trips the following day, Monday, when at midday we were, taken out, marched back to 'La Bosielle,' had a tin of Bully Beef and a couple of biscuits thrown to us, a roll call which amounted to about 130 lads of our Battalion and the[n] at about 4 o'clock we were off again bound for the front line and over the top with the best of Luck. The remainder of our Btn were still back at Gordon's Dump etc. Well I don't mind admitting that I had a comical taste in my mouth, on that long march to the trenches, with death flying flagrants all around us; as Fritz had a very uncomfortable Artillery barage right back. Well when we got into our front line it was about 6 oclock with Fritz almost sniping with Wizz Bangs and a few rifles thrown in. Well our Bomber's and B Coy went over on our left, and got there position, we going over later on, and digging in; by midnight things were fairly quiet, lasting until about about [sic] 9'am, when Fritz began to let us know that he also had a guernsey. Well he shelled heavily all through that day, putting up a very heavy barrage on our supports, and when it began to get dark we were one mass of flares from Fritzs star pistols, inter-mixed with lights for Artillery work, which still continued as Fritz was very jumpy, but to our miscomfort. We were relieved at 2am of Wednesday morning, by the 2nd Div. and we soon made fast tracks for safety, which we found after passing over which were a lovely trench 36 hrs before was now nothing but one mass of debris and scrap iron.

Well we arrived down just behind chalk, at [sic] 4am, where our A.M.C. were working we got a cup of tea, which to us, dead beat, tasted something delicious, we then moved back to La Bosielle staying there for a few hours, and then back to Alberts, and out of the hundred and sixty or so which went up that night between thirty and forty of us answered the Roll Call. Well we moved back again at mid-day after a bit of a wash and shave, end of August, and getting our packs. We were then bound for Doullen's (to entrain to Bey[the rest of this word is cut off] about forty miles away, which we reached in about four days time. We then went in the Line at Ypres. Well I'll now close, I could write another dozen pages, but I haven't

the time, I'm now in Annexe Col [the rest of this word is cut off]
No 1 General Hospital France, Etretat, but I'm leaving Today Dec.
12, 1916 for the Bas[the rest of this word is cut off] and then on to
the Btn. I only left the B[the rest of this word is cut off] ten days
ago, but I only came away with Influenza, and I'm as Good as Gold
again now. I'll now conclude, with the Fondest Love and Kisses to
all at home.

From

Leslie.

NOTE: *The influenza that Leslie caught was in fact he had his leg
blown off in the trenches.*

———— • ————

MAY SINCLAIR (1863–1946) was a novelist and philosopher, born in
Cheshire. The excerpt below is from *A Journal of Impressions in Belgium*
(1915), based on her experiences in the Munro Ambulance Corps in
1914.

[Monday 28 September, 1914.]
In the afternoon Mademoiselle F. called to take me to the Palais
des Fêtes. We stopped at a shop on the way to buy the Belgian Red
Cross uniform – the white linen overall and veil – which you must
wear if you work among the refugees there.

Madame F. is very kind and very tired. She has been working here
since early morning for weeks on end. They are short of volunteers
for the service of the evening meals, and I am to work at the tables

for three hours, from six to nine p.m. This is settled, and a young Red Cross volunteer takes me over the Palais. It is an immense building, rather like Olympia. It stands away from the town in open grounds like the Botanical Gardens, Regent's Park. It is where the great Annual Shows were held and the vast civic entertainments given. Miles of country round Ghent are given up to market-gardening. There are whole fields of begonias out here, brilliant and vivid in the sun. They will never be sold, never gathered, never shown in the Palais des Fêtes. It is the peasants, the men and women who tilled these fields, and their children that are being shown here, in the splendid and wonderful place where they never set foot before.

There are four thousand of them lying on straw in the outer hall, in a space larger than Olympia. They are laid out in rows all round the four walls, and on every foot of ground between; men, women and children together, packed so tight that there is barely standing-room between any two of them. Here and there a family huddles up close, trying to put a few inches between it and the rest; some have hollowed out a place in the straw or piled a barrier of straw between themselves and their neighbours, in a piteous attempt at privacy; some have dragged their own bedding with them and are lodged in comparative comfort. But these are the very few. The most part are utterly destitute, and utterly abandoned to their destitution. They are broken with fatigue. They have stumbled and dropped no matter where, no matter beside whom. None turns from his neighbour; none scorns or hates or loathes his fellow. The rigidly righteous *bourgeoise* lies in the straw breast to breast with the harlot of the village slum, and her innocent daughter back to back with the parish drunkard. Nothing matters. Nothing will ever matter any more.

They tell you that when darkness comes down on all this there is hell. But you do not believe it. You can see nothing sordid and nothing ugly here. The scale is too vast. Your mind refuses this coupling of infamy with transcendent sorrow. It rejects all images but the one image of desolation which is final and supreme. It is as if these forms had no stability and no significance of their own; as if they were locked together in one immense body and stirred or slept as one.

Two or three figures mount guard over this litter of prostrate forms. They are old men and old women seated on chairs. They sit upright and immobile, with their hands folded on their knees. Some of them have fallen asleep where they sit. They are all rigid in an attitude of resignation. They have the dignity of figures that will endure, like that, for ever. They are Flamands.

This place is terribly still. There is hardly any rustling of the straw. Only here and there the cry of a child fretting for sleep or for its mother's breast. These people do not speak to each other. Half of them are sound asleep, fixed in the posture they took when they dropped into the straw. The others are drowsed with weariness, stupefied with sorrow. On all these thousands of faces there is a mortal apathy. Their ruin is complete. They have been stripped bare of the means of life and of all likeness to living things. They do not speak. They do not think. They do not, for the moment, feel. In all the four thousand – except for the child crying yonder – there is not one tear.

And you who look at them cannot speak or think or feel either, and you have not one tear. A path has been cleared through the straw from door to door down the middle of the immense hall, a narrower track goes all round it in front of the litters that are ranged under the walls, and you are taken through and round the Show. You are to see it all. The dear little Belgian lady, your guide, will not let you miss anything. '*Regardez, Mademoiselle, ces deux petites filles. Qu'elles sont jolies, les pauvres petites.*' '*Voici deux jeunes mariés, qui dorment. Regardez l'homme; il tient encore la main de sa femme.*'

You look. Yes. They are asleep. He is really holding her hand. '*Et ces quatre petits enfants qui ont perdu leur père et leur mère. C'est triste, n'est-ce pas, Mademoiselle?*'

And you say, '*Oui, Mademoiselle. C'est bien triste.*'

But you don't mean it. You don't feel it. You don't know whether it is '*triste*' or not. You are not sure that '*triste*' is the word for it. There are no words for it, because there are no ideas for it. It is a sorrow that transcends all sorrow that you have ever known. You have a sort of idea that perhaps, if you can ever feel again, this sight will be worse to remember than it is to see. You can't believe what you see; you are stunned, stupefied, as if you yourself had been crushed and numbed in the same catastrophe. Only now and then a face upturned (a face that your guide hasn't pointed out to you) surging out of this incredible welter of faces and forms, smites you with pity, and you feel as if you had received a lacerating wound in sleep.

Little things strike you, though. Already you are forgetting the faces of the two little girls and of the young husband and wife holding each other's hands, and of the four little children who have lost their father and mother, but you notice the little dog, the yellow-brown mongrel terrier, that absurd little dog which belongs to all nations and all countries. He has obtained possession of the warm centre of a pile of straw and is curled up on it fast asleep. And the Flemish family who brought him, who carried him in turn for miles rather than leave him to the Germans, they cannot stretch themselves on the straw because of him. They have propped themselves up as best they may all round him, and they cannot sleep, they are too uncomfortable.

More thousands than there is room for in the straw are fed three times a day in the inner hall, leading out of this dreadful dormitory. All round the inner hall and on the upper storey off the gallery are rooms for washing and dressing the children and for bandaging sore feet and attending to the wounded. For there are many wounded among the refugees. This part of the Palais is also a hospital, with separate wards for men, for women and children and for special cases.

Late in the evening M. P— took the whole Corps to see the Palais des Fêtes, and I went again. By night I suppose it is even more '*triste*' than it was by day. In the darkness the gardens have taken on some malign mystery and have given it to the multitudes that move there, that turn in the winding paths among ghostly flowers and bushes, that approach and recede and approach in the darkness of the lawns. Blurred by the darkness and diminished to the barest indications of humanity, their forms are more piteous and forlorn than ever; their faces, thrown up by the darkness, more awful in their blankness and their pallor. The scene, drenched in darkness, is unearthly and unintelligible. You cannot account for it in saying to yourself that these are the refugees, and everybody knows what a refugee is; that there is War – and everybody knows what war is – in Belgium; and that these people have been shelled out of their homes and are here at the Palais des Fêtes, because there is no other place for them, and the kind citizens of Ghent have undertaken to house and feed them here. That doesn't make it one bit more credible or bring you nearer to the secret of these forms. You who are compelled to move with them in the sinister darkness are more than ever under the spell that forbids you and them to feel. You are deadened now to the touch of the incarnate.

On the edge of the lawn, near the door of the Palais, some ghostly roses are growing on a ghostly tree. Your guide, M. P—, pauses to tell you their names and kind. It seems that they are rare.

Several hundred more refugees have come into the Palais since the afternoon. They have had to pack them a little closer in the straw. Eight thousand were fed this evening in the inner hall.

In the crush I get separated from M. P— and from the Corps. I see some of them in the distance, the Commandant and Ursula Dearmer and Mrs. Lambert and M. P—. I do not feel as if I belonged to them any more. I belong so much to the stunned sleepers in the straw who cannot feel.

Nice Dr. Wilson comes across to me and we go round together, looking at the sleepers. He says that nothing he has seen of the War has moved him so much as this sight. He wishes that the Kaiser could be brought here to see what he has done. And I find myself clenching my hands tight till it hurts, not to suppress my feelings – for I feel nothing – but because I am afraid that kind Dr. Wilson is going to talk. At the same time, I would rather he didn't leave me just yet. There is a sort of comfort and protection in being with somebody who isn't callous, who can really feel.

But Dr. Wilson isn't very fluent, and presently he leaves off talking, too.

Near the door we pass the family with the little yellow-brown dog. All day the little dog slept in their place. And now that they are trying to sleep he will not let them. The little dog is wide awake and walking all over them. And when you think what it must have cost to bring him—

C'est triste, n'est-ce pas?

As we left the gardens M. P— gathered two ghostly roses, the last left on their tree, and gave one to Mrs. Lambert and one to me. I felt something rather like a pang then. Heaven knows why, for such a little thing.

——— • ———

ROBERT GRAVES (1895–1985) was a poet and novelist. He was born in London to an Irish father and German mother. He served in the Royal Welch Fusiliers. Graves's wartime experiences are described in his 1929 autobiography *Goodbye to All That*. In the extract below, soldiers examine remnants of the lives of the inhabitants of an abandoned village. It is dated 24 June 1915; Graves was billeted at Vermelles at the time.

This is a very idle life except for night-digging on the reserve line. By day there is nothing to do. We can't drill because it is too near the German lines, and there is no fortification work to be done in the village. To-day two spies were shot. A civilian who had hung on in a cellar and had, apparently, been flashing news; and a German soldier disguised as an R. E. corporal who was found tampering with the telephone wires. We officers spend a lot of time practising revolver-shooting. Jenkins brought out a beautiful target from the only undestroyed living-room in our billet-area. It was a glass case full of artificial fruit and flowers, so we put it up on a post at fifty yards' range. He said: 'I've always wanted to smash one of these damn things. My aunt had one. It's the sort of thing that *would* survive an intense bombardment.' For a moment I felt a tender impulse to rescue it. But I smothered it. So we had five shots each, in turn. Nobody could hit it. So at last we went up to within twenty yards of it and fired a volley. Someone hit the post and that knocked it off into the grass. Jenkins said: 'Damn the thing, it must be bewitched. Let's take it back.' The glass was unbroken, but some of the fruit had come loose. Walker said: 'No, it's in pain; we must put it out of its suffering.' He gave it the *coup de grâce* from close quarters.

There is an old Norman church here, very much broken. What is left of the tower is used as a forward observation post by the artillery. I counted eight unexploded shells sticking into it. I went in with Jenkins; the floor was littered with rubbish, broken masonry, smashed chairs, ripped canvas pictures (some of them looked several hundreds of years old), bits of images and crucifixes, muddied church vestments rotting in what was once the vestry. Only a few pieces of stained glass remained fixed in the edges of the windows. I climbed up by way of the altar to the east window and found a piece about the size of a plate. I gave it to Jenkins. 'Souvenir,' I said. When he held it up to the light it was St Peter's hand with the keys of heaven; medieval glass. 'I'm sending this home,' he said. As we went out we met two men of the Munsters. They were Irish Catholics. They thought it sacrilegious for Jenkins to be taking the glass away. One of them said: 'Shouldn't take that, sir; it will bring you no luck.'

[Footnote: Jenkins was killed not long after.]

—— • ——

HAVILDAR ABDUL RAHMAN was a Punjabi Muhammadan whose censored letter, below, was sent to Naik Rajwalk Khan of the 31st Punjabis at Fort Sandeman, Zhob District, Baluchistan. Rahman was fighting in France for the British Forces as part of the colonial army, in the 59th Scinde Rifles, 8th Company. Written in Urdu the letter was censored by a British officer; it is available to read because the censor would make reports in which excerpts would be translated and transcribed.

[20th May 1915]

For God's sake don't come, don't come, don't come to this war in Europe. Write and tell me if your regiment or any part of it comes and whether you are coming with it or not. I am in a state of great anxiety; and tell my brother Muhammad Yakub Khan for God sake not to enlist. If you have any relatives, my advice is don't let them enlist. It is unnecessary to write any more. I write so much to you as I am pay havildar and read the letters to the double company commander. Otherwise there is a strict order against writing on this subject. Cannons, machine guns, rifles, and bombs are going day and night, just like the rains in the month of Sawan (July – August). Those who have escaped so far are like the few grains left uncooked in a pot. That is the case with us. In my company there are only 10 men. In the regiment there are 200. In every regiment there are only 200 or 280.

———— • ————

DIARY OF AN UNKNOWN RAMC ORDERLY, Western Front, 1916. The following is taken from the Imperial War Museum Archives. Little is known of the anonymous author other than that he was an orderly working at the Somme.

Wed. 19. [April 1916]
> V. WET.
> Sleep all day. Heavy shelling. On night duty in 'Lone Barn'.
> Very busy all night, see some terrible sights. Bad case of
> feet blown off.
[...]

Fri. 5. [May]
> FINE. Have a drastic letter from Madge. On day nursing
> in officers' ward in hospital at Essars near Bethune. Go to
> Bethune for first time with Ernie. Have a very nice time.
[...]

Wed.17. [May]
> V. HOT. Change from day to night work. Busy nursing in
> officers' wards. Have letter from Madge saying she wishes
> only to be friends. We do not agree on several points.
[...]

Fri. 19. [May]

V. HOT. a.m. Write a final letter to Madge.

2 p.m. Go for a walk by the La Bassee canal to Essars with Frank.

Have a tune in CEMS hut.

[...]

Sat. 3. [June]

FINE.

Sleep all day.

Write a final letter to Madge.

[...]

Wed. 14. [June]

WET. V. COLD.

Have letter from Madge saying she will not accept me only as a friend. On night duty.

Thurs. 15. [June]

WET.

On night duty.

Write long letter to Madge.

[...]

Wed. 21. [June]

FINE.

9.0 a.m. Go for walk to Locon with E. M. Ware and I see Frank. Learn that Madge has a boy in the A.S.C.

[...]

Fri. 21. [July]

    V. FINE.

    Go to gas school & go through gas chamber containing gas
    five times stronger than the enemy send over.

    6. p.m. Go to Bethune theatre with D. Earl.

[...]

Sun. 13. [August] Orderly on Motor Amb. at Balliel near St Pol.

    V. HOT.

    At Ballieu near St Pol.

    a.m. Clean Car Big post 9 letters 1 Madge.

    p.m. Take patients on car to St Pol hospital. Have tea at
    canteen.

[...]

Wed. 13. [September]

    FINE.

    Leave Vauchelles and go with car up the line to Cookers
    A.D.S. On the edge of Thiepval Wood. Sleep in dug outs.
    Pretty scenery. Heavy bombardment.

[...]

Sun.8. [October] In the trenches stretcher bearing at Thiepval.
Go over parapet. Knocked down many times by shells.

    V. WET.

    Leave car at workshop and return to Amb. Put on nursing
    & clerking duties with Sykes, in evacuating ward Clairfoy.
    6 p.m. Go to Acheux with Sykes, and see Frank.

Sat. 14. [October]

FINE.

In trenches and German dug outs (Thiepval). Big attack. Go up first line at midnight and get the wounded. Heavily shelled. Up all night. Schawben redoubt won.

Memo. Go up the trenches bearing for first time. In German dug outs in Thiepval. Advance. Many dead lying about. Most awful experience of my life.

Accompanying the written war memories W. G. Seymour sent to the BBC in 1963, he included 'a small photograph of myself holding a kitten that we got from a wild cat litter out of a dug-out in 1917'.

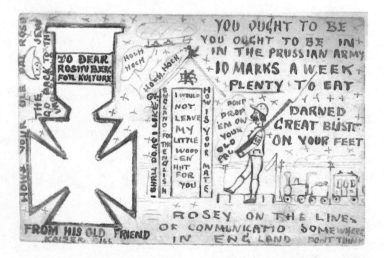

This is a 'white feather' postcard given to a male civilian on the grounds that he was believed to be a coward. His refusal to enlist is aggressively linked with support for the enemy. The German Iron Cross has been cut out from the card. It is held at the Imperial War Museum.

BETWEEN BORDERS

How the war divided us

W. H. RIDDELL submitted this letter to the BBC following its invitation in 1964 for memories of people who had given or received white feathers. He was a conscientious objector.

19. 5. 64

The Secretary

B.B.C.

Bristol

Dear Sir,

With reference to the enclosed newspaper cutting, would my experience be useful to you.

In Feb 1916 I applied for exemption from military service on religious grounds. My appeal was heard at the Wimbledon Tribunal. I was directed to find work of national importance under the Pelham Committee.

Under the Society of Friends I found work market gardening at Evesham and left London in July 1916 as this was agreed to.

One morning I was crossing the Avon bridge at Evesham to go to work at Bengeworth.

Here I was challenged by three young women who promptly tried to put a white feather in my lapel.

Of course, I did not agree with them neither would I accept their gift, whereupon they decided to throw me over the bridge into the river, which I understand is about fifteen feet deep at this point. This developed into an awkward struggle with me on the losing side.

Of course I prayed as never before for I was getting desperate when unnoticed by me two dogs about six feet away began a disagreement which developed into a dogfight whereupon the girls left me.

I went onto a farm at Wickamford after three months so never met them again I am glad to say.

Yours faithfully

W. H. Riddell.

———— • ————

VERNON LEE (the pen name of Violet Paget, 1856–1935) was a writer, born in France. As a child, she also lived in Germany, Switzerland and Italy and was fluent in four languages. The passage below was published in *Jus Suffragii: Monthly Organ of the International Woman Suffrage Alliance* on 1 January, 1915.

I was at the Temple on Christmas Eve for Bach's music. The shimmering double church was full of old and elderly men, of women of all ages, with a sprinkling of soldier-lads, brought along, on what may be their last Christmas in this world, by their mothers and sisters and sweethearts. Everyone – but it was perhaps that my own eyes and heart were opened – everyone seemed so altered from other perfunctory times, grave, sincere, aware of all it meant.

With the first rasping notes of the organ, tearing the veil of silent prayer, there came before my mind, as when a cloud-rent suddenly shows depths of solemn moonlit sky, the fact that *There* also, *There* beyond the sea and the war chasm, in hundreds of churches of Bach's own country (I can see the Thomas-Kirche at Leipzig, where he was Cantor, and the church of his birthplace, Eisenach), *There*, at this very moment, were crowds like this one at the Temple, listening to this self-same Christmas Music. *There* also elderly men, stay-behinds, and many, many women, old and young, and a sprinkling of soldier-lads brought for that, maybe, last Christmas at home and on Earth. Praying like these silently kneeling around me, and praying for the same mercies: Give us, O God, strength to live through these evil times, or, if so be, die to some purpose; suffer not, O Lord, who seest our hearts, that we be crushed in this war not of our making; teach us to forgive the cruel folk who hate us; give us such peace as will never be broken. Forgive us, deliver us; remember, O Father, the peace and good-will which were promised with Thy Son.

Something like that, articulate or not, is welling up with unshed tears and silent sobs in those kneeling crowds, behind those screening hands, both on this side and on yonder, of the shallow seas and the unfathomable ocean of horror and hatred. They are united, these English and those German crowds, in the same hopes and fears and prayers, even as, unsuspecting, they are united in the same sequences of melody, the same woofs of harmonies wherewith, across two hundred years, that long dead but undying organist of Leipzig enmeshes, draws together, nooses and nets our souls to lift them, clarified, close embraced, nay consubstantial, into the presence of the new born, the eternally reborn, Hope of the World.

They are thinking and feeling the same, those German and these English crowds. They are played into unanimity not only by Bach with his tunes and counterpoints, but by the ruthless hands of our common calamity. The same heroic, or resigned, or despairing modes; saddest of all, perhaps, the brief snatches of would-be cheerfulness, and beneath all individual, all articulate differences, the unanalysable harmonies of collective sorrow.

They have come, those German women like these English ones, to seek rest in this church and this music after their day in hospitals and relief offices and committee rooms. They also have brought along with them their soldiers, their boys or their lovers, home perhaps for the last time; brought them from old peaceful habit, or because one can feel nearer together, without the unnerving fear of words and glances, here in this church, side by side, embracing in the music and in God. And, the service over, they will many of them, German women like English, go back to their homes, light up the Christmas tree, pull the paper caps and the favours out of the crackers, and laugh and play, so that the children at least may forget the war, and remember only that the Christ Child has been born once more. German and English, the same burdens have been brought to the church, been laid down in the prayer and the music; the same burdens have been shouldered again. Never have we and they been closer together, more alike and akin, than at this moment when War's cruelties and recriminations, War's monstrous iron curtain, cut us off so utterly from one another.

United, moreover, in the common feeling of Christmas. For a symbol turns the simple fact we can singly know into the myriad applications we can together feel. And the Child Christ, whom, orthodox or unorthodox, we are all celebrating, was not born once, but is born always, over and over again. He lies in every cradle, the incarnate, unblemished hope of every land and every generation. And He is the Redeemer because every new life, like every new day after the winter solstice, like the wheat quickening in the winter furrow, is the redemption of our Present by our Future, the deliverance by our Hope from our Despair. Enmity dies and is forgotten, being accidental, changeable, sterile, and against the grain of life. But peace and goodwill on earth is born for ever anew, because it is born of the undying needs of our common humanity.

That is the message of Bach's Christmas music, his cosmic thunders hushed into pastoral flutings; the message of the long-deceased German organist to us English who listen; the message to us listening English back to Bach's fellow-countrymen united with us in listening and in sorrowing and hoping.

———— • ————

JOHN REED (1887–1920) was a left-wing journalist, born in Portland, Oregon. He died in Russia, and is buried at the Kremlin Wall. In 1912 he began writing for *The Masses*, a radical magazine. From 1913–14 he reported on the Mexican Revolution. Upon the outbreak of the First World War he travelled to Europe and published journalism based on his observations and encounters with eyewitnesses. The following passages are from his 1916 book *The War in Eastern Europe*.

Late one night we walked through the deserted quarter of docks and warehouses, so filled with shouting movement by day. From a faintly lighted window came the sound of pounding and singing, and we peered through the grimy pane. It was a water-front saloon, a low-vaulted room with a floor of hard-packed earth, rough table and stools, piles of black bottles, barrel-ends and one smoking lamp hung crazily from the ceiling. At the table sat eight men, whining a wavering Oriental song, and beating time with their glasses. Suddenly one caught sight of our faces at the window; they halted, leaped to their feet. The door flew open – hands reached out and pulled us in.

'*Entrez! Pasen Ustedes! Herein! Herein!*' shouted the company, crowding eagerly about as we entered the room. A short, bald-headed man with a wart on his nose pumped our hands up and down, babbling in a mixture of languages: 'To drink! To drink! What will you have, friends?'

'But *we* invite *you*—' I began.

'This is my shop! Never shall a stranger pay in my shop! Wine? Beer? *Mastica?*'

'Who are you?' asked the others. 'French? English? Ah – Americans! I have a cousin – his name Georgopoulos – he live in California. You know him?'

One spoke English, another harsh maritime French, a third Neapolitan, a fourth Levantine Spanish, and still another pidgin-German; all knew Greek, and the strange patois of the Mediterranean sailor. The fortunes of war had swept them from the four corners of the Middle World into this obscure back-water on the Salonika docks.

'It is strange,' said the man who spoke English. 'We met here by chance – not one of us has ever known the other before. And we are all seven carpenters. I am a Greek from Kili on the Black Sea, and he is a Greek, and he, and he – from Ephesus, and Erzeroum, and Scutari. This man is an Italian – he lives in Aleppo, in Syria – and this one a Frenchman from Smyrna. Last night we were sitting here just like now, and he looked in at the window like you did.'

The seventh carpenter, who had not spoken, said something that sounded like a German dialect. The proprietor translated:

'This man is Armenian. He says all his family is killed by the Turks. He tries to tell you in the German he learned working on the Bagdad Railway!'

'Back there,' cried the Frenchman, 'I leave my wife and two kids! I go away hiding on a fisherboat—'

'God knows where is my brother.' The Italian shook his head. 'The soldiers took him. We could not both escape.'

Now the master of the house brought liquor, and we raised our glasses to his beaming countenance.

'He is like that,' the Italian explained with gestures. 'We have no money. He gives us food and drink, and we sleep here on the floor, poor refugees. God will certainly reward his charity!'

'Yes. Yes. God will reward him,' assented the others, drinking. The proprietor crossed himself elaborately, after the complicated fashion of the Orthodox Church.

'God knows I am fond of company,' he said. 'And one cannot turn away destitute men in times like these, especially men of pleasing talents. Besides, a carpenter gains good wages when he works, and then I shall be repaid.'

'Do you want Greece to go to war?' we asked.

'No!' cried some; others moodily shook their heads.

'It is like this,' the English-speaking Greek said slowly: 'This war has driven us from our homes and our work. Now there is no work for a carpenter. War is a tearing down and not a building up. A carpenter is for building up—' He translated to the silent audience, and they growled applause.

'But how about Constantinople?'

'Constantinople for Greece! Greek Constantinople!' shouted two of the carpenters. But the others broke into a violent argument.

The Italian rose and lifted his glass. '*Eviva* Constantinople Internazionale!' he cried. With a cheer everybody rose. 'Constantinople Internazionale!'

'Come,' said the proprietor, 'a song for the strangers!'

'What was that you were singing when we came?' demanded Robinson.

'That was an Arab song. Now let us sing a real Turkish song!' And throwing back their heads, the company opened their noses in a whining wail, tapping with stiff fingers on the table while the glasses leaped and jingled.

'More to drink!' cried the excited innkeeper. 'What is song without drink?'

'God will reward him!' murmured the seven carpenters in voices husky with emotion.

The Italian had a powerful tenor voice; he sang '*La donna è mobile*,' in which the others joined with Oriental improvisations. An American song was called for, and Robinson and I obliged with 'John Brown's Body' – which was encored four times.

Later dancing displaced music. In the flickering light of the fast-expiring lamp the proprietor led a stamping trio in the *kolo*, racial dance of all the Balkan peoples. Great boots, clumped stiffly down, arms waved, fingers snapped, ragged clothes fluttered in brown shadow and yellow radiance… Followed an Arab measure, all swaying bodies and syncopated gliding steps, and slow twirlings with closed eyes. At an early hour of the morning we were giving the company lessons in the 'boston,' and the turkey trot… And so ended the adventure of the Seven Carpenters of Salonika.

[...]

The handsome great sleeping-cars bore brass inscriptions in *svelte* Turkish letters and in French, 'Orient Express' – that most famous train in the world, which used to run from Paris direct to the Golden Horn in the prehistoric days before the war. A sign in Bulgarian said 'Tsarigrad' – literally 'City of Emperors' – also the Russian name for the eastern capital that all Slavs consider theirs by right. And a German placard proclaimed pompously, 'Berlin-Constantinopel' – an arrogant prophecy in those days, when the Constantinople train went no farther west than Sofia, and the drive on Serbia had not begun.

We were an international company: three English officers in mufti bound for Dedeagatch; a French engineer on business to Philoppopolis; a Bulgar military commission going to discuss the terms of the treaty with Turkey; a Russian school-teacher returning to his home in Burgas; an American tobacco man on a buying tour around the Turkish Black Sea ports; a black eunuch in fez, his frock coat flaring over wide hips and knock knees; a Viennese music-hall dancer and her man headed for the café concerts of Pera; two Hungarian Red Crescent delegates, and assorted Germans to the number of about a hundred. There was a special car full of bullet-headed Krupp workmen for the Turkish munition factories, and two compartments reserved for an *Unterseeboot* crew going down to relieve the men of U-54 – boys seventeen or eighteen years old. And in the next compartment to mine a party of seven upper-class Prussians played incessant 'bridge': government officials, business men, and intellectuals on their way to Constantinople to take posts in the embassy, the Regie, the Ottoman Debt, and the Turkish universities. Each was a highly efficient cog, trained to fit exactly his place in the marvellous German machine that ground already for the Teutonic Empire of the East.

The biting irony of life in neutral countries went with us. It was curious to watch the ancient habit of cosmopolitan existence take possession of that train-load. Some ticket agents with a sense of humour had paired two Englishmen with a couple of German embassy attachés in the same compartment – they were scrupulously polite to each other. The Frenchman and the other Britisher gravitated naturally to the side of the fair Austrian, where they all laughed and chattered about youthful student days in Vienna. Late at night I caught one of the German diplomats out in the corridor gossiping about Moscow with the Russian teacher. All these men were active on the firing-line, so to speak, except the Russian – and he, of course, was a Slav, and without prejudices…

But in the morning the English, the Frenchman, and the Russian were gone – the breathing-place between borders of hate was past – and we fled through the grim marches of the Turkish Empire.

—— • ——

ELEANOR BARTON (1872-1960) was President of the Women's Co-operative Guild. On 4 August 1914 there was an international meeting of women and demonstration against the war in London. At 11p.m. that day hostilities were declared between Britain and Germany. The following story was told by Barton at that meeting and was included in an article in *Votes for Women*.

She [Barton] told how, coming up from Sheffield, an old sailor, fifty years of age, was put into the carriage by his friends, and afterwards two young Germans got in. On the platform was the eldest son of the old salt in such a terrible state of grief that he had to be supported, as he came to see his old father off to war. Strong men and women wept together. As the train passed out of the station one of the Germans, a young married man, stood up and put out his hand to the old man, and said, 'By God, we are enemies; give me your hand – it is not my fault.' They shook hands, and the old salt replied, 'It is hell, my lad. Why could not it have been settled by arbitration? I have travelled all over the world, have given thirty years' service to the navy in China and Japan, and have never made an enemy of a foreigner, but plenty of friends.'

—— • ——

OPEN LETTERS FROM THE WOMEN OF ENGLAND, GERMANY AND AUSTRIA A few months after the demonstration described above, Jus Suffragii published this 'Open Christmas Letter', addressed 'TO THE WOMEN OF GERMANY AND AUSTRIA'. It was entitled, 'On Earth Peace, Goodwill towards Men'; which was of course intended to include 'Women' as well. In March 1915 the reply was published in the journal. Each letter concluded with a long list of names.

TO THE WOMEN OF GERMANY AND AUSTRIA
Open Christmas Letter
SISTERS, –
    Some of us wish to send you a word at this sad Christmastide,

though we can but speak through the Press. The Christmas message sounds like mockery to a world at war, but those of us who wished and still wish for peace may surely offer a solemn greeting to such of you who feel as we do. Do not let us forget that our very anguish unites us, that we are passing together through the same experiences of pain and grief.

Caught in the grip of terrible Circumstance, what can we do? Tossed on this turbulent sea of human conflict, we can but moor ourselves to those calm shores whereon stand, like rocks, the eternal verities – Love, Peace, Brotherhood.

We pray you to believe that come what may we hold to our faith in Peace and Goodwill between nations; while technically at enmity in obedience to our rulers, we own allegiance to that higher law which bids us live at peace with all men.

Though our sons are sent to slay each other, and our hearts are torn by the cruelty of this fate, yet through pain supreme we will be true to our common womanhood. We will let no bitterness enter in this tragedy, made sacred by the life-blood of our best, nor mar with hate the heroism of their sacrifice. Though much has been done on all sides you will, as deeply as ourselves, deplore, shall we not steadily refuse to give credence to those false tales so freely told us, each of the other?

We hope it may lessen your anxiety to learn we are doing our utmost to soften the lot of your civilians and war prisoners within our shores, even as we rely on your goodness of heart to do the same for ours in Germany and Austria.

Do you not feel with us that the vast slaughter in our opposing armies is a stain on civilisation and Christianity, and that still deeper horror is aroused at the thought of those innocent victims, the countless women, children, babes, old and sick, pursued by famine, disease, and death in the devastated areas, both East and West?

As we saw in South Africa and the Balkan States, the brunt of modern war falls upon non-combatants, and the conscience of the world cannot bear the sight.

Is it not our mission to preserve life? Do not humanity and commonsense alike prompt us to join hands with the women of neutral countries, and urge our rulers to stay further bloodshed?

Relief, however colossal, can reach but few: Can we sit still and let the helpless die in their thousands, as die they must – *unless* we rouse ourselves in the name of Humanity to save them? There is but one way to do this. We must all urge that peace be made with appeal to Wisdom and Reason. Since in the last resort it is these which must decide the issues, can they begin too soon, if it is to save the womanhood and childhood as well as the manhood of Europe?

Even through the clash of arms we treasure our poet's vision, and already seem to hear

'A hundred nations swear that there shall be

Pity and Peace and Love among the good and free.'

May Christmas hasten that day. Peace on Earth is gone, but by renewal of our faith that it still reigns at the heart of things, Christmas should strengthen both you and us and all womanhood to strive for its return.

We are yours in this sisterhood of sorrow.

OPEN LETTER IN REPLY TO THE OPEN CHRISTMAS LETTER FROM ENGLISHWOMEN TO GERMAN AND AUSTRIAN WOMEN

To our English sisters, sisters of the same race, we express in the name of many German women our warm and heartfelt thanks for their Christmas greetings, which we only heard of lately.

This message was a confirmation of what we foresaw – namely, that women of the belligerent countries, with all faithfulness, devotion, and love to their country, can go beyond it and maintain true solidarity with the women of other belligerent nations, and that really civilised women never lose their humanity.

If English women alleviated misery and distress at this time, relieved anxiety, and gave help irrespective of nationality, let them accept the warmest thanks of German women and the true assurance that they are and were prepared to do likewise. In war time we are united by the same unspeakable suffering of all nations taking part in the war. Women of all nations have the same love of justice, civilisation, and beauty, which are all destroyed by war. Women of all nations have the same hatred for barbarity, cruelty, and destruction, which accompany every war.

Women, creators and guardians of life, must loathe war, which destroys life. Through the smoke of battle and thunder of cannon of hostile peoples, through death, terror, destruction, and unending pain and anxiety, there glows like the dawn of a coming better day the deep community of feeling of many women of all nations.

May this feeling lay the immovable foundation for the building up of German, English, and international relations, which must finally lead to a strong international law of the peoples, so that the peoples of Europe may never again be visited with such wars as these.

Warm sisterly greetings to Englishwomen who share these feelings!

———— • ————

MAUDE ONIONS worked as a signaller (in the Women's Army Auxiliary Corps) in France during the First World War. Her book, *A Woman at War: Being Experiences of an Army Signaller in France 1917–1919*, from which this extract is taken, was first published privately in 1928 and released publicly the following year. It is pacifist in tone, dedicated both to one of her friends and 'to EVERY WOMAN (irrespective of nationality or creed) who hates war and loves peace'.

I like to look back to eight o'clock on the morning of November 11th, 1918, because it was then that I tapped out the official message to the armies in the field, which helped to bring peace to a war-weary world.

'Hostilities will cease at 11.00 November 11th aaa. Troops will stand fast at the line reached at that hour which will be reported to Army Headquarters aaa. Defensive precautions will be maintained aaa. There will be no intercourse of any description with the enemy aaa. Further instructions to follow.'

In the little Signal Office at Boulogne nothing happened at eleven o'clock, nothing except a silence, and an involuntary glance at the clock. Outside, nothing happened. It was the first great silence of armistice. It was as though France had just heaved a vast sigh of relief. It was not until the afternoon that any signs of rejoicing became evident. Then, as I made my way down to the quay side, on the stroke of three, every siren and hooter was let loose, every church bell clanged out – a deafening roar. But not a sound, not a movement, came from the hundreds of human beings who thronged the streets. The stricken soul of France seemed to have lost even the desire to rejoice.

A deafening noise, the flags of the Blighty boat ran up, and for the first time for four weary years she sailed without an escort. Some of us tried to cheer, but voice failed. Then suddenly through the noise and din, the sobbing of a woman, a few yards away – 'Finis – finis – incroyable…'

Almost unconsciously, I found myself in the little military cemetery behind the congested streets of the town, where our men were buried three deep, for land was dear in France, and where the graves had been so beautifully kept by the loving hands of a khaki girl. I could not distinguish the names, for the mist of tears.

As I turned to go from that scene of peace, I stumbled and almost fell over something on the ground, a broken piece of wood, that had sunk so deep that it was scarcely visible. I knelt down to examine it, and it was with difficulty that I was able to decipher the lettering. It was the grave of a German soldier.

Cautiously, afraid of being seen, I stooped and placed some flowers at the foot of the broken cross.

Somewhere, a woman was sorrowing.

—— • ——

STEFAN WESTMANN was a sergeant in the 29th Division of the German Army. He was interviewed in 1963 for the BBC *Great War* series. This is taken from the Sound Archive of the Imperial War Museum and was edited by Max Arthur in association with the Imperial War Museum, also reproduced in *Forgotten Voices of the Great War*.

While the Prince Regent of Bavaria launched an attack on Neuve Chapelle on January the 25th, this was only a feint to get the enemy to concentrate on the wrong area. Our attack was launched against the French and British trenches on the south of the Aire-La Bassée canal.

We got orders to storm the French position. We got in and I saw my comrades start falling to the right and left of me. But then I was confronted by a French corporal with his bayonet to the ready, just as I had mine. I felt the fear of death in that fraction of a second when I realised that he was after my life, exactly as I was after his. But I was quicker than he was, I pushed his rifle away and ran my bayonet through his chest. He fell, putting his hand on the place where I had hit him, and then I thrust again. Blood came out of his mouth and he died.

I nearly vomited. My knees were shaking and they asked me, 'What's the matter with you?' I remembered then that we had been told that a good soldier kills without thinking of his adversary as a human being – the very moment he sees him as a fellow man, he's no longer a good soldier. My comrades were absolutely undisturbed by what had happened. One of them boasted that he killed a *poilu* with the butt of his rifle. Another one had strangled a French captain. A third had hit somebody over the head with his spade.

They were ordinary men like me. One was a tram conductor, another a commercial traveller, two were students, the rest farm workers – ordinary people who would never have thought to harm anybody.

But I had the dead French soldier in front of me, and how I would have liked him to have raised his hand! I would have shaken it and we would have been the best of friends because he was nothing but a boy – like me. A boy who had to fight with the cruellest weapons against a man who had nothing against him personally, who wore the uniform of another nation and spoke another language, but a man who had a father and mother and a family. So I woke up at night sometimes, drenched in sweat, because I saw the eyes of my fallen adversary. I tried to convince myself of what would've happened to me if I hadn't been quicker than him, if I hadn't thrust my bayonet into his belly first.

Why was it that we soldiers stabbed each other, strangled each other, went for each other like mad dogs? Why was it that we who had nothing against each other personally fought to the very death? We were civilised people after all, but I felt that the thin lacquer of civilisation of which both sides had so much, chipped off immediately. To fire at each other from a distance, to drop bombs, is something impersonal, but to see the whites of a man's eyes and then to run a bayonet into him – that was against my comprehension.

——— • ———

E. M. FORSTER (1879–1970) is best known for his novels *A Room with a View* (1908), *Howards End* (1910) and *A Passage to India* (1924). During the war, he worked in Alexandria, Egypt, as a Red Cross searcher: the job entailed interviewing wounded soldiers in hospital in order to locate the missing. The article below, 'Reconstruction in the Marne and the Meuse', was published shortly before he took on this role and was initially published in the *Westminster Gazette* on 30 August 1915.

Anyone who attended a picture-palace in the early months of the war may remember an ingenious device that illustrated the battle of the Marne and the subsequent German retreat to the Aisne. The Germans, represented by little black blocks and an occasional eagle, were seen leaping and sliding across the map of France towards Paris, their prey. Outside Paris the Allies, shown as shaded blocks, checked them, the turning movements were executed, and then the eagles slipped back eastward, pursued by the strains of 'Rule, Britannia' and the 'Marseillaise.' It was an interesting film, and brought home to the ordinary man the strategical side of the September invasions. But there is one side of invasion it could not bring home: the destructive. France is not a map, but France, and the German armies do not advance over white paper and retreat leaving it white, but into civilisation that they leave a desert. Each of those little black blocks leaves a stain behind – more than a stain, a festering sore that eats inwards and spreads. Invasion is more than the destruction of property, it is more even than murder and pain. It is the herald of spiritual death. The survivors, when the tide of horror retreats, feel that it is sure to return, and that even if it does not, life is not worth living again. Before it came they could not imagine anything else. They have had an experience of which we, in our isled security, can have no conception; their mental state is now as far removed from ours as if it was on the other side of the grave.

What is being done for those survivors, for those who lay in the line of that German retreat between the Aisne and the Marne? France is a first-class power, with a past as splendid as our own and a reputation for humanity as great, and at first sight it seems impertinent for English people to offer her any assistance in connection with her war victims. But it must be remembered that on France falls the brunt of the war in the west – a war in which England has hitherto played a minor part. France is not negligent, nor is she poor, but she is busy, desperately busy. Though she can provide much of the stuff, e.g. materials to build huts, horses and petrol for transport, hotels and houses for hospitals, she cannot provide time and she cannot provide labour, because all her energies are employed in expelling the Germans. Consequently, she has been willing to accept the offer of the Society of Friends to work in the evacuated departments of the Marne and the Meuse, and the reports that they have issued – now about a dozen in number – give a vivid account of the destruction and of the attempts at reconstruction.

'Imagine,' writes one of the workers, 'a village in England – one that you are acquainted with: it may even be your home – with some 700 houses, of which 650 have been burned to the ground, and then you will be able to form some idea of what is S— now. The inhabitants left in astounding bewilderment, hardly able to believe that the German army was so close, and so in the hurry and scramble to get away they left everything behind them, innocently expecting to find their belongings again when they returned, scarcely crediting the Germans with such viciousness as led them to burn S— to the ground. And so when they returned a few days after the German retreat, conceive their sorrow and chagrin on finding their homes razed to the ground and all trace of their possessions gone. All their hay and crops – no sight sadder than the grey heaps of powdered ashes – cattle, rabbits, and everything, burnt or destroyed. How I admire their courage as I see them grubbing about amongst their ruins, searching for some lost thing, or beginning – where would you begin? – to clear away the débris?'

The Society of Friends begins by sending out investigators, who are usually women who have been trained in social work. In accordance with their reports the other workers follow. Nurses visit patients in their own homes, builders erect huts for the peasants (who *must* get back to their ground and have nowhere to live in), and there is a growing department of agricultural relief. These are the four main divisions of activity, and about 125 volunteers from England are at present engaged in them. 'It is not only the material help given,' writes the secretary of the Relief Committee (Miss Ruth Fry): 'the most important aspect of it all is the courage raised anew in these much-tried sufferers, to whom the coming of these helpers is a very impressive sign of the reality of our friendship.' And she tells how the children in a ruined village will, at the investigating visit, stand about, bored and apathetic, as if life contains nothing but stagnation and despair, and how, when the Friends return, girt with a pleasing bustle of medicine bottles, or agricultural implements, or planks, the children will gradually recover interest and end by screaming at the motor-cars, as all well-conducted children should. 'Were the Germans to reoccupy the districts tomorrow, our work would not be wasted, because we have kept the people from idleness for a little and helped them to regain hope.'

The work began in November, and at first the medical side predominated: for instance, a Maternity Hospital for the Marne refugees was organised at Châlons. Miss Pye, one of the organisers, thus describes a patient whom she went to fetch by car:

In spite of the fact that we were unknown to Madame L., of a foreign county, arriving late in the dusk of a winter evening, she rose up, laid down her sewing, put on her hat and cloak, and came away with us into the dark. It was her first baby. Her husband, a compositor in Reims before he was called up, had been seriously wounded four months before, and since then she had had no news at all. She spoke during the long ride back of their happy life together, then of his being called out, of the horrors of the bombardment, and her six weeks' nightly sojourn in the cellars. She spoke of the Germans in Reims, but said they were 'très gentils,' and that many of her friends had found the same. One she met had been so sad, and had wept over having to fight and leave his wife and children. She showed him the picture of her husband, and he wished her good fortune and his safe return. Her courage was splendid. She said, 'If he never comes back to me I must bring up my child and work for him; one must have courage these days; one has moments, but it is no good to weep, it only brings weakness.' Just before a little daughter was born to her the news came that her husband was dead.

Her courage never failed. 'For my dear little girl I want to be strong,' she said.

In the later reports it is agriculture that figures. The two departments are almost entirely rural, and a great effort is being made to continue their life. Most of the farm machines have been destroyed by fire – that is to say, they survive, but the iron is so soft that it bends at a touch – and to replace them about eighty mowing machines have been distributed among the villages on the co-operative system (an innovation among the French peasantry, this; in some districts there was opposition); while the Agricultural Relief of Allies Fund is helping the Friends to provide reapers and binders for the forthcoming harvest. This harvest was sown by Frenchwomen last autumn, who went out into the fields immediately after the German retreat and, as though they were themselves some process of nature, carried on the labour of countless generations, and prolonged the fertility of France into another spring. In comparison with their courage, their patriotism, what are the instruments of destruction? Like Madame L., they nurse the inviolable hope, they are tending the life of the earth, and it is to help them in this faith, beside which war is a phantom, that the Society of Friends is working.

To an outsider, this insistence on hope, this attempt at *spiritual* reconstruction, whatever the fortunes of battle, seems particularly characteristic of the Quaker mind. The supreme evil of war is surely not death, but despair – the feeling that the incursion of the soul into matter has been a mistake, that we may just as well sit brooding among the ashes of happiness and beauty, that it is useless to work, useless to give help and even to receive it. We know this feeling even in England, where the war has touched us comparatively little. As casualty list succeeds casualty list, the whole of civilisation seems sliding; and what must it be for the French, who have known war's full physical horror? Against such despair the Quaker fights. He believes that though civilisation may slide, the power of which civilisation is only a partial expression stands firm, being rooted in humanity. Or – to adapt that image of the cinematograph and its shifting blocks – he believes that no space that the armies of love have once traversed is ever the same again. There is always a radiant trace, always a lingering glory, always a glow that strengthens inwardly and is ready to shine outwardly as soon as clouds lift and the battle smoke thins under the winds of time.

———— • ————

EDITH WHARTON (1862–1937) was born in New York and won the Pulitzer Prize for *The Age of Innocence* (1920). Her war writing includes *Fighting France: From Dunkerque to Belfort* (1915), *The Marne* (1918), and *A Son at the Front* (1923). While in Paris, she volunteered for relief work for refugees from Belgium and Northern France. In 1916 she compiled an anthology called *The Book of the Homeless*, proceeds from which would benefit war refugees. The excerpt below is from Wharton's preface, in which she tells an anecdote about a 'little acrobat' displaced from his home.

Last year, among the waifs swept to Paris by the great torrent of the flight from the North, there came to the American Hostels a little acrobat from a strolling circus. He was not much more than a boy, and he had never before been separated from his family or from his circus. All his people were mummers or contortionists, and he himself was a mere mote of the lime-light, knowing life only in terms of the tent and the platform, the big drum, the dancing dogs, the tight-rope and the spangles.

In the sad preoccupied Paris of last winter it was not easy to find a corner for this little figure. But the lad could not be left in the streets, and after a while he was placed as page in a big hotel. He was given good pay, and put into a good livery, and told to be a good boy. He tried . . . he really tried . . . but the life was too lonely. Nobody knew anything about the only things *he* knew, or was particularly interested in the programme of the last performance the company had given at Liège or Maubeuge. The little acrobat could not understand. He told his friends at the Hostels how lonely and puzzled he was, and they tried to help him. But he couldn't sleep at night, because he was used to being up till nearly daylight; and one night he went up to the attic of the hotel, broke open several trunks full of valuables stored there by rich lodgers, and made off with some of the contents. He was caught, of course, and the things he had stolen were produced in court. They were the spangled dresses belonging to a Turkish family, and the embroidered coats of a lady's lap-dog. . .

I have told this poor little story to illustrate a fact which, as time passes, is beginning to be lost sight of: the fact that we workers among the refugees are trying, first and foremost, to *help a homesick people*. We are not preparing for their new life an army of voluntary colonists; we are seeking to console for the ruin of their old life a throng of bewildered fugitives. It is our business not only to feed and clothe and keep alive these people, but to reassure and guide them. And that has been, for the last year, the task of the American Hostels for Refugees.

———— • ————

SHER BAHADUR KHAN was a Punjabi Musalman fighting in France in the Secunderabad Cavalry Brigade. The letter below, originally written in Urdu transcribed by the Censor of the Indian Mails, was written to Raja Gul Nawaz Khan in Jhelam, India.

[9th January 1916]

I have seen strange things in France. The French are sympathetic and gracious people. Some time ago we were established for about three months in a village. The house in which I was billeted was the house of a well-to-do man, but the only occupant was the lady of the house, and she was advanced in years. Her three sons had gone to the war. One had been killed, another had been wounded and was in hospital, and the third was at that time in the trenches. There is no doubt that the lady was much attached to her sons. There are miles of difference between women of India and the women of this country. During the whole three months, I never once saw this old lady sitting idle, although she belonged to a high family. Indeed during the whole three months she ministered to me to such an extent that I cannot adequately describe her kindness. Of her own free will she washed my clothes, arranged my bed, polished my boots for three months. She used to wash down my bedroom daily with warm water. Every morning she used to prepare and give me a tray

with bread, butter, milk and coffee. I was continually wishing to find
a way to reimburse her the expense; but however much I pressed
her, she declined. When we had to leave that village the old lady
wept on my shoulder. Strange that I had never seen her weeping for
her dead son and yet she should weep for me. Moreover, at parting
she pressed on me a five-franc note to meet my expenses en route.

—— • ——

ERNST TOLLER (1893-1939) was a German-Jewish playwright. When
war broke out he joined the German Army but was later imprisoned
for his part in organising a munition workers' strike. He ended the
war a socialist and a pacifist and six years after the publication of I Was
a German: An Autobiography (1933) he committed suicide. The extracts
below are from 'At the Front' and 'The Military Prison'.

And suddenly, like light in the darkness, the real truth broke in upon
me; the simple fact of Man, which I had forgotten, which had lain
deep buried and out of sight; the idea of community, of unity.

A dead man.

Not a dead Frenchman.

Not a dead German.

A dead man.

The barred window divided the eternal grey of the winter sky into
little gloomy squares. If I pulled myself up to the sill I could see on
the other side of the courtyard the white court-martial house, where
the uniformed curtailers of the rights of man measured out grey

prison years. The ground-floor window had friendly white curtains. The porter lived there. And once, at one of the windows, two hands parted the curtains and a girl looked out curiously at the courtyard. Our eyes met, and her head disappeared, but the gentle agitation of the curtains betrayed her presence.

The next day at the same time I was again at my grating, and the girl was again at her window; every day at the same hour the friendly ritual was repeated. When the sentries approached and danger threatened she waved to me; she invented a language of expressive gestures; her smiles and glances were the vowels, her hands and shoulders the consonants.

Then one evening the bolt clashed back in the door of my cell, and the warder called me by name.

'Am I to be taken to another prison?' I asked.

'Out you get!' he snapped.

I followed him along the corridor and into his office.

And there, under the warm gaslight, was the girl of the window, leaning on the table. I stared at her uncomprehendingly; a wave of colour swept her cheeks and she lowered her eyes in confusion.

I was bewildered and apprehensive.

Apparently the porter's daughter was a friend of this warder, and knew, as everybody in the neighbourhood knew, that the military prison was being used for political prisoners – romantic adventurers, twentieth-century Robin Hoods who robbed the rich to help the poor, fools who preached peace when the nations were at war, and when even the priests had declared that God with His angel hosts watched over our army; the sort of people, in short, one reads about in newspapers; dangerous people, interesting people.

And so this girl had determined to see one of these fascinating creatures for herself. When she asked her lover, however, to smuggle her secretly into the prison he simply laughed at her. But the next evening, when he climbed up to her room as usual, he found the shutters of the windows barred; there was no answer when he knocked. Raging inwardly, he had to give it up, for he could already hear voices in her parents' bedroom.

'Why didn't you let me in last night, Marie?' he asked next day.

'Because I didn't want to.'

'Can I come to-night?'

'Yes, if you show me one of those poor men.'

He offered no more resistance. On the following Sunday he was on duty, with nobody else in the office. The military guard he bribed with cigarettes. And thus it was that I found myself face to face with my girl.

'Well, there is your man,' said the warder. 'And now I hope you're satisfied.'

He sat down at the table, took out a mouth-organ from his pocket and began to play it, up and down, up and down.

'If you're going to play, we may as well dance,' I said.

'None of your lip!' he said.

'Go on playing,' said the girl.

The warder thought of the barred bedroom window, gave a wry smile, and started up a waltz.

'May I have the honour?'

'Thank you,' said the girl. And we danced round the table to the music of the warder's mouth organ; when we came to the wall where the chains and fetters and handcuffs were hanging I kicked out at them, and we danced on to the accompaniment of their metallic clashing.

Suddenly the music broke off; the warder turned and listened intently.

'Aren't you going to play any more?' the girl asked threateningly.

'Shut up, you silly fool! The boss is coming. This'll cost me my job! Into your cell, you!' And turning to the girl: 'You too!'

He pushed me out of the room, and I ran back to my cell, the girl following; the moment the door closed behind us she fell into my arms and we kissed. But the warder was soon with us again.

'False alarm. Come on out of there! That'll do for to-day.'

—— • ——

ROSA LUXEMBURG (1871–1919) was a revolutionary socialist, theorist and letter writer, born in Poland but living much of her life in Germany. She founded the radical left-wing Spartacus League with Karl Liebknecht (she is writing to his wife in the letters below). Luxemburg was imprisoned for her agitation against the war. She and Karl Liebknecht were rearrested and assassinated on 15 January 1919 by the Freikorps, a paramilitary organisation seeking to quash the Spartacist uprising. Luxemburg's body was thrown into the Landwehr canal in Berlin.

Breslau, Mid-November, 1917.

My beloved Sonichka,

I hope soon to have a chance of sending you this letter at long last, so I hasten to take up my pen. For how long a time I have been forced to forbear my habit of talking to you – on paper at least. I am allowed to write so few letters, and I had to save up my chances for Hans. D. [Dr Hans Dieffenbach, a friend killed in the war] who was expecting to hear from me. But now all is over. My last two letters to him were addressed to a dead man, and one has already been returned to me. His loss still seems incredible. But enough of this. I prefer to consider such matters in solitude. It only annoys me beyond expression when people try, as N. tried, 'to break the news' to me, and to make a parade of their own grief by way of 'consolation'. Why should my closest friends understand me so little and hold me so cheaply as to be unable to realise that the best way in such cases is to say quickly, briefly, and simply: 'He is dead'?

…How I deplore the loss of all these months and years in which we might have had so many joyful hours together, notwithstanding all the horrors that are going on throughout the world. Do you know, Sonichka, the longer it lasts, and the more the infamy and monstrosity of the daily happenings surpasses all bounds, the more tranquil and more confident becomes my personal outlook. I say to myself that it is absurd to apply moral standards to the great elemental forces that manifest themselves in a hurricane, a flood, or an eclipse of the sun. We have to accept them simply as data for investigation, as subjects of study.

Manifestly, objectively considered, these are the only possible lines along which history can move, and we must follow the movement without losing sight of the main trend. I have the feeling that all this moral filth through which we are wading, this huge madhouse in which we live, may all of a sudden, between one day and the next, be transformed into its very opposite, as if by the stroke

of a magician's wand; may become something stupendously great
and heroic; *must* inevitably be so transformed, if only the war lasts
a few years longer... Read Anatole France's *Les dieux ont soif.* My
main reason for admiring this work so much is because the author,
with the insight of genius into all that is universally human, seems
to say to us: 'Behold, out of these petty personalities, out of these
trivial commonplaces, arise, when the hour is ripe, the most titanic
events and the most monumental gestures of history.' We have to
take everything as it comes both in social life and in private life; to
accept what happens, tranquilly, comprehensively, and with a smile.
I feel absolutely convinced that things will take the right turn when
the war ends, or not long afterwards; but obviously we have first to
pass through a period of terrible human suffering.

[...]

Your Rosa

Breslau, Mid December, 1917.

Karl has been in Luckau prison for a year now. I have been thinking
of that so often this month and of how it is just a year since you
came to see me at Wronke, and gave me that lovely Christmas tree.
This time I arranged to get one here, but they have brought me such
a shabby little tree, with some of its branches broken off – there's
no comparison between it and yours. I'm sure I don't know how I
shall manage to fix all the eight candles that I have got for it. This
is my *third* Christmas under lock and key, but you needn't take it to
heart. I am as tranquil and cheerful as ever. Last night I lay awake
for a long time. I have to go to bed at ten, but can never get to

sleep before one in the morning, so I lie in the dark, pondering many things. Last night my thoughts ran thiswise: 'How strange it is that I am always in a sort of joyful intoxication, though without sufficient cause. Here I am lying in a dark cell upon a mattress hard as stone; the building has its usual churchyard quiet, so that one might as well be already entombed; through the window there falls across the bed a glint of light from the lamp which burns all night in front of the prison. At intervals I can hear faintly in the distance the noise of a passing train or close at hand the dry cough of the prison guard as in his heavy boots, he takes a few slow strides to stretch his limbs. The gride of the gravel beneath his feet has so hopeless a sound that all the weariness and futility of existence seems to be radiated thereby into the damp and gloomy night. I lie here alone and in silence, enveloped in the manifold black wrappings of darkness, tedium, unfreedom, and winter – and yet my heart beats with an immeasurable and incomprehensible inner joy, just as if I were moving in the brilliant sunshine across a flowery mead. And in the darkness I smile at life, as if I were the possessor of charm which would enable me to transform all that is evil and tragical into serenity and happiness. But when I search my mind for the cause of this joy, I find there is no cause, and can only laugh at myself.' – I believe that the key to the riddle is simply life itself, this deep darkness of night is soft and beautiful as velvet, if only one looks at it in the right way. The gride of the damp gravel beneath the slow and heavy tread of the prison guard is likewise a lovely little song of life – for one who has ears to hear. At such moments I think of you, and would that I could hand over this magic key to you also. Then, at all times and in all places, you would be able to see the beauty, and the joy of life; then you also could live in the sweet intoxication, and make your way across a flowery mead. Do not think that I am offering you imaginary joys, or that I am preaching asceticism. I want you to taste all the real pleasures of the senses. My one desire is to give you in addition my inexhaustible sense of inward bliss. Could I do so, I should be at ease about you, knowing that in your passage through life you were clad in a star-bespangled cloak which would protect you from everything petty, trivial, or harassing.

. [...]

> Write soon, darling Sonichka.
> Your Rosa

Never mind, my Sonyusha, you must be calm and happy all the same. Such is life, and we have to take it as it is, valiantly, heads erect, smiling ever – despite all.

—— • ——

EDWARD WILLIAMSON MASON was imprisoned several times during the war for his resistance to joining the army (conscription was introduced in 1916); he also refused alternative service. He served his first sentence at Durham Prison. He sent the letter below, written on 14 December 1916, from the army camp at Catterick. Mason was born in London, and left school at fourteen to work in a tailor's shop. He met Henry Litchfield Woods, to whom most of his letters were addressed, in an East End Socialist hall. The letter below was published in the 1918 volume *Made Free in Prison*.

CATTERICK,
Thursday, 14th December.

If you look with the eye of faith over the portal of the huge gates at Wormwood Scrubs, you will see a message written up for all prisoners of conscience about to enter into the silence. The message is obscurely written for the ordinary criminal, he always reads it as – 'Abandon hope, all ye who enter here.' But to the prisoner of conscience the message is pikestaff clear, and he reads – 'Abound in hope, all ye who enter here.' That is what he reads if his heart is full of faith and courage and void of all repining and regret. I must admit that when I first saw the message I misread it, and entered the portal as an ordinary criminal, but I have since discovered my error, and when I see the scroll in a few days' time I shall read it aright.

Dante saw the first legend written above the gates of Hell. Many people think prison is Hell, and so it is if you like to allow it to be so. Believe me, dear friend, it is so no more to me.

I have made my plans for living in Wormwood Scrubs and am ready for anything. I believe I shall gradually become absorbed in a deep tranquillity. To many, prison is a gnawing monotony, a corroding silence that preys upon the heart. To explore your own mind day after day, week after week, month after month, to hear your own thoughts reverberating in the empty silence of your weary brain, what horror! But that horror can be exorcised by calm meditation, books, poetry, and a cheerful and hopeful resolution.

If our militarists could realise what formidable and relentless men they are forging, I think the absolutists would be released. A man who has withstood imprisonment for his principles is not going to relapse into lethargy after his release. After the War we will renew the war. At present we are in our dug-outs (cells) and trenches (prisons), undergoing a bombardment of two-year shells and alternative service bombs, but it is surprising how few casualties are sustained. At first the alternative service bombs did a great deal of damage, but now I believe the lads are getting over the shock. The enemy is dismayed at his two-year shells doing so little damage to our morale. Beneath their impact our temper is being strengthened, and when we can resume active hostilities our *élan* will be irresistible.

Remember that, our separation apart, I shall suffer not at all. I want to assure you most firmly that all will be well with me.

—— • ——

CIVILIAN PRISONERS AT KNOCKALOE Swiss physician Adolf Lukas Vischer (1884–1974) quoted the testimonies below in his study *Barbed Wire Disease: A Psychological Study of the Prisoner of War* (1919). The book consists of his reflections and research into the impact of imprisonment on the mind of the prisoner of war. He was interested in how their situation, and consequent psychological health, differed from that of those in 'ordinary' prisons. Below are two extracts he reproduces from *Lager-Echo*, a Journal of the Civilian Prisoners' Camp at Knockaloe on the Isle of Man.

We live in a kingdom of thorns, and the points that prick us on all sides are to us like a nightmare. Do you imagine that these thorny obstacles that hem us in on all sides are soothing to our spirits?

Make the experiment, and imagine a picture of a man pointing a formidable revolver at you in such a way that from whatever angle you look at the picture, you stare down the black muzzle. Hang up this picture in your sitting room, a copy of it in your bedroom, and another in your office. At the end of twenty-four hours you will take a hatchet and give that man such a blow that, dumbfounded, he will drop the murderous weapon. Three times you will strike, and then you will sweep up the fragments and cast them on the rubbish-heap. Physically, the prisoner is powerless. But in spirit he gnaws unceasingly at the roots of the thorny hedge.

(*Lager-Echo*, Knockaloe, No. 7, 18 August 1917)

There are many things of which we can see and hear too much, but most of all our dear companions. In despair, thousands of us have wished ourselves far away on a mountain top. Solitude! Music of the spheres for a prisoner of war who has dragged out two or three years amidst a swarm of men, behind double rows of wire-fencing. Oh! only to be out of this crowded desert. Just for ten minutes to be on a solitary storm-tossed mountain top, on the chilliest glacier, in a mad whirlwind – anywhere, even where danger lies, to get away from the sight and sound and smell of mankind, and to be able to think one's thoughts. Here it is like an ant-heap (a nest of termites, as [Gaston] Riou calls it), a hive of bees... This long period of the closet contact finally reduces one to look on one's companions as on the dismembered carcasses in a butcher's shop... Our characters are now like a book that all can read, and the pages are soiled by constant handling.

(*Lager-Echo*, Knockaloe, No. 9, 26 September 1917)

—— • ——

'G. H. M.' was in Ruhleben internment camp for civilian prisoners of war, located to the west of Berlin. Prisoners there had been captured when working or travelling in Germany or in the North Sea at the outbreak of the war. The inmates had their own camp journal, in which this story was first published. A transcribed version, together with the biographical note included below, can be found in the Imperial War Museum.

A CHRISTMAS TRAGEDY

George Scrooge clambered into his bunk in a particularly bad temper. Not that one can blame a man for having a fit of the blues once in a while, but this was Christmas Eve, and nobody ought to be ill-humoured on Christmas Eve, no matter where he is. Of course Scrooge was convinced that there never had been such tiresome fools as his box mates, and his box mates were equally convinced that Scrooge had taken too much rations for supper; but, however that may be, Scrooge crawled under the blankets, swore at everybody in general, and pulled the curtain across the bed.

Now it is important to note that fact, because when Scrooge woke up an hour later, the curtain was drawn back. 'Extremely annoying!' He was now in a worse temper than ever, so he stuck his head out in order to be rude, when he noticed – the moon was shining through the window – that the two Figures seated at the table were no box mates of his. This of course rather took him aback, and he wasn't rude in the way he meant to be. 'W-who the deuce are you?' he spluttered. One of the Figures rose up – it was a merry fellow in a bottle-brown coat, with a cigar and a packet of toffee in his hand,

and it gazed at Scrooge with a watery leer. 'Keep your pecker up,' it carolled; 'I am the g[h]ost of your first Ruhleben Xmas!' Scrooge gaped, when the second Figure approached the bed, breathing weak tea – and rum – onto his face. 'And I am the ghost of your second Ruhleben Xmas,' it wheezed. 'I am a gay dog, I am – see?' and it danced up and down the box shouting boisterously. 'Oh cut it out!' said Scrooge, and pulling the curtain he turned over and went to sleep. But not for long. He woke up feeling very cold and miserable, and saw that the curtain was again drawn back.

This time the box was full of shapes – grey melancholy spectres that fixed him with weary eyes. 'Go away!' he said, as firmly as he could. The spectres did not move.

A little shiver ran down Scrooge's spine, and he tried again more pleasantly. 'Don't let me keep you if you wish to be off, you know.'

Still the spectres did not move.

Scrooge felt distinctly uncomfortable, and the worst of it was, he began to doubt whether he hadn't, perhaps – after all – and the doubt became a certainty, and slipping his feet into a pair of clogs, he tried to whistle.

The spectres did not move as he passed out of the box, but the corridor, too, was full of the sad grey shapes.

'This is worse than I supposed,' muttered Scrooge, and he hurried outside.

More spectres – they thronged the yard, they filled the square from the Casino to the Captain's office, they were gathered in the Grand Stands, they blocked the Promenade – from one end of the Camp to the other, there was no escaping them.

Then Scrooge's nerve forsook him.

'Who are all ye?' he shrieked. A wail rose from all the shadowy forms, a wail so plaintive and sinister that Scrooge's very heart stood still. 'We are the ghosts of the Ruhleben Xmases to [c]ome!'

In the morning four men carried Scrooge to the Lazaret [sanatorium].

G. H. M.

A young Scotch boy of 20 yrs of age – having spent a year when 16 yrs old – in Germany – to learn the language, – returned there in the summer of 1914 to make a long bicycle trip. – While doing so the war broke out, & the lad was promptly interned at the Ruhleben camp, – where he suffered all sorts of hardships. The family's friend, here in Zürich, sent him his <u>first</u> Christmas box – & in it put some home-made 'toffy' – which greatly pleased him. By the second Christmas he had 'a mental break-down' from what he had undergone – & was put in a sanatorium – where he is <u>still</u> – in Germany – of course. Towards the last weeks in Ruhleben he <u>wrote</u> this pathetic tale – showing the <u>visions</u> he had from hunger & ill health – before he <u>entirely</u> broke down – & it being published in the prisoners' journal, it was <u>signed</u> with his initials, – which were recognised by his Scotch friend <u>here</u>, & this faithful copy given me.

—— • ——

T. E. LAWRENCE, popularly known as Lawrence of Arabia (1888–1935), was born in Wales and educated in Oxford. During the First World War he worked as an intelligence officer and liaison officer, shaping policy in the Middle East; he mobilised the Arab revolt (1916–

18) against the Ottoman Turks, allies of Germany. He left for England after the capture of Damascus (Syria) in October 1918. The passage below is from his autobiography *Seven Pillars of Wisdom* (privately printed in 1926, published in 1935).

I was sent to these Arabs as a stranger, unable to think their thoughts or subscribe to their beliefs, but charged by duty to lead them forward and to develop to the highest any movement of theirs profitable to England in her war. If I could not assume their character, I could at least conceal my own, and pass among them without evident friction, neither a discord nor a critic but an unnoticed influence. Since I was their fellow, I will not be their apologist or advocate. To-day in my old garments, I could play the bystander, obedient to the sensibilities of our theatre . . . but it is more honest to record that these ideas and actions then passed naturally. What now looks wanton or sadic seemed in the field inevitable, or just unimportant routine.

Blood was always on our hands: we were licensed to it. Wounding and killing seemed ephemeral pains, so very brief and sore was life with us. With the sorrow of living so great, the sorrow of punishment had to be pitiless. We lived for the day and died for it. When there was reason and desire to punish we wrote our lesson with gun or whip immediately in the sullen flesh of the sufferer, and the case was beyond appeal. The desert did not afford the refined slow penalties of courts and gaols.

Of course our rewards and pleasures were as suddenly sweeping as our troubles; but, to me in particular, they bulked less large. Bedouin ways were hard even for those brought up to them, and for strangers terrible: a death in life. When the march or labour ended I had no energy to record sensation, nor while it lasted any leisure to see the spiritual loveliness which sometimes came upon us by the way. In my notes, the cruel rather than the beautiful found place. We no doubt enjoyed more the rare moments of peace and forgetfulness; but I remember more the agony, the terrors, and the mistakes. Our life is not summed up in what I have written (there are things not to be repeated in cold blood for very shame); but what I have written was in and of our life. Pray God that men reading the story will not, for love of the glamour of strangeness, go out to prostitute themselves and their talents in serving another race.

A man who gives himself to be a possession of aliens leads a Yahoo life, having bartered his soul to a brute-master. He is not of them. He may stand against them, persuade himself of a mission, batter and twist them into something which they, of their own accord, would not have been. Then he is exploiting his old environment to press them out of theirs. Or, after my model, he may imitate them so well that they spuriously imitate him back again. Then he is giving away his own environment: pretending to theirs; and pretences are hollow, worthless things. In neither case does he do a thing of himself, nor a thing so clean as to be his own (without thought of conversion), letting them take what action or reaction they please from the silent example.

In my case, the effort for these years to live in the dress of Arabs, and to imitate their mental foundation, quitted me of my English self, and let me look at the West and its conventions with new eyes: they destroyed it all for me. At the same time I could not sincerely take on the Arab skin: it was an affectation only. Easily was a man made an infidel, but hardly might he be converted to another faith. I had dropped one form and not taken on the other, and was become like Mohammed's coffin in our legend, with a resultant feeling of intense loneliness in life, and a contempt, not for other men, but for all they do. Such detachment came at times to a man exhausted by prolonged physical effort and isolation. His body plodded on mechanically, while his reasonable mind left him, and from without looked down critically on him, wondering what that futile lumber did and why. Sometimes these selves would converse in the void; and then madness was very near, as I believe it would be near the man who could see things through the veils at once of two customs, two educations, two environments.

———— • ————

W. E. B. DU BOIS (1868–1963) was an African-American writer, activist, and leader and one of the founders of the NAACP (National Association for the Advancement of Colored People), formed in 1909. The articles below were published in the NAACP journal, *The Crisis*. For many years after the war Du Bois worked on, but did not publish, a history of the black troops in the conflict entitled *The Black Man and the Wounded World*.

Close Ranks

This is the crisis of the world. For all the long years to come men will point to the year 1918 as the great Day of Decision, the day when the world decided whether it would submit to military despotism and an endless armed peace – if peace it could be called – or whether they would put down the menace of German militarism and inaugurate the United States of the World.

We of the colored race have no ordinary interest in the outcome. That which the German power represents today spells death to the aspirations of Negroes and all darker races for equality, freedom and democracy. Let us not hesitate. Let us, while this war lasts, forget our special grievances and close our ranks shoulder to shoulder with our own white fellow citizens and the allied nations that are fighting for democracy. We make no ordinary sacrifice, but we make it gladly and willingly, with our eyes lifted to the hills.

[July 1918]

Returning Soldiers

We are returning from war! *The Crisis* and tens of thousands of black men were drafted into a great struggle. For bleeding France and what she means and has meant and will mean to us and humanity and against the threat of German race arrogance, we fought gladly and to the last drop of blood: for America and her highest ideals, we fought in far-off hope: for the dominant southern oligarchy entrenched in Washington, we fought in bitter resignation. For the America that represents and gloats in lynching, disfranchisement, caste, brutality and devilish insult – for this, in the hateful upturning and mixing of things, we were forced by vindictive fate to fight, also.

But today we return! We return from the slavery of uniform which the world's madness demanded us to don to the freedom of civil garb. We stand again to look America squarely in the face and call a spade a spade. We sing: This country of ours, despite all its better souls have done and dreamed, is yet a shameful land.

It *lynches*.

And lynching is barbarism of a degree of contemptible nastiness unparalleled in human history. Yet for fifty years we have lynched two Negroes a week, and we have kept this up right through the war.

It *disfranchises* its own citizens.

Disfranchisement is the deliberate theft and robbery of the only protection of poor against rich and black against white. The land that disfranchises its citizens and calls itself a democracy lies and knows it lies.

It encourages *ignorance*.

It has never really tried to educate the Negro. A dominant minority does not want Negroes educated. It wants servants, dogs, whores and monkeys. And when this land allows a reactionary group by its stolen political power to force as many black folk into these categories as it possibly can, it cries in contemptible hypocrisy: 'They threaten us with degeneracy; they cannot be educated.'

It *steals* from us.

It organizes industry to cheat us. It cheats us out of our land; it cheats us out of our labour. It confiscates our savings. It reduces our wages. It raises our rent and steals our profit. It taxes us without representation. It keeps us consistently and universally poor, and then feeds us on charity and derides our poverty.

It *insults* us.

It has organized a nation-wide and latterly a world-wide propaganda of deliberate and continuous insult and defamation of black blood wherever found. It decrees that it shall not be possible in travel nor residence, work nor play, education nor instruction for a black man to exist without tacit or open acknowledgment of his inferiority to the dirtiest white dog. And it looks upon any attempt to question or even discuss this dogma as arrogance, unwarranted assumption and treason.

This is the country to which we Soldiers of Democracy return. This is the fatherland for which we fought! But it is *our* fatherland. It was right for us to fight. The faults of *our* country are *our* faults. Under similar circumstances, we would fight again. But by the God of Heaven, we are cowards and jackasses if now that the war is over, we do not marshal every ounce of our brain and brawn to fight a sterner, longer, more unbending battle against the forces of hell in our own land.

We *return*.

We *return from fighting*.

We *return fighting*.

Make way for Democracy! We saved it in France, and by the Great Jehovah, we will save it in the United States of America, or know the reason why.

[May 1919]

———— • ————

MARINA YURLOVA was born in Russia around 1900. In 1914, still a young teenager, she joined the Cossack Army, fighting alongside the men. In 1919 she emigrated to the United States via Japan and became a dancer. The excerpt below is from her memoir, *Cossack Girl* (1934). Here she describes a test of the limits of her comradeship with the male soldiers: her close proximity to them while they are undressing brings new feelings of 'modesty' and 'shame': 'That is what four walls can do to you', she reflects.

Our soldiers ran true to form in the building of their quarters – little rude huts, with ten men assigned to each. And they could easily have made them five times as large, with a whole army on hand to build them.

And now a new problem arose. It was one thing to sleep near my 'brothers,' wrapped in a blanket under the open sky; it was quite another to share these cramped quarters with them.

My first night will serve as an example for the rest. It had been raining all day, but we had gone through our drills just the same, and had come back to Kosel's hut, and hung our uniform coats up to dry.

Supper was over. The windows were tightly shut. The air was foul with the fumes of *mahorka* – a crude peasant tobacco – and the stench of unwashed bodies. I lay curled up in my bunk, watching the men with an entirely new feeling: modesty. That is what four walls can do to you.

The oil lamps were lit, and a stove was burning. Kosel had found a pack of cards, so greased and dirty that the figures on them were barely visible, and the men were playing for matches instead of money. You don't have anything to spare out of a few shillings a month; but the disputes were just as loud and the play just as intense as if a million roubles hung in the balance.

After that they took to singing songs and telling stories. They were very good to me, those men; for though – since Kosel and the commander had made no objections to me – they had come to take me for granted, they were very careful to whisper any story that wasn't fit for me to hear. The two noisiest there were the huge Gritsko and Fedka, a red-haired good-for-nothing about half his size, and all they argued about was the amount of liquor each could swallow without feeling it.

But this is the scene that I remember still with a sort of horror. My nine companions had decided at last to hunt for insects, and there they all were, crouched around the stove, which was burning fiercely in the centre of the hut. First they took off their blouses and singed the seams, then they pulled off their shirts...

The lamplight threw grotesque, great shadows on the walls, and gleamed on their white skins and hairy chests. I'd never seen a half-naked man before and lay in my bunk, staring at them with horrified fascination. Their conversation was brief and monotonous; they were so intent on their task that they had forgotten all about me. Outside a dog howled miserably, and a thin, drizzling rain pattered on the roof.

The stove threw a red glow on Kosel's matted chest.

Nothing makes you so lonely as shame. I was suddenly conscious, as I lay there, of the predicament I was in; of my girl's body – for the first time in my life, I think; of the strangeness of my surroundings – that I, a colonel's daughter, should be here, in this place that smelled so horribly of bad air and bad tobacco, of singeing shirts, of damp foot wrappings hanging up to dry, of unwashed bodies and feet.

Somebody – it was the great Gritsko, I think – rose slowly to his feet, muttering to himself, stretching his arms. He was quite naked.

I pushed my fist into my mouth and bit on it until it bled. Then I crawled from my bunk and stumbled to the door – out into the night, into the rain and mud.

When I came back at last, chilled and miserable, they had all gone to sleep. There was still a glow from the stove, and I thought I could safely take my own clothes off now to dry them, and to hunt for insects as the men had done. But my shirt was only half off my head when somebody snored loudly and twisted over in his sleep, and I scrambled into my shirt again, and went and curled up, shivering, in my bunk.

When at last I fell asleep, I had a dream of Kosel.

He had the body of a goat, four legs, and a great shaggy coat of fur.

A naked Gritsko was driving him round and round the hut...

———— • ————

ISABELLE RIMBAUD (1860–1917), was the sister of the French poet Arthur Rimbaud. She describes evacuating Roche with her husband Pierre after its invasion in August 1914, and the bombing of Reims the following month, in her book In the Whirlpool of War (1918).

Monday, August 3.

The village becomes emptier every hour of men under forty-eight years of age. At the same time there is a change in the moral atmosphere: hatreds die down and enemies become reconciled. There is no more slandering a neighbour, no more desire to do him an ill turn; but gentle speech instead. The fires of envy and vanity die out in look and soul. In the families of called-up men the farewells are heart-breaking, as if something irrevocable were happening; and all arrangements are made on this understanding.

Emile is gone.

Men of the field army are beginning to pass along the road.

[...]

Monday, August 31st

[...]

We start off again at about one o'clock. Just outside Berru the view embraces a large panorama of woods, cultivated lands and vineyards, scattered over with smiling villages. The hill becomes steep; now we are among woods, and tall trees interlace their branches above us, making a dome of coolness ahead. We pass through Berru and Cernay forests, in which the Reims folk spend their Sundays in summer-time. To-day these splendid glades, which have witnessed so many merry picnics, harbour a multitude of refugee families who have gone round the hill. This halting-place is a moving sight, with its panic and despair. Ah! The forest re-echoes no longer with the laughter and play of former days! From its depths come sounds of misery and fear, the sobbings of children, and curses. The poor wretches have with them droves of cows and sheep, which, watched by small boys, bellow and bleat in reply to the nervous neighing of horses. Small heaps of ashes and embers on the fouled earth, broken branches, and an indescribable look of devastation speak of the bivouacs of former nights and foretell those nights to come. No ties of fellowship seem to bind these groups together. They are, as it were, tribes come each from a different locality, each bringing with it its own peculiar load of misery. There is no intercourse between tribe and tribe: each has enough to do in looking after its own people. Their sufferings on the road, the tragedies they have lived through or feared, have deprived these unfortunates of all taste for neighbourliness. The selfish instinct of self-preservation is their only stimulus and guide. The rich, who have carriages, never offer a lift to the poor who go on foot; and the latter don't think of asking for one. They hardly worry themselves about the excessive weight of their bundles, though they dream of throwing them away or lightening them.

[...]

Friday, September 4

[...]

Our hostess knows every one here, and everybody knows her. She speaks to one, answers another, ventures on to the street in defiance of orders, keeps stopping. This gets on Pierre's nerves. 'I think,' says he, 'that we shouldn't stay here among all this crowd. It is unwise to do so. Let us go straight to the Royal Square, or go home again.' The words are hardly out of his mouth when a mighty explosion raises the echoes! Nobody takes any notice. We are abreast of Saint-Jacques Church when a second explosion occurs. That makes people turn round and ponder. 'There! they are celebrating their entry by blank fire.' But the haughty Prussian officers, who keep on passing, begin to frown and look astonished. We reach the Theatre. A third explosion! This time loud cries are heard. Looking behind us, we see the lower end of the Rue de Vesle filled with dust and smoke; the sunshine is dimmed by it. Everybody begins to run. From all sides people shout at us: 'They are bombarding us; take cover; get back home!' In the Royal Square the inquisitive people round the statue of Louis xv., who had climbed up on to the plinth, scatter in all directions, saying that the Germans have signalled them to get to cover. Mothers with babies rush off, uttering piercing cries; children sob and won't walk; men pommel and push the women riveted to the spot by fear. The streets are emptied in a twinkling, while the shells follow one another methodically and fall with a great uproar. We are much upset, my husband and I. As we don't know our way about Reims and cannot see any vehicle able to carry us, we instinctively take the first street to the right that we come to – the Rue du Clôitre, which takes us to the apse of the Cathedral. Thence, by the Rue Robert-de-Coucy, we head for the Parvis, hurrying along our friend, whose serenity seems as great as ever. 'Impossible, my dears,' she says; 'my heart trouble prevents me going fast. Go ahead without me.' We offer her our arms; but she refuses decidedly, pretending that it is too warm to hurry. We can't dream of leaving her, but how trying it is! I involuntarily quicken my pace and find myself a few yards ahead of the others. In the middle of the street, facing the gate of the Beau Dieu, two ecclesiastics in long cloaks, with still unmoved faces, have stopped and are coolly looking at the top of the north tower, partly hidden by a cloud of dust and screened by scaffolding, out of which fly a number of birds as large as pigeons. Strange objects, which at first I take to be bits of broken bottles, patter and jump on the pavement. I step forward to pick up one of these curious objects, and my hand has already been stretched out towards it when I realise its nature. It is death stalking about me. I feel afraid, and remain motionless, petrified, my eyes fixed mechanically on the sculptures of the lower part of the Cathedral, whose every detail now appears to me to stand out with extraordinary clearness. A short, haggard workman is dragging by the elbow a young woman who weeps and wraps her apron about a small child clasped in her arms. The man shouts at me: 'Get away! They're aiming at the Cathedral!'

—— • ——

TESTIMONY FROM FRENCH DEPARTMENTS UNDER OCCUPATION *The Deportation of Women and Girls from Lille* (1916) begins with an address compiled by the French government seeking to alert neutral governments to German violations of international law. The Minister of Foreign Affairs articulated concerns about the treatment of French citizens in departments under occupation. Excerpts of letters and depositions were gathered by the Ministry of War and added to the document.

Annexe 14.

Letter from X, at Lille, 1st May, 1916, to Mme L. G., at Paris-Passy.

'This week has been terrible for our unhappy town; 1,200 to 1,500 people have been carried off every night, escorted by soldiers with fixed bayonets and bands playing, machine guns at the corners of the streets, principally girls and young women of all sorts, also men from 15 to 50, sent off promiscuously in cattle trucks with wooden benches, for unknown destinations and employments, nominally to work on the land. You can imagine the despair and agony of their relations. We learn this afternoon that the horrible business is over and our quarter has been spared.

I had come to sleep at home for the first time in two years, in the attempt to save my maid. I am at last going to sleep without the fear of being wakened in the middle of the night to go and open the door to an invasion of soldiers. There will be nobody left except mothers with children under 14, or old men. In the middle of all this the Town Hall was burnt out one night, as if by magic. The deported people, however, showed truly French courage; they kept back their tears, and the trains left the station to the sound of the Marseillaise. The worse things are, the nearer to deliverance it seems to us we are coming.'

Annexe 21.

Letter signed R., not dated, and addressed to Madame B., in Paris.

'My dear C.,

I suppose the people in France already know of all the trials through which we are passing, even more painful than the last. We have come out of this last one again scot free, and have stayed here, both of us, till a new order comes.

We spent a terrible Easter week here; this is what happened. On Wednesday the 19th of this month, a placard warning the population that there were going to be deportations by order in the invaded territory, that each person was to furnish himself with household utensils and had the right to 30 kilogrammes of luggage. You can imagine the panic in the town.

Two days of waiting passed and at last, on the night of Friday 21st to Saturday 22nd, the streets of one district were blocked by the police at 3 in the morning and the alarm given in each house, with the order to keep in the passage with all luggage. They had brought for this vile duty soldiers, or rather brutes, from another locality simply in order that there should not be any friendliness or weakness towards families who would have begged for mercy. Then, according to the number of people living in the house, the brute made his choice. They carried off girls of the family, servants, men of all sorts and of all ages. They attacked chiefly the working class, which unfortunately always suffer the most; lads and girls of good family who were caught in the raid were released; the same was the case with people seriously ill, but for them application had to be made and often they were put into the train before exemption was granted.

From the 22nd to the 29th, inclusive, 9,890 were deported; a reprieve was granted for Easter day.

All these poor people wondered where and why they were being taken away; there were, I can assure you, sad pictures, but always the cheerful side as well, for one heard groups singing, some patriotic songs, others popular tunes, and as they were kept at the station the whole day some groups played cards, while waiting for their departure. One could even say that the greater number were cheerful, or rather put on a good face against their misfortune, to the bewilderment of the Boches, who were amazed to see the French character not recoiling before any sacrifice.

In spite of that, it is painful to be at their mercy, for everything about them is false, and one wonders what is the object of this deportation and in what state of health and morale these people will come back.

Then, as a climax to our misfortunes, on Easter night, a fire, due to some unknown cause, entirely destroyed the Town Hall; fortunately the essential things were saved, but what a tragic night!!'

Annexe 153.

M. Albert Camille L——, aged 17, no profession, deported from A—— (Oise), in January, 1915: – 'Directly the Germans came, we really suffered from hunger. We only had 120 grammes of foul black bread. As to meat, we only had the refuse thrown away by the soldiers, and we had to pay very high even for that.

'The Boches encouraged the population to cultivate the land; they even sold us potatoes for seed; then, when the crop was ready, they took it all without even giving requisition vouchers. The corn they worked at themselves without troubling about the boundaries of the fields; they demanded repayment of the price of this work, then harvested it all and took it. It was absolutely forbidden for us to have any corn or meat in our houses on pain of imprisonment.

'The Germans took prisoner about 40 civilians, between 18 and 45, in our village. Ten are shut up in the factory of C. They are employed on forced labour. All the trees in this district are cut down. There is not a walnut tree left.' [Walnut was used to make rifle butts.]

———— • ————

MARY BRITNIEVA was born in St Petersburg in 1894. Her mother was English. She served as a nurse on the Eastern Front, and wrote about her experiences in her memoir *One Woman's Story* (1934). The memoir is dedicated to her husband who had been executed by the Bolsheviks during the revolution.

It was in 1916 that the Russian Red Cross applied for permission from the German Authorities to send a mission consisting of a small medical staff to visit the prisoner of war camps in Germany and Austria. Sister Vera M., one of the outstanding nurses of our sisterhood, was chosen to accompany the Mission.

They could not have made a better choice: Sister Vera was not only one of our best nurses – she had a wonderful personality which made itself felt the moment one saw her. Tall and stately, she had a beautiful and typically Russian face which seemed to radiate kindness and sympathy, her manner was charming and simple, and she had a special way of speaking to the soldiers which at once endeared her to them – it was so obvious that she knew, understood and loved them with all her great heart. To me she always seemed to personify Russia itself – her looks, her manner, her speech were so typical of our country.

The consent of the German authorities having been obtained, the members of the Mission left Sweden and Denmark and were away for several months.

When I next saw Sister Vera she had many interesting and moving stories to tell me, but one especially remained in my memory as an example of quite outstanding idealism and devotion. I will try to write it down as I heard it from her.

It happened in Galicia, in one of the small concentration camps visited by the Mission. The prisoners – about fifty of them – were working in the fields, and Sister Vera went out to them. There was a fallen tree lying by the side of the field, and here they all collected around her, eager to see and hear the 'Sestritza' who had brought them tidings from their far-away homes. First she said a few words to them, words of comfort and hope, and then they asked her individual questions and handed her letters or asked her to carry out various commissions. Afterwards, they sang Russian folk-songs and finally they all prayed aloud and chanted parts of the beautiful Orthodox Church service. It was evening, the sun was setting and its glowing rays bathed the quiet field, adding to the sense of peace and of beauty that prayers and singing had evoked in the hearts of those poor outcasts. The time came for Vera to return to headquarters and, one by one, the men filed past to shake hands and to wish her godspeed. One of the men stretched out a hand that was terribly mutilated – all the fingers were missing and only part of the thumb remained. 'How did that happen,' asked Vera horrified, 'was it a shell?' The man flushed and drew back shyly, hiding his hand behind his back. 'No, it didn't happen at the front,' he muttered and turned away. But Vera's interest was aroused and she repeated her question. The man hung his head and stood silent – but here his companions broke in '…go on, tell the Sister, Petruha, there's nothing to be ashamed of, tell her how it happened.'

Vera had a good look at him. What she saw was a simple, homely and good-natured peasant face with a reddish beard and kind, child-like grey eyes. She drew him gently towards her, and sitting down on the tree trunk, said encouragingly:

'Sit down next to me, Petruha, and tell me how it happened – I want you to tell me yourself.' Petruha smiled shyly and began his tale:

'You see, Sestritza, I was taken prisoner in East Prussia with several others and we were all put to work in a factory. I was made a stoker. All day long I shovelled coal into a furnace with never a thought in my head: I was unaccustomed to the work, and my back and arms ached, but after a few days, when I had got more used to things, my mind began to work again, and suddenly I realized that I was doing wrong: "Oh, God" – I thought in terror – "here am I actually helping to make shells and bullets for the enemy! – Shells and bullets destined to kill my own brothers, to kill our brave allies whom we have promised to help. No, I must not do it. I must not! I cannot be a traitor to them all – let them punish me, let them do what they like to me, but I cannot lose my very soul." And this thought, constantly in mind, I had no peace that night, and the next morning, when we were led down to the factory, I refused to work. I was led away and they suspended me from a beam by my wrists, my toes just touching the ground. I hung like that for twelve hours and it was terribly painful. When they took me down, they put me in hospital, and I remained there for three weeks. At the end of that time I was pronounced well enough to resume work and they sent me back to the same factory. Once again they put me down to stoke the boilers and again I refused to work, it was the only way in which I could save myself from being a foul traitor, for now I realized more clearly than ever that every shovelful of coal put on by me helped to make that which meant death, yes, Sestritza, *death*, to my brothers. And I couldn't kill my own blood and flesh. They led me away and suspended me as before, but this time I hung for twenty-four hours. The blood rushed through my head, my ears felt as if they would burst and I bled by the nose – it was painful agony… They took me to hospital again and I lay there for three months. But I recovered and I was taken back to the same factory. As I was being marched along the road, my soul was full of anguish and I prayed and prayed to the Lord to give me strength so that I should not give in, for I knew that if I did, my soul would perish – I would have sold it to the devil. But as we neared the gate, a terrible fear came over me – I knew too well what would happen when I refused to work: again they would hang me up by my wrists and probably add other punishments this time and I feared that I might not be able to bear it all, so I prayed to the Lord for help that He might in His mercy show me some way out.

When we entered the gate and were being marched across the yard, I suddenly saw something that shone brightly lying on a tree-stump that stood in the middle of the yard; after a few paces I saw that it was an axe, a beautiful new axe. There it lay reflecting the sunshine almost as a mirror would and, as this thought occurred to me, I suddenly seemed to feel that a voice inside of me had spoken to me pointing out the way. It was the answer to my prayer. God had had that axe put there to help me. I broke away from the line of prisoners and ran swiftly to the tree-stump, I made the sign of the cross and saying to myself: 'For Faith, Tsar and Country,' I seized the axe in one hand, and placing the other on the stump, with one blow I chopped off my fingers.'

NOTHING is to be written on this side except the date and signature of the sender. Sentences not required may be erased. If anything else is added the post card will be destroyed.

[Postage must be prepaid on any letter or post card addressed to the sender of this card.]

I am quite well.

I have been admitted into hospital

{ *sick* } *and am going on well.*

{ *wounded* } *and hope to be discharged soon*

I am being sent down to the base.

I have received your { *letter dated* _____
{ *telegram* ,, _____
{ *parcel* ,, _____

Letter follows at first opportunity.

I have received no letter from you

{ *lately*

{ *for a long time.*

Signature } *Peace*
only }

Date _____

Wt. W65—P.P.948. 8000m. 5-18. C. & Co., Grange Mills, S.W.

This is an example of a Field Service postcard that was issued to soldiers for sending home. In place of a signature the soldier who sent this postcard, Albert E. Peto, has inscribed the word 'Peace'. He probably sent this postcard on, or close to, the date of the Armistice on 11 November 1918. It is held at the Imperial War Museum.

These train tickets to towns in German possession were found by R.E. Roller in the ruins of Ypres station in 1916 and sent to his uncle. The letter that accompanied them is included in this section.

WHITE SPOTS

Searching for what
was lost

HENRY WILLIAMSON (1895–1977) was born in Brockley, London. His book *Tarka the Otter* (1927) won the Hawthornden Prize. He was a territorial soldier before the First World War started, and served until demobilised in 1919. He wrote seven books about the war: *The Wet Flanders Plain* (1929), *The Patriot's Progress* (1930) and five parts of his fifteen-volume work *A Chronicle of Ancient Sunlight* (1951–69). In 1963 Gordon Watkins, a producer at the BBC, asked Williamson to contribute to the *Great War* series. He was eventually interviewed, but his initial response was to send a postcard agreeing to a meeting yet saying: 'I've waited since 1919 to write these novels – now they are all in print and I am FREE' (18 July). This is a later letter.

16th Oct[obe]r 1963

Ox's Cross,
BRAUNTON,
N. DEVON
Dear Watkins

The fact is, I lived, and smouldered, to write my 1914–18 world since 1919: planned to start in 1929; found myself encumbered; went to settle family cars etc on a farm in 1937, still horribly frustrated; saw it all come again & finally broke down (1945) – to retire here to this hut with its flaming open hearth and find myself lonely & 'finished'. By 1949 life had changed and thenceforward it was all write write write, seven days a week and often all Xmas Day – for 13 years on end, when my mainstay, the bride of 1949, broke & left & all was to do again with little or nothing left to do. And in the period of 13 years I 'held the Great War in the hollow of (my) hand', as George D. Painter wrote to me – and then it was over &

done with. Gone back into limbo. So I have really nothing left to say – like (one supposes) Siegfried Sassoon, Robert Graves, and others of the hosts of the (articulate) soldiers of that time when the lyric perished on the Somme, leaving a waste land to the scholars who never knew the Western front, that great lurid wound stretching from the sands of Belgium's coast to the Alps – never ceasing to weep from gangrenous dawn to those sunsets of the Salient with the [the next word is unclear] of pus and blood.

I am past it – all lies within covers of the five novels – there ain't no more left to say – but the <u>happy release</u> of Xmas Day 1914 might just be possible – & the little-known details –

From, Henry Williamson.

I shall be up on 1 Nov for a 1914 Old Comrades dinner – the few survivors of the London battalion I served with as a rifleman in the autumn of that year, in the 4th Division. HW

———— • ————

A. A. LONG was a sergeant in the Royal Engineers. Below is an excerpt from a long letter he wrote to his wife on 3 March 1919 while on active service, in which he describes an automobile tour he took of the battlefields in Belgium and Northern France.

We decided to push on to the region occupied by the Germans in their attacks on Ypres, and made for the Zonnebeke road. Never shall I forget the sight on getting well clear of Ypres. As mentioned before, the country here was quite flat & typical of this part of Flanders. A wide belt of land stretched for miles north & south with not a single

whole tree left standing, not a building to be seen – desolation &
barrenness on every hand – yet with every evidence of the awful
struggles which must have taken place. We halted about half way
between Ypres & Zonnebeke & walked over some of the ground
where desperate fights had gone on. Judging from the appearance
of the place it is inconceivable that any man could possibly have
come through alive. Evidently this particular spot had been occupied
at different times by both British & German troops – the way the
defences faced showed this. Barbed wire entanglements, twisted cut
about by shrapnel, are still there, whilst one comes across more or
less wrecked German 'pill-boxes' showing that our gunners had done
their work well. Smashed dug-outs (filthsome holes) in plenty, and
destroyed trenches are, of course, to [be] seen all round. We have
heard repeatedly of the mud of low-lying Flanders. It must be seen for
one to realise fully what it is like. Even now, long after the churning
of it has ceased, one has to pick one's way very carefully to avoid
sinking to the tops of one's boots in the greasy stuff. It is impossible to
conceive how men managed to exist in the waterlogged trenches and
the muddy reeking dug-outs, under fire all the while. Three bent &
battered tanks were lying derelict nearby & I climbed into one which
had had half one side blown off. The steel is twisted all shapes, but
of course it must have been subjected to shelling for a long time after
being disabled. The litter of a modern battlefield is lying all about –
broken rifles, bayonets, hand-grenades – still dangerous, stick-bombs,
shell cases, unexploded ('dud', as they are called) shells – those I saw
being mostly German & all pointing towards Ypres – helmets, boots,
equipment, &c. &c. everywhere, the latter suggestive of some tragic
happening to the owner. In one place a complete soldier's pack left

behind told its own story. Human bones were lying about the shell holes. Protruding from the side of one shell hole the rims of two steel German helmets were visible. One of our fellows pulled one helmet out & that had a story of its own. The crown had a long deep dent evidently caused by a piece of shell which had penetrated the steel & must have killed the wearer instantly. What struck the onlooker most I think was the manner in which the ground has been cut up by the shells. The shell holes just here were literally edge to edge, & one had to make one's way along the 'rims'. Ordered trenches & pathways were completely obliterated, whilst further afield were tremendous holes (now filled with water, making sizeable ponds) suggestive of mine craters. And amongst all this confusion I came across one of the first signs of spring – a piece of henbit in blossom & this made me think of you & home in our beautiful Bassett, & Lord's Wood.

We did not need to stop here long, for what we saw in a limited area was typical of the rest of the open battlefields. We returned to the car & had lunch which we had brought with us, afterwards continuing our journey through the old lines occupied by the enemy. We soon reached the spot where the village of Zonnebeke once stood – now a heap of rubble. Thence we went on a road along part of the famous Passchendaele Ridge and leading (as the map indicated) to Becalaere. This place was distinguished by the name on a board, all other evidence of a village having stood there being completely absent! We were now well in the German area & signs of Fritz's hasty retirement began to appear everywhere. Stacks of unused shells, rifle & machine gun ammunition, were left on the road sides, heaps of war material of all sorts laid about – while here & there stood a smashed gun – & in one case he had abandoned a steam road roller – this last being unable to travel fast enough!

Saddest of all were the crosses we passed which were scattered about the fields in ones & twos &, occasionally, a small group of four or more in an out-of-the-way corner. All signified hasty burial, some our own men, others German soldiers. On one cross was scrawled '2 unknown soldiers'! Several crosses were lying about anyhow – these, if originally marking graves, had been blown from the spot they were intended to mark. I only noticed one cemetery which had been knocked about by shells & this one had suffered badly, the headstones &c. being scattered about the place.

Parties of Chinese & German Prisoners were met now & again, these, although not working at the time, being engaged on clearing the battlefields. This will be a slow process & will take years to complete – the whole area being so huge & the work involved enormous.

[...]

I cannot say I enjoyed the trip, for the sights, to me, were too fraught with tragedy. I could not look upon the devastation & chaotic condition of the countryside without thinking of all the slaughter & bitter suffering resulting from the awful events which had occurred in the area visited. And one is forced to reflect that man has indeed sunk very low to use his superior intellect in fashioning means of dealing death and destruction all round. All this in an enlightened age – and to what purpose? Man is indeed a refined savage, and war is a hideous spectre born of the devil. If this war is the last and the world becomes the better for it – well and good; if not, God help the world!

—— • ——

KURT TUCHOLSKY (1890–1935) was a journalist, satirist and social critic, born in Berlin. He studied law at university, and was conscripted into the German army in 1915. He served on the Eastern Front and by the end of the war had become a pacifist. 'The White Spots' ('Die Flecke'), reprinted in full below, was published in 1919. In 1933 his books were amongst those burnt by the National Socialist Party in front of Berlin University. He emigrated to Sweden in 1929, where, entering a profound depression and suffering from ill-health, he committed suicide on 21 December 1935.

In the Dorotheenstrasse in Berlin stands a building that was formerly the Military Academy. At a man's height there is a granite border that runs around the house, slab after slab.

These slabs look peculiar: they have white spots; the brown granite is light in many places – what can it be?

White spots, is that what they are? They ought to be reddish ones. This is where the German casualty lists were posted in the 'great' years.

This is where those terrible sheets of paper were posted, new ones almost everyday, those endless lists with names, names, names… I own a copy of Number One of these documents; on it the military units are still carefully noted, there are a few dead on this first list; Number One was very brief. I don't know how many more appeared after it – but there were well over a thousand. Name after name – and each time it meant that a human life had been snuffed out or that a human being was 'missing', crossed out for the time being, or wounded, or maimed.

That's where they were posted, where these white spots are now.

Hundreds of silent people crowded around them, people who had their dearest ones out there and who were trembling that they might read one name among all the thousands. What did they care about all the Müllers and Schulzes and Lehmanns who appeared on these lists! Let thousands upon thousands perish – as long as *he* wasn't among them. And it was on this mentality that the war battened. And it was because of this mentality that it could go on like this for four long years. Had we all risen – all as one man – who knows how long it would have lasted.

People have said that I don't know the way a German can die; I know it well enough. But I also know how a German woman can weep – and I know how she weeps today, now that she slowly, excruciatingly slowly, realises what her man has died for. What he has died for…

Am I rubbing salt on wounds? I should like to burn the celestial fire into wounds. I should like to cry out to the mourners: He died for nothing, for a madness, for nothing, nothing, nothing!

In the course of the years these white spots will gradually be washed away by the rain and disappear. But those other spots cannot be effaced. There are traces engraved on our hearts that will not go away. And each time I pass the Military Academy, with its brown granite and white spots, I silently say to myself: Promise it to yourself. Make a vow. Be active. Work. Tell the people. Liberate them from national madness, you, with your small power. You owe it to the dead. The white spots cry out. Do you hear them? They cry: No more wars!

— • —

C. BRUCE TABERNER served as a corporal on the Ypres Front in 1917. On 15 October 1963 he replied to the BBC's call for memories of the First World War. Taberner sent an anecdote, entitled 'The Fir Cone'.

Shelled shocked on the Ypres front in August 1917 – and spending some time in the hospital at Etaples – in the same ward was an Australian who had lost his memory due to shell shock and his speech was affected. One day the sister asked me would I care to take this Australian for a stroll in the grounds. I did – and he took my hand like a child of three – it was pitiable to see him – a big six foot of a man. As we strolled along the path he suddenly stopped – looked down and picked up a large fir cone. He handled it carefully – and I'm sure he was reminded of a hand grenade because he threw it overarm like a bowler – and then he ducked. I retrieved the cone and put it in my pocket – and still holding my hand we returned to the hospital. Later he was specially interviewed by doctors – along with others – but what happened I never knew – all I do know is that when he returned to the ward he was a new man – lively – jolly with his memory restored. I still have that fir cone – mounted at home – and although this is a vivid memory after 46 years it was an experience that touched me with compassion at the time. And I sometimes wonder if that fir cone had a bearing in bringing back his memory – who knows.

——— • ———

G. C. CLENCH served in the Navy as an Engine Room Artificer. In response to the BBC's call for memories from the war, he sent the following letter and an account of another disaster he witnessed in Scapa Flow that was printed in the *Daily Herald* thirty years earlier, as part of the series 'The War Story I Shall Tell My Son'.

G. C. CLENCH H.M. NAVY
ENGINE ROOM ARTIFICER (M1558)
NORTH SEA MAINLY
BATTLE SHIP H.M.S. CONQUEROR
AUG 4th – NOV 11th 1918

Usk

Mon.

8th Aug 1963

Dear Sirs,

Ten years from now I am making probably my last trip to North Scotland for a fortnight, to see if any vestige is left of the ill fated H.M.S. 'Natal' at Invergordon, sunk by internal explosion at Nigg Bay, nr. Invergordon, during Christmas week in 1915.

I date this event by the fact that vivid memories of my being there and witnessing this event were caused by near tragedy to my own ship a few weeks earlier on a vile black night at sea in the Pentland Firth. The Grand Fleet were returning from North Sea patrol to base at Scapa, during the night, in frightful weather and my ship collided with the stern of the next ahead, tearing a hole 90 ft long & 11 ft wide, back from our starboard bow under the water line and another hole of similar dimensions above the water line. We were very much down in the bows and a very lame duck when we finally dropped anchor in Scapa.

228 | A BROKEN WORLD

Temporary repairs at Scapa, then the 90 odd miles to Invergordon, where we were hoisted by the floating dock before proceeding a few weeks later to Birkenhead for the major repair work.

While undergoing emergency repairs in the floating dock at Invergordon one afternoon, perambulating the deck high above water level with clear vision down Cromarty Firth towards the North Sea. At approx 3.30 p.m. I saw a great sheet of flame blast from the side of H.M.S. 'Natal' – the masts canted over as the stricken cruiser heeled over and sank, leaving but a small portion of the hull just visible. Later a steel superstructure, sufficient to carry a beacon warning light was fitted, as if to remind us of what could happen to us at any time, a constant reminder each time we entered or left Cromarty Firth.

The 'Natal' blazed out at 3.30 p.m. If memory gives my facts aright – at 3 p.m. a large party of children left that ship after having a Xmas party aboard. It was also said at the time that six women, still aboard, perished in the disaster. Facts I cannot substantiate but records surely could.

In conclusion. I am hoping for a clear day at Scrabster or John-o-Groats to view the Pentland Firth, the Orkneys, where there is no trace of H.M.S. 'Vanguard' – no marker buoy exists of the second and greater disaster that occurred – that I too was forced to see. A last visit to the Pier (if still there) at Invergordon, where in 1916, I last shook hands with my brother, before each of us left for our respective ships two days before Jutland – he to his death on H.M.S. 'Defence' – myself to survival for, to date, another 47 years. Why? Perhaps partly for this. To jog some people's memories of little known events of the Great War and the untimely end of those who were uselessly blasted to eternity on:-

    H. M. Ships 'Bulwark' at Chatham

             'Natal' at Invergordon

             'Vanguard' Scapa Flow

                            Yours Faithfully

                            G. C. Clench

P. S. I enclose first account published in 1933 as published by 'Daily Herald', of the end of 'H. M. Vanguard' which may or may not interest your department. I wish no monetary gain from what I have been able to say, contending that it is a 'must' as far as I am concerned and if details are lacking – I have been as brief as possible, for I am still a busy and active man at 69.

No acknowledgement is called for or required.

                  G C

WEDNESDAY, DAILY HERALD

NOVEMBER 8, 1933

THE WAR STORY I SHALL TELL MY SON

Blown Up – With a Thousand Men Aboard

Our readers' war memories are bringing to light some of the little known, or totally suppressed, episodes of the war.

To-day's £1 prize winner is one of them. It is from G. C. C., of Usk, Monmouth, and is as follows: –

A glorious summer's night, completing the day's regatta of a battle squadron, the water calm and placid, the Grand Fleet lying grim – at anchor in Scapa Flow.

Coming on deck for a breather before retiring below, I was struck with the peace of it all – yet we were at war.

Turning down the after gangway, I had reached the bottom step, when the air was torn asunder by a terrific explosion, and our ship seemed to be heeling over.

Gathering my scattered senses, I turned and ran on deck, endeavouring to find out what happened.

A few cables' length away the air and sea were aflame, and what a second before had been the proud battleship Vanguard was nowhere to be seen.

Flaming cordite was dropping through the sky, crackling and hissing like giant fireworks as it struck the water and fizzled out. On the water where she should have been, burning oil fuel and wreckage added further to this indescribable scene of horror.

That night of war in Scapa claimed nearly a thousand men and two million pounds' worth of man's labour in one second on its rapacious altar.

Are the nation's magazines going to blow up again with the same senseless futility as those of H.M.S. Vanguard?

——— • ———

BOND OF SACRIFICE In 1917 the National War Museum (now the Imperial War Museum) released an invitation for relatives of officers who had fallen in the war to send a photograph and biographical details relevant to their military service. These would be printed in a publication entitled 'Bond of Sacrifice'. The Museum also organised a much broader and longer-lasting initiative, under the same title, which sought to collect photographs of other ranks and women. Below are some responses to both requests.

24 July 1917

'WE WANT YOUR PHOTOGRAPH.'

The National War Museum having been established by order of the Cabinet, the Committee are most anxious to collect Portraits of Officers and will be very grateful if these may be sent unmounted with a short note giving name, Rank, date of Commission, Decorations and other details of interest.

Photographs should be sent to the Secretary, National War Museum, H.M. Office of Works, S.W. 1.

1st August, 1918

Dear Madam,

I am directed by the Committee of the Imperial War Museum to thank you very heartily for sending to us the photograph of your son, 2nd Lieut. E. R. Leary, together with the short typed memoir.

Both will be carefully preserved here, until such time as the Nation shall erect a fitting Valhalla, wherein to commemorate the deeds of our fallen heroes.

I enclose an Official Letter of thanks, and remain,

Yours faithfully,
Keeper of Photographs.

London

March 13 1919

Dear Sir,

Will you kindly accept my very best thanks for your letter acknowledging our Dear Boys Photo

Amidst the turmoil these little things go a considerable way towards driving the dark clouds away & I am proud to know that our 'Sonny' has a little corner of his own in the Museum

His mother joins me in thanking you for the lovely sentiments expressed

Yours faithfully

Harry Quibell

JH Sikes & M.A.

[August 1917]

Sir

I noticed in the news that you would like the Photos of Officers and those who have won distinctions, well don't you think it an insult to our brave lads, who have fought, who have done more than their share in the War and not been promoted, they do quite as much as officers, no doubt more, for instance I am a soldier's wife, my husband joined in Nov 1914, arrived in France Mar 22nd 1915, went through the July 1st advance on the Somme front and [h]as been wounded on Aug 22nd 1916 and he is still doing his bit, don't you think it more honourable to have the likes of my husband, if only Pte.

Yours Mrs Bodman

Birmingham

May 31. 1918.

Sir,

In yr. letter to the papers <u>re records of dead soldiers.</u> do you mean you want <u>any</u> officer's record?

We have lost two dears sons, R. W. Somers-Smith K. R. R.

& J. R. Somers-Smith L. R. B. M. C.

do you mean ordinary boys like this – or only very distinguished officers – ?

If so, could you let me know exactly <u>what you want</u>?

As they were both good [word unclear] do you want to hear about that? or only the military record. I could get a friend of ours, to write it up properly, if I knew exactly <u>what</u>.

yours faithfully

M. F. Somers-Smith

London

March 8th 1919

Sir

I enclose a photo of my late Husband Dennis Murphy. I shall like him to be with others that have helped in this war. He was a good man and the best of Husbands their for I want to do all I can so that he shall not be forgotten. I can quite understand that they cannot all be on show at once, as you have photos of so many dear ones. What sad people and unhappy homes this war [h]as made. I have a baby girl year and two months which is a great comfort to me, but nothing can take the place of one so dear as my Husband

Yours truely

Ethel Murphy

——— • ———

MRS S. E. CHESSUM donated these notes to the Imperial War Museum where they are part of the Bond of Sacrifice Collection. Her son, Clarence Godwin Chessum, was killed in action on March 13 1917. She sends flower seeds to the Front; even if her son does not see them grow, they might, she writes, provide 'cheer' to others. The notes are difficult to read. At times she seems to be transcribing the words of her son; at others she is reporting incidents from his life. Memories are written on tiny scraps of paper, and some of them are transcribed here.

Mr Secretary,

Dear Sir I have sent some of the incidents of my dear Son's life have no relics. you may find a use for them. His loss can never be made up. was almost always with us. I had 8 children 4 sons 1. doing N.S. at Admiralty (clerical) 1. 17th Essex Regt just shifting from Weybourne C. 1. here, Munitions and the one killed. Daughters in Australia. we were 9 round the table, now. I am only one, not able to go out, or up long. age 68. 1. Nephew W Dormer has been killed. 1. Gassed. 1 Alfred Dormer been in a great deal of action I think over 2 years. a brother of my Son's Wife has sent a few coins and little curios. he is in Salonica soon coming home. his Wife died this morning 6 children left. 1 Boy on high seas. excuse me troubling you with all this but it's life as it is. Yours Respectfully.

(Mrs) S.E. Chessum.

Oct. 1917.

My Dear Son sent me these, he did like so when had read them. He must have felt it. He told me once I'll never leave you Mother, but did <u>not</u> <u>delay</u> at the call of duty. said I know Mother if you felt it your duty you would not flinch.

I sent some flower seeds for him to put in somewhere amongst the trees. it maybe some other lonely soldier, will see something of them, & be a voice to him. of <u>Cheers</u>.

he wrote saying. I have put them in. but do not suppose shall see them grow up. but some other sore head may be cheered.

Christian Herald.

<u>July 4. 1918</u>.

In connection with the War. Visiting the Battlefield of Warlencourt.

The position held by the German artillery was one calculated to impress us with the <u>heroism</u> and the <u>devotion</u> of <u>our men</u>.

The memory of the Durhams will be immortal in this connection. and hard-headed Britishers as we all were in the party. It was with dimmed eyes that we turned away from the memorial erected on the mound, and passed on in silence, to view the trenches. on our way back. passed a little well-kept Cemetery. some distance from Albert.

Copied July 4 1918.

Clarence Godwin Chessum.
4.9.7.0.6.14. Durham Light Infantry.
killed in action
March 13. 1917.

A Workman. Bookbinder, but a great lover of nature. His greatest delight when out of Hoxton, where he worked, was to take the children & wife to the country by Riverside.

[...] months in Brighton he got up to have an hour on the end of Peir [sic] before 6 when work began. (was working <u>there</u>) and in the evening went round the country and said what beauty there was to be seen in England, if people would only look up own country first, instead of run[n]ing off to some foreign.

In Edmonton, belonged to Rifle Club in the evening, practiced and won his cross guns. so he filled up all spare hours wherever happened to be. and kept the best side of the Public H. (outside).

In the Camp at [word unclear] looked for, and soon found a quiet little spot. none of the others went, but he was so fond of the quiet country, and a River for a swim. (nearly all the year round) he wrote me, he was never tired of hearing the water running over the Stones.

there was young cattle grazeing there. used to stand round looking at him writing. once he just found one starting to eat his Handkerchief, he had hung to dry after his swim. (his only towel) he drove them off, but they did not go far. then stood looking. they have beautiful eyes.

One day he had laid thinking of us all no doubt. then a voice at his side said, would you like a cup of tea? (what a treat,) did not know any one was near even. that was the best ever was. when he took the cup back. he found the Captain was not far off. had a Picnic. he said did it go down good. ? My boys grateful face, and smile told. as he said yes. so then he was handed some biscuits we never forgot it here at home.

Once another thing he enjoyed there. in that quiet spot. some nice little cakes made by Mrs Rose. after the tea was over the cakes left were sold. I had some, and just came right, as he was starting

[...] he could to all the [paper ripped here; missing words] he could. The poor little ones, knew [the words 'Biscuits' and 'Fruit' are written above and below 'knew'] from when he was having a frugal meal. sitting in St Sepulchres churchyard, used to like to go there, rather than a closely packed room. (having Dinner). away on Holiday took a poor ragged boy about with him, all day, in the country. to the boys delight. went in to Sea together was pleased [to] make the Boy happy.

———— • ————

CHARLES ROYSTON JONES was a private with the 1/15th Battalion London Regiment, who was killed in the Battle of the Somme on 15 September 1916. In 1920 Charles's parents, Charles and Amelia Jones, took a pilgrimage to the battlefields. The fragments below are taken from a notebook they made about their son which included letters, newspaper cuttings, poems, maps, and a description of their tour.

The Last Letter

Sun 10 Sept (On the Move)   France

Rec Wed 13 Sept

Dear Father

Just a few lines to let you know I am quite in the 'pink' & to thank you for your last long letter, which I enjoyed very much. I have received everything sent including the last parcel (the contents tell mother were quite all right & had not been damaged).

When there is anything serious, I shall write every two days or so. We are at present out of the line. The books you sent were very enjoyable. Please thank my sister for the photograph sent – I am writing separately when I have time.

Hoping you are very well

Yours sincerely

<u>Roy</u>

P. S. I want some safety rasor [sic] blades as soon as poss, as I have run out of them. Also a new shirt. Many thanks by the way for all the attention to my 'wants' which you have given. I really can't thank you enough & I am indeed very grateful.

Please give my love to Mother.

(In answer letter was sent with 5 Fc Note 13/9/16)

Field Service Post-Cards. (The Somme)

Tuesday Sept 12.

Received Friday

I am quite well. I have received your letter dated 3.9.16
Letter follows at first opportunity.

Royston Jones

The Last Card

Thursday Sept 14th   Rec Mon Sept 18th
(The Somme)

I am quite well. I have received your letters of the 8th of September.
Letter follows at first opportunity.

Roy

(Birthday Parcels were sent as follows)

Mother's 15/9/16

Father's 18/9/16   Birthday Card & 5 Fcs on 19/9

Millicent's 19/9/16

Lillian 20/9/16

The Moving Finger writes; and having writ,
Moves on: nor all thy Piety nor Wit
Shall lure it back to cancel half a Line,
Nor all thy Tears wash out a Word of it.
(Omar Khayyam)

'A Cloud, a Mist, and a blinding Rain
And the World was never the same again'

'And the stately ships go on
To their haven under the hill,
But O for the touch of a vanished hand
And the sound of a voice that is still!'

[Newspaper cutting]
No. 3638, Pte. C. ROYSTON JONES, London Regt., who
has been killed in action, was the son of Mr. and Mrs. Jones,
of Stoke Newington. He volunteered from the Civil Service
early in 1915, and went to the front in October of the same
year. He saw a good deal of fighting and had some narrow
escapes until September 15, when he was killed in taking a
German trench. His sergeant of platoon writes: 'I knew him as
a keen and willing soldier, and a true friend. His musical gifts
charmed and brightened us all when away from the "line".
It was a glorious end to the beautiful life of one loved and
respected by us all.'

Many enquiries were made and letters from comrades were received,
with regard to the last scenes. It seems that after getting through
High Wood, the battalion pushed on to Flers.

On the morning of the 19th No 2 Platoon were holding a
communication trench which had previously been held by the
Germans and that stretched away partly to the new German lines.

They were due to be relieved the same day. But the Germans
made a surprise attack at dawn and they were unable to escape & a
number of them were cut off & shot down in getting away. Some of
them feigned death whilst on the ground & were fired at whilst they

lay there. Amongst these seems to have been our own poor dear boy.

His small pay book was found & seen by us at the A. P. D. It was soaked & stained with blood & wet. (It rained a great deal about the time of the battle.)

He makes a note that he had been [word unclear] on 16/6/16, and the last payment was 10 francs on August 28th. He had evidently fallen on his left side and laid there for some time, as his pay book had been in the left side pocket & his sword bayonet handle had made a deep impression right into the covers of the book evidently by the weight of his body being on it & pressing it in. He probably lay in the open till after the regiment was relieved, (for they retook the lost ground) & was buried by a party of the battalion that took the ground over. This was either the Northumberlands or the Durhams.

[…]

'Requiem.'

Favourite lines of Roy's by R. L. S[tevenson]

Under the wide and starry sky
Dig the grave and let me lie;
Glad did I live and gladly die,
And I laid me down with a will.

This be the verse you grave for me.
'Here he lies where he wished to be,
Home is the sailor, home from the sea
And the hunter home from the hill.'

[…]

We had now traversed the triangle Bapaume, Albert, Peronne. Bapaume which encloses the Battlefields of the Somme in which the British had half a million casualties & lost some of the noblest boys she ever produced. After the battle Sept 15.16 Roy may have looked over from outside High Wood & seen the villages on this very road I had just passed through. We continued our journey to Arras. Night was falling & through the mists & shadows one fancied they could he[a]r the tramp-tramp tramp of ghostly feet & see again as in a vision the loved faces of those heroic boys of ours, whom we had loved & lost, and who had made such an awful sacrifice for us. We would have been happy indeed if we could have saved them by our sacrifice but alas! The Fates ruled otherwise – Vale & Farewell

C. A. J.

8/8/20

—— • ——

R. E. ROLLER found three railway tickets to towns in German possession in 1916, in the ruins of Ypres Station. He mounted and framed these tickets and sent them to his uncle. The following letter was glued to the back.

Dec 21st 1918.

Dear Uncle Arthur

When I was with my battery at Ypres in Belgium in the beginning of 1916, I happened one day to be passing near Ypres Station, which was a spot always to be avoided owing to the barrage which the Huns put down pretty well continually; if not on the station itself very near to it; and I thought I would go and have a look at the station, of course there was very little semblance of a station left but I managed to discover the remains of the booking office, where after a good deal of scrummaging round I found three return tickets to different towns all of them bearing on the War and also occupied by the enemy then, these tickets I kept out of curiosity and now this year I have had them roughly mounted in a frame and am sending them to you as a Xmas present, their intrinsic value is of course nil, but thought you might like to have them from an interesting point of view as they are not the usual kind of 'souvenir' one sees and get[s] so tired of.

Also getting them very nearly cost me a broken leg as while I was in what remained of the booking office, the Germans started their usual barrage quite near and the concussion of one of the explosions brought down one of the heavy beams from above me falling just behind the spot where I was kneeling missing my extended leg by about six inches which was rather a close shave.

The tickets are extremely dirty but have not had them cleaned as that is the condition in which I found them.

—— • ——

WILLIAM HATCHELL BOYD was born at Clonliffe, Dublin on 30 September 1887. He worked as an accountant until he entered the army in 1915. He became a 2nd lieutenant in the 5th Battalion, Royal Dublin Fusiliers. He contributed to military attempts to suppress the Sinn Féin rebellion in April 1916 and the following July went to France. On 9 September he was killed by a shell during the capture of Ginchy.

The newspaper cutting below commemorates Lieutenant Thomas Kettle; William Hatchell Boyd's death is relegated to a sentence. It first appeared in the Dublin *Freeman's Journal* on October 23 1916, and was written by a 'Dublin Officer'. The cutting was sent to the Imperial War Museum, along with a short biography; the donors underlined the lines relating to Boyd.

Second Lieutenant James Emmet Dalton, of the Royal Dublin Fusiliers, who has been awarded the Military Cross for conspicuous bravery in the field, is the son of Mr. J. F. Dalton, who is well-known in Dublin Nationalist and Commercial circles. He is only 18 years of age, and joined the army in January last. He arrived in France on the 1st September, and at once went into the firing line. He was awarded the Military Cross for the following, according to the official record:

At the capture of Ginchy, on the 9th September, 1916, bravery and leadership in action; when owing to the loss of officers the men of two companies were left without leaders he took command and led these companies to their final objective. After the withdrawal of the 47th Brigade and the right flank of his battalion was in the rear he carried out the protection of the flank, under intense fire, by the employment of machine guns in selected commanding and successive positions. After dark, whilst going about supervising the consolidation of the position, he, with only one sergeant escorting, found himself confronted by a party of the enemy consisting of one officer and 20 men. By his prompt determination the party were overawed and, after a few shots, threw up their arms and surrendered.

In a number of letters written to his parents and breathing a fine Christian spirit, the young officer speaks very modestly of his brave deed, and says that in the war he is fighting for Ireland. In one of these communications he describes the death of Lieutenant Thomas Kettle.

BOOK ON THE IRISH DIVISION

'Between the 2nd and 5th October,' he wrote, 'I spent some pleasant hours with Lieutenant Kettle. He was writing a book about the war and the Irish Division, namely, the 16th: On the night of the 5th we marched for three hours in terrible rain on an awfully uneven road until we came to "Trones Wood", which is opposite Guillemont. On the morning of the 7th we lost 200 men and seven officers at Guillemont by the Boch shell fire. We returned to Trones Wood and Tom took over command of "B" Company, whilst I became second in command of "A" Company.

'During the morning of the 8th Tom and I were discussing the losses we had sustained when an orderly arrived with a note for each of us saying "Be in readiness, Battalion will take up A and B position in front of Ginchy tonight at 12 midnight."

'I was with Tom when he advanced to the position that night, and the stench of the dead that covered our road was so awful that we both used some foot powder on our faces. When we reached our objective we dug ourselves in, and then, at 5 o'clock p.m. on the 9th, we attacked Ginchy. I was just behind Tom when we went over the top. He was in a bent position, and a bullet got over a steel waistcoat that he wore and entered his heart. Well, he only lasted about one minute, and he had my crucifix in his hands. . . <u>Then Boyd took all the papers and things out</u> of Tom's pockets in order to keep them for Mrs. Kettle, but <u>poor Boyd was blown to atoms in a few minutes</u>. The Welsh Guards buried Mr. Kettle's remains. Tom's death has been a big blow to the regiment, and I am afraid that I could not put in words my feelings on the subject.'

In another letter Lieut. Dalton states – 'Mr. Kettle died a grand and holy death, the death of a soldier and a true Christian.'

—— • ——

MASS-OBSERVATION DIARISTS   The Mass-Observation project was set up in 1937 by Tom Harrisson, Charles Madge and Humphrey Jennings. They recruited volunteer writers who would contribute details of their everyday lives. Included below is an excerpt from Madge and Harrisson's book *Britain by Mass-Observation* (1939) about behaviour during the Armistice Silence on 11 November 1937. This was an unusual year as the service at the Cenotaph was interrupted by the shouts of ex-serviceman Stanley Storey. A newspaper report of this incident, published in the *Manchester Guardian*, is included here and is followed by a diarist's report (not part of the project, but found in the Imperial War Museum); then a Day Survey from one of the Mass-Observers.

When M-O decided to make a survey of the Silence, it was without any preconceived ideas about it. 1,000 observers were simply asked to describe exactly what happened to them between 10.30 and

11.30 on the morning of November 11, 1937. They sent in reports, which are analysed in this section.

The survey, as it turned out, revealed the widespread feeling that the ceremony was already out-of-date and should be stopped. But this feeling would have remained voiceless without the intervention of ex-serviceman Stanley Storey. His shouts broke the silence. They were heard by millions who were listening in to the Cenotaph service. Next day this entitled Hannen Swaffer in the *Daily Herald* to write: 'Armistice Day's formal Empire service at the Cenotaph, with its Two Minutes' Silence, should never be held again! Yesterday's happenings made this even more obvious.'

Five observers were near the Cenotaph, but only two of them knew that anything had happened. Of 56 who were listening in, 44 heard the interruption. The story was well told by the *Manchester Guardian*:

'...An instant after the last wreath was in place, Big Ben struck the first note of eleven, the maroons sounded, and the silence fell like a curtain.

For a few seconds the air was empty of every sound except the rustling of the plane leaves. And then suddenly there was a commotion on the pavement outside the Home Office and behind the line of Cabinet Ministers. The rigid line of sailors at the edge of the crowd was abruptly broken, and a thick-set, fair-haired man, bare-headed, and wearing a mackintosh, rushed out into the roadway, shouting in a high tormented voice, "All this hypocrisy!" and after it another phrase which sounded like "Preparing for war".

He ran forward in a direction which would have taken him past the Prime Minister, but half a dozen policemen burst through the gap after him and brought him down in a struggling heap about two yards away from Mr. Chamberlain. They piled themselves on top of him until he was invisible, and tried to muffle his shouts. But again one heard faintly from beneath the heap his cry of "All this hypocrisy", and another incoherent sound in which one could only distinguish the word "war".

The Silence still held everybody else rigid and dumb. Mr. Chamberlain never moved, though all this was happening just behind him. The King turned his head slightly towards the disturbance for an instant, then looked to his front again and stood motionless. The sailors whose rank had been broken re-formed it silently. A police officer cantered up to see that everything necessary was being done, and the policemen on the ground got to their feet and dragged the interrupter back into the crowd, where they laid him down and kept him quiet. Not another sound or movement came from all those thousands of people; the Silence still held them.

When at last it came to an end the police could be seen escorting the man away through the crowd towards Downing Street, where he was taken to an ambulance station. They were supporting rather than escorting him, for he seemed almost unconscious by this time and made no more noise.

The crowd through which he passed remained orderly, so far as one could distinguish from a roof on the other side of the street, though there was a certain amount of shouting which was drowned by the roll of drums that followed the end of the Silence. A few excitable people are said to have shouted 'Kill him!' but so far as one could judge there were not many people who made any noisy protest.

Afterwards one learned that the man was one Stanley Storey who had been confined to an asylum last February and had escaped in September. At the time, of course, this was not known, and his shout seemed rather the agonized cry of one who had found the strain of the moment and of his own convictions too much to be borne. As such it heightened one's own feelings almost intolerably. There must be few people who can attend the celebrations of Armistice Day without having to thrust into the background of their minds the fear that all the suffering of twenty years ago has not prevented more sufferings to come...'

From *Britain by Mass-Observation*,

arranged and written by Charles Madge and Tom Harrisson (1939)

Nov 11th.

Armistice Day. The Cenotaph Service was broadcast and for the first time the silence was broken. A fanatic, escaped from a Mental Hospital, rushed up towards the King at the beginning of the silence shouting something about war & hypocrisy but was quickly removed. We heard it all on the wireless & wondered whatever was happening. In my opinion it's about time this stopped, or else cut out of this glorious business of triumphant marching & bugles blowing etc. We listened to the Albert Hall do. It was wonderful – all the usual war choruses and jolly good bands – but much the best thing of all was during the service when two boys sang the first verse of 'O Valiant Hearts'. There is nothing in music I like better than a fine boy's voice, & these were so clear & beautiful, & they kept together so well that it sounded like one.

When I think of a million young men killed in one blow it makes me squirm. Why can't these people who want war think of it. And today if one person is shot there is an inquest & great fuss & punishment. A million die & yet it seems that even another million will have to be slaughtered. I remember Rev. Fowler saying in Rye Pulpit – 'There is <u>no</u> glory in war!' & how true.

Miss M. Cooke, diary, 11 November 1937, Imperial War Museum

Croxon

D. S. 46

Grimsby

Armistice Day.

I cannot buy a poppy, for I have not got a penny. not so rich. <u>11. o' clock</u>, what an unearthly silence. My thoughts are upon my little children in School, their heads will be bowed in reverence to our beloved dead. It is all very sad for the relatives of the fallen, for it seems a pity to keep on reopening an old wound, causing a heartache. I don't think any body really wishes to remember the war and its horrors. I am thinking and worrying about my child's wet feet, hoping that her leaking shoe will not soak her foot, wet feet mean bronchitis for her, unless I can stop it with my favourite medicine. Her father served throughout the war in the Royal Navy as minesweeper; his three medals I would exchange for a pair of shoes for his child. If he were here he would say I had done right.

Somebody has just knocked at my door, (the silence is over) a gentleman with a poppy in his buttonhole has called from the County Court. He makes sure I am Mrs – He asks if this is all the home I have (looking round). It consists of three old chairs, a table, a couple of pictures, our bed. Of course they are not worth the taking. they would not raise 2/6 in the saleroom. So I am very grateful for small mercies. This warrant is for a water rate due on the house which we occupied previous to living here nearly a year ago, the amount of rate owing was 8s. 9d. now they bring it to 16 shillings some people endeavour to get rich quick. Nice time to distress any body, armistice day.

There are a few words upon a poppy day appeal poster to this effect. Our glorious dead will not rest if we do not observe – I cannot remember the exact words, but I have often wondered wether [sic] my husband has rested at the particular times when his little children's bed has been put in the gutter, not only once – Now, I turn to my Bible, in one chapter of James which reads <u>Pure religion and undefiled</u> before God and the Father is this, to visit the fatherless and the widows in their affliction, and to keep himself unspotted from the world. It would not be God's laws to turn a widow and little children on to the street. because they have very little money.

E. Croxon

———— • ————

ALBERT and ERNEST FLETCHER were former servicemen who also responded to the BBC's call for war memories in 1963. Their anger at being forgotten by the country for which they fought is evident from this letter.

FLETCHER
WOKING
SURREY
SEPT 9th

SIRS

I WEAR <u>MONS</u> <u>STAR</u> SO DO MY <u>BROTHER</u> LATE <u>DORSETS</u> I AM LATE <u>QUEENS</u> <u>ROYAL</u> <u>WEST</u> <u>SURREY</u> WE COULD TELL YOU QUITE A LOT ABOUT GRATITUDE ETC AND BEING THROWN ON THE <u>RUBBISH</u> <u>HEAP</u> BY A <u>GRATEFULL</u> <u>COUNTRY</u>

WE ARE ALWAYS AT HOME <u>OLD</u> <u>AGE</u> <u>PENSIONERS</u> AND FORGOTEN, RUBBING OUR WOUNDS

Yours faithfully
Albert and Ernest
Fletcher

—— • ——

SIEGFRIED SASSOON AND TONY ESSEX The following letters were exchanged between the poet Siegfried Sassoon (1886–1967) and the BBC television producer Tony Essex between 1963 and 1964. Essex was trying to persuade Sassoon to contribute lines of poetry to the documentary series, *The Great War*; the suggestion was that he write introductory verses to accompany the opening credits of each episode.

October 22nd 1963

Siegfried Sassoon Esq., C.B.E.

Heytesbury House

Warminster

Wiltshire

Dear Mr. Sassoon:

Some time ago we had a delightful lunch with Edmund Blunden. After lunch he was calling upon you. I am quite sure he will have told you of our massive project here at the BBC, that of making 26 half hour (or longer) films telling the social, political and military History of the Great War. Apart from all the film and photographs available, we are also hoping to make extensive use of the great poetry, literature and paintings of the time, and one day your agent will doubtless be hearing from us about those poems of yours we seek to use. The whole series should be magnificent; it is certainly the biggest and most moving undertaking the BBC has ever tackled.

I am writing to ask if you could make a personal and vital contribution to our series by creating an introductory verse for each of the 26 films in our series?

I intend to open each film with a composite scene of 'Grief' (by Rodin) overlooking a battlefield, and want a six-line verse which starts on the theme of 'I saw a million men etc...' and ends on the theme of 'they went laughing to death' or words to that effect. The middle two lines should change with each programme, and be in keeping with the subject of that programme, a full list of which will be sent to you if you feel you can undertake this task for us.

I do not need to tell you how honoured we would be to publish a new poem by you during the course of our series, and so I await your feelings on the matter with eager interest.

Yours sincerely:

Tony Essex Producer: 'The Great War'

HEYTESBURY HOUSE

WILTSHIRE

Warminster

24.10.63

Dear Mr Essex.

E. B. [Edmund Blunden] told me about your undertaking, Naturally I would wish to be of any help possible, though I am no longer an active writer. I have never been able to produce verse to order, and am by no means sure that what you plan could be done properly by <u>anyone</u>. But if you will send me the schedule of programmes I will think it over, & consult EB, who might collaborate with me. It would have to be <u>unrhymed</u>. But would not an eloquent prose caption be more suitable? Any kind of <u>poetizing</u> would be out of key, of course.

Yours sincerely,

S.

I do not employ an agent.

The BBC. deals with me direct.

November 8, 1963

Siegfried Sassoon Esq., C.B.E.

Heytesbury House

WARMINSTER

Wiltshire

Dear Mr Sassoon,

Thank you for your letter of October 24th. I am grateful that you will consider our task, and attach a list of themes of each of our twenty-six programmes. The second copy is for Edmund Blunden to whom I note you will be writing.

I had a feeling I was asking rather a lot, but hope you can have a try at this – prose would not really be suitable (although, I take your point about it not rhyming – it really isn't necessary that it should).

What I want is something Michael Redgrave can speak at the beginning of each film which will set the theme of the particular programme and introduce the subsidiary title which will appear as the verse ends. This verse will also be printed in the 'Radio Times', week by week, so that viewers will know the theme and mood of the film they are about to see.

I look forward to hearing that you might be able to manage something, and am most grateful to you for your interest.

Yours sincerely,

TONY ESSEX

Producer: 'The Great War'

Programme 1: This programme defines the political structure of Europe, and how jealousies, dreams of power, inter-family disputes, the shift of economic balance and an interlacing of alliances gradually create a situation where War becomes inevitable. The programme ends with the assassination at Sarajevo.

Programme 2: This programme traces the events from the Sarajevo assassination to the outbreak of war. It shows how, in stages, in the key nations, military leaders, because they are ready, gradually take over the formulation of their nation's policy thus making a clash of arms unavoidable. Even the Kaiser drew back at the last moment, but it was too late, and fighting broke out, over a period of days, throughout Europe.

Programme 3: This programme shows how Servia [sic] and Belgium captured the imagination by heroic resistance against tremendous power. In the West the Schleiffen [sic] Plan unfolds, the French amid appalling losses, press deep into a vast trap prepared for them, the British Army lands and marches into a lesser trap, and the youth of Europe flocks to join in before it is all over.

Programme 4: This programme studies the gradual loss of direction and impetus in the German strategy, how the Eastern assaults grind to a standstill, and how, in the West, by adroit side-stepping under the control of Joffre, the Allied Armies survive Mons and the Retreat etc. and reform to open the Battle of the Marne.

[...]

16th December 1963

Dear Mr. Sassoon,

Just a note as I wonder how you feel about our project and if it is possible that in due course you may be able to come up with something.

More important, I write for all of us here to wish you a very Happy Christmas and a healthy, prosperous New Year.

Yours sincerely,

Tony Essex

Producer, 'Great War' Series

Siegfried Sassoon Esq., C.B.E
Heytesbury House,
WARMINSTER,
Wiltshire.

23rd January 1964

Dear Mr. Sassoon,

I wonder if you are yet able to let me know how you feel about writing for our project? I hate to appear to be pressing you, but as you probably know, the mad world of television is filled with schedules, deadlines and so on.

Very sincerely,

Tony Essex

Producer, 'The Great War' series

Heytesbury House,

24-1-64

Dear Essex.

I assumed that my silence would be taken as dissent! Blunden agreed with me that your idea is impracticable – anyhow for him and me. Six respectable lines of generalisation might be produced, but the alteration each time of the middle lines seems to me near to absurdity. I can only imagine such cracks as

> /And now we do our best to show
> What Haig arranged with Clemenceau—/
>> or
> And here Lloyd George pulls off his task with
> Doing the dirty on old Asquith—/

Apologies for ribaldry, and best of luck.

Yours sincerely,

S

30th Jan 1964

Dear Mr. Sassoon,

Thank you for your note (and for the couplets!)

Put like that, I agree the idea sounds a bit off, but I hasten to assure you this was not quite what I had in mind!! However, I accept your decision sadly and wish you well.

Very sincerely,

(Tony Essex)

Producer, 'The Great War'

—— • ——

ARTHUR MEE (1875–1943) was a journalist and writer, born in Nottinghamshire. The work from which the passage below has been drawn, *Enchanted Land: Half-a-Million Miles in the King's England* (1936), was a piece of travel writing which surveyed the counties of England. One chapter charts his visits to small memorials up and down the country: 'the visible mark of the Great War in every place.' He concludes the chapter by writing of the 'Thankful Villages'; they were given this title because all their men returned.

Now and then on the tour through our ten thousand villages there has come to us the thrill of joyfulness to find no sad memorials, and twenty times and more we have come upon a village thankful for all its men came back. The thrill came to us first in Somerset after we had been riding for miles on the hills that look down on Bath, and in our minds the small place called Woolley stands out as the first of England's Thankful Villages.

It stands superbly on a ridge, but we must wind and wind and wind through a maze if we would find this little place; there is just room to get the car between the hedges without hurting the grass-hoppers, and at last we see it shining like a gem on a sunny day, a tiny church between two barns.

We have seen a book in which the writer said that of Woolley there is nothing to say, but never again will that be said, for of Woolley there is this to say, that this hamlet of thirteen houses sent thirteen men to war and every one came back.

[…]

Here they stood on one great day, the men from the red fields of France, the parched sands of Mesopotamia, and the stony wilds of Palestine. Here they stood while the old rector welcomed them home, the 13 families crowding the 18 pews. We could find no shop in Woolley, no inn, no school, no letter-box, but we found a plain brass tablet of thankfulness for the safe return of their 13 men. One was wounded at Ypres, one won the Croix de Guerre for rescuing French wounded, and one was gassed; but every man came home again – home to one of the rarest hamlets in this precious countryside, home to this village thankful, to these 13 houses with not one vacant chair.

It would be good to think that our Thankful Villages had all some visible token of their thankfulness, but often there is nothing; the village has just its memory that the men came back. But if we come to Rodney Stoke in Somerset we find a village proudly expressing its thankfulness that it offered 17 men and four women to England and all came safely home. Nowhere else have we found the spirit of thankfulness expressed as in a lovely window here, facing the door as we came in, with these grateful words:

To the glory of God and in thankful remembrance of the safe return of all the men connected with this parish who by land and sea served their King and Country in the Great War.

Facing it is a roll of honour with the names of seventeen men and four women: Dora and Eveleen Coleridge Smith, Sarah Chappell, and Ethel Barber. The first two were the rector's daughters, both nursing abroad; the others nursed at home.

[…]

It has been a sad pleasure to come upon these Thankful Villages of which no other record exists than the one we have been able to make. Except in these few villages there is probably in every town and city and hamlet in the kingdom one

In every wood and field and lane,
Who will not pass this way again.

These are the 23 Thankful Villages we have been able to discover where all the men came back; they are in 12 counties, and we give the number of the men who came back to them:

In Yorkshire: Cayton 43; Catwick 30; Norton-le-Clay 16; Cundall 12. In Bedfordshire: Stanbridge 33. In Gloucestershire: Coln Rogers 33; Brierley 14; Little Sodbury 6. In Cambridgeshire: Knapwell 23. In Wiltshire: Littleton-Drew 22. In Somerset: Stocklinch 19; Rodney-Stoke 17; Woolley 13; Aisholt 8; Tellisford 3; Chelwood 4; Stanton Prior 3. In Northants: Woodend 19. In Derbyshire: Bradbourne 18. In Lincolnshire: Bigby 10. In Notts: Wigsley 7; Maplebeck 2. In Leicestershire: Willesley 3.

Cayton, one of the Yorkshire villages in this list, has perhaps the record for thankfulness, for as many as 43 men went and 43 came back. As for Little Sodbury in Gloucestershire, those who believe that all things are guided in this world will like to remember that it was in an attic there that William Tyndale sat reading his Bible, and was inspired to present to the English people the noblest possession the centuries have vouchsafed to them. Four centuries after Tyndale, Fate has been kind to the village of his dreams. At Tellisford the lords of the manor have been rectors for 150 years and have kept the heart of the village friendly and beautiful. A flagged path brings us to the church between the low stone walls of a garden and a farm, covered in springtime with the matchless arabis and aubretia. Out of our English chalice of beauty has come no fairer place.

It has been surprising to find that the remarkable experience of these Thankful Villages has already been forgotten in some of them. Would it not be a lovely thing if in each one there could be some mark of gratitude for this shining ray of fortune which befell them when England was in the Valley of the Shadow?

———— • ————

RONALD BLYTHE (1922–) is a writer best known for his book *Akenfield: Portrait of an English Village* (1969). It is loosely based on interviews with villagers; each chapter tells one of their life stories; together they build a composite picture of a village in rural East Anglia. The passage below tells the story of Leonard Thompson, a 71-year-old farmworker.

Len and his wife live in a solitary house which stands not more than a yard off the Roman road. The foundations of the house must rest in the ditch made by the road-builders when they dug out earth for the camber. The mixture of fragility and tenacity which marks the cottage is somehow indicative of Len himself. Although there is nothing particularly frail about him in the physical sense – he is a little brown bull of a man with hard blue eyes and limbs so stretched by toil that they seem incapable of relaxing into retirement – he has stood firmly in the apocalyptic path of events which have wrenched the village from its serfdom. He is astute, unsentimental and realistic. He is neither proud nor regretful to have endured the bad times.

[...]

There were ten of us in the family and as my father was a farm labourer earning 13s. a week you can just imagine how we lived. I will tell you the first thing which I can remember. It was when I was three – about 1899. We were all sitting round the fire waiting for my soldier brother to come home – he was the eldest boy in the family. He arrived about six in the evening and had managed to ride all the way from Ipswich station in a milk-cart. This young man came in, and it was the first time I had seen him. He wore a red coat and looked very lively. Mother got up and kissed him but Father just sat and said, 'How are you?' Then we had tea, all of us staring at my brother. It was dark, it was the winter-time. A few days later he walked away and my mother stood right out in the middle of the road, watching. He was going to fight in South Africa. He walked smartly down the lane until his red coat was no bigger than a poppy. Then the tree hid him. We never saw him again. He went all through the war but caught enteric fever afterwards and died. He was twenty-one.

[...]

I left school when I was thirteen, on April 20th when the corn was low, I helped my mother pulling up docks in the Big Field for a shilling an acre, which my mother took.

[...]

When the farmer stopped my pay because it was raining and we couldn't thrash, I said to my seventeen-year-old mate, 'Bugger him. We'll go off and join the army.' It was March 4th 1914. We joined the army a few hours after we had made our decision. We walked to Ipswich and got the train to Colchester. We were soaked to the skin but very happy. At the barracks we kissed the Bible and were given a shilling. The recruiting sergeant said, 'You can't go home in all this rain, you can sleep in a bed in the recruiting room.' In the morning he said, 'Go home and say good-bye, and here's ten shillings each for your food and fares. Report back on Monday.'

In my four months' training with the regiment I put on nearly a stone in weight and got a bit taller. They said it was the food but it was really because for the first time in my life there had been no strenuous work. I want to say this simply as a fact, the village people in Suffolk in my day were worked to death. It literally happened. It is not a figure of speech. I was worked mercilessly. I am not complaining about it. It is what happened to me.

We were all delighted when war broke out on August 4th. I was now a machine-gunner in the Third Essex Regiment. A lot of boys from the village were with me and although we were all sleeping in ditches at Harwich, wrapped in our greatcoats, we were bursting with happiness. We were all damned glad to have got off the farms. I had 7s. a week and sent my mother half of it. If you did this, the government would add another 3s. 6d. – so my mother got 7s. My father died early this year and my mother lived on this 7s. a week for the whole of the war, adding a scrap to it by doing washing, and weeding in the fields. Neither of my parents lived long enough to draw the Old Age Pension. I can remember, when work was short, a group of unemployed young men coming to where some old men were sugar-beeting, which is the worst job there is, and shouting, 'Now that you grandfathers have got the pension' – it was 5s. a week – 'why don't you get out of the field and give us a chance?' These 'old' men were only in their fifties but the hardness of their lives had made them ancient.

All this trouble with the village fell behind us now. I was nineteen and off to the Dardanelles, which is the Hellespont, I discovered. I had two boys from the village with me. We'd heard a lot about France so we thought we'd try Turkey. The band played on the banks of the river as we pulled out of Plymouth and I wondered if we would ever come home again. We were all so patriotic then and had been taught to love England in a fierce kind of way. The village wasn't England; England was something better than the village. We got to Gib and it was lovely and warm. Naked Spanish boys dived round us for coins. There were about fifty nurses on the top deck and they threw tanners. You could see they were having an eye-opener. We stopped to coal-up. The dust blew all over the decks and all over us. We were packed like sardines and eating rubbish again. Water and salt porridge for breakfast. Beans and high salt pork for dinner. The pork was too bad for land-men to eat so we threw it into the coaldust and the coolies snatched it up and thrust it into their mouths, or put it into sacks to take home for their families.

We arrived at the Dardanelles and saw the guns flashing and heard the rifle-fire. They heaved our ship, the *River Clyde*, right up to the shore. They had cut a hole in it and made a little pier, so we were able to walk straight off and on to the beach. We all sat there – on the Hellespont! – waiting for it to get light. The first things we saw were big wrecked Turkish guns, the second a big marquee. It didn't make me think of the military but of the village fêtes. Other people must have thought like this because I remember how we all rushed up to it, like boys getting into a circus, and then found it all laced up. We unlaced it and rushed in. It was full of corpses. Dead Englishmen, lines and lines of them, and with their eyes wide open. We all stopped talking. I'd never seen a dead man before and here I was looking at two or three hundred of them. It was our first fear. Nobody had mentioned this. I was very shocked. I thought of Suffolk and it seemed a happy place for the first time.

Later that day we marched through open country and came to within a mile and half of the front line. It was incredible. We were there – at the war! The place we had reached was called 'dead ground' because it was where the enemy couldn't see you. We lay in little square holes, myself next to James Sears from the village. He was about thirty and married. That evening we wandered about on the dead ground and asked about friends of ours who had arrived a month or so ago. 'How is Ernie Taylor?' – 'Ernie? – he's gone.' 'Have you seen Albert Paternoster?' – 'Albert? – he's gone.' We learned that if 300 had 'gone' but 700 were left, then this wasn't too bad. We then knew how unimportant our names were.

I was on sentry that night. A chap named Scott told me that I must only put my head up for a second but that in this time I must see as much as I could. Every third man along the trench was a sentry. The next night we had to move on to the third line of trenches and we heard that the Gurkhas were going over and that we had to support their rear. But when we got to the communication trench we found it so full of dead men that we could hardly move. Their faces were quite black and you couldn't tell Turk from English. There was the most terrible stink and for a while there was nothing but the living being sick on to the dead. I did sentry again that night. It was one-two-sentry, one-two-sentry all along the trench, as before. I knew the next sentry up quite well. I remembered him in Suffolk singing to his horses as he ploughed. Now he fell back with a great scream and a look of surprise – dead. It is quick, anyway, I thought. On June 4th we went over the top. We took the Turks' trench and held it. It was called Hill 13. The next day we were relieved and told to rest for three hours, but it wasn't more than half an hour before the relieving regiment came running back. The Turks had returned and recaptured their trench. On June 6th my favourite officer was killed and no end of us butchered, but we managed to get hold of Hill 13 again. We found a great muddle, carnage and men without rifles shouting 'Allah! Allah!', which is God's name in the Turkish language. Of the sixty men I had started out to war from Harwich with, there were only three left.

We set to work to bury people. We pushed them into the sides of the trench but bits of them kept getting uncovered and sticking out, like people in a badly made bed. Hands were the worst; they would escape from the sand, pointing, begging – even waving! There was one which we all shook when we passed, saying, 'Good morning', in a posh voice. Everybody did it. The bottom of the trench was springy like a mattress because of all the bodies underneath. At night, when the stretch was worse, we tied crêpe round our mouths and noses. This crêpe had been given to us because it was supposed to prevent us from being gassed. The flies entered the trenches at night and lined them completely with a density which was like moving cloth. We killed millions by slapping our spades along the trench walls but the next night it would be just as bad. We were all lousy and we couldn't stop shitting because we had caught dysentery. We wept, not because we were frightened but because we were so dirty.

We didn't feel indignant against the Government. We believed all they said, all the propaganda. We believed the fighting had got to be

done. We were fighting for England. You only had to say 'England'
to stop any argument. We shot and shot. On August 6th they made
a landing at Suvla Bay and we took Hill 13 again, and with very few
casualties this time. We'd done a good job. The trench had been lost
yet again, you see. When we got back for the third time we found a
little length of trench which had somehow missed the bombardment.
There were about six Turkish boys in it and we butchered them right
quick. We couldn't stay in the trench, we had to go on. Then we ran
into machine-gun fire and had to fall flat in the heather, or whatever
it was. Suddenly my mate caught fire as he lay there. A bullet had
hit his ammunition belt. Several people near jumped up and ran
back, away from the burning man and the machine-gun fire. I could
hear the strike of the gun about a foot above my head. I lay between
the burning man and a friend of mine called Darky Fowler. Darky
used to be a shepherd Helmingham way. I put my hand out and
shook him, and said, 'Darky, we've got to go back. We *must* go back!'
He never answered. He had gone. I lay there thinking how funny it
was that I should end my life that night. Then my mate began to go
off like a firework – the fire was exploding his cartridges. That did
it! I up and ran.

There is nobody can say that you have killed a man. I shot
through so many because I was a machine-gunner. Did they all die?
– I don't know. You got very frightened of the murdering and you did
sometimes think, 'What is all this about? What is it for?' But mostly
you were thinking of how to stay alive. The more the killing, the
more you thought about living. You felt brave and honoured that you
should be fighting for England. You knew that all the people at home
were for it. We believed we were fighting for a good cause and so,

I expect, did the Turks. You didn't think personally. You can't say you *shot* a man, although you know you hit him, because there were so many guns going at the same time. But I should think that I killed several.

After Gallipoli I went to France. I went through the Somme and through the battle of Arras, after which I was captured. It was 14th April 1917. We ran and gave ourselves up, there was nothing more we could do. The Germans lined us up and marched us off. I thought, 'We're safe now. We're out of it...' I didn't know what was going to happen. If I had I would sooner have gone through all the fighting again. It was the worst thing which ever happened to me in my life. We were taken to Lille, where the Germans had to make us ill and wretched in a week in order to march us through the town, so that they could say to the people, 'Look at the great British army, look what it has been reduced to!' We were driven into dark dungeons, straight off the battlefield, starved, made filthy and in only *six days* we were ill and we looked like scarecrows. The Germans knew how to do this to men. After the parade about 300 of us were packed into a half-built mansion and there we lived on pearl barley boiled in coppers and bread or cake made of weed-seed. Then we were put into a forest to make charcoal and sometimes the Germans shot into our legs as we marched. We never knew what they would do next. They chose boys to thrash. I don't know why I was chosen but I was a favourite for this thrashing and was always being taken off for a beating. George Holmes, a farmer's son from the village, was one of the people who died from the ill-treatment.

At Christmas 1917 they took us to Germany, right down to Kiel. It was snowing and we were in rags. No shoes. They gave us wooden clogs. We dug on the Kiel railway, making a track to the Baltic for the big guns. Many people died. On November 5th 1918 some German sailors arrived and set us free. They cut all the barbed wire and left just one guard in charge. 'You can leave if you like,' they said. 'The war will soon be over. There is going to be a revolution, so keep off the roads. You could go and help the farmers pick up potatoes. That would be sensible.'

So this is what we did. And when the war ended, there we were, Germans, Poles, Russians and Englishmen, working in the fields and realising that there was damn little growing in them.

[…]

I am old now. I read library books about the Great War – my war. The one I am reading now is called *The Sword-Bearers*. I have these deep lines on my face because I have worked under fierce suns.

————— • —————

At Jim's grave

Aug 1926

Brother Tom Sams
ex RN

Jim Sams served as a sapper with the Royal Engineers Signal Company. He was killed in action on the Western Front on 29 March 1918. His brother, Tom Sams, served in the Royal Navy. Tom took a pilgrimage to see his brother's grave in 1926 and sent three postcards, one of which read:

Dear Dad,

Two friends and myself are spending a week here. I am taking a wreath up to lay on poor Jim's grave. It does bring it home very forcibly. Will write again,

Love from
Tom

POST CARD

CARTE POSTALE.

Communication—Correspondance   Address—Adresse

STAMP
HERE

JIM'S GRAVE

VILLERS - AU - BOIS · CEMETARY

It is indeed a beautifull and peacefull spot

Brother Tom 1926

AFTERWORD

War writers are often anthologists: collectors of stories, voices and images. Miscellany can speak of experiences not made sense of, or a decision not to force them into an overarching meaning. Included in this collection is May Sinclair's account of a tour of a 'dreadful dormitory' for refugees. She describes being unable to find the right words to encapsulate what she sees. She is frustrated by, and yet cannot quite abandon, her guide's question: '*C'est triste, n'est-ce pas?*' ('It's sad, isn't it?'). She is 'stunned, stupefied', and this is shown in her initial inability to provide a satisfactory answer. She cannot say how the scene makes her feel, because she cannot feel: her senses are 'numbed'. Yet the title of her published collection, *A Journal of Impressions in Belgium*, gives a hint of what will awaken them. Sinclair ultimately finds that in order to feel she must stop trying to contain her view in an abstract word or idea: 'The scale is too vast.' She must instead narrow her gaze. 'Little things strike you,' she says.

The detail Sinclair fixes on is an 'absurd little dog' lying in the straw, surrounded by a Flemish family who have sacrificed their own comfort in order to make a bed for him. Other writers in this collection have similarly sifted their memories for salient images and episodes; 'the diamonds of the dustheap', to coin a phrase Virginia Woolf used on 20 January 1919 to describe the hoped-for yields of making a diary. Were diamonds there already, awaiting retrieval, or did pressure have to be exerted upon rawer materials? Sinclair's detail is not arbitrary. Selection brings shape and significance to experience: it is one way of making life intelligible. The detail Sinclair picks out from the scene resonates with ideas – though, as with much fiction, she leaves the work of articulating them to readers. Could the impression she selects be expressive of resilience? The refugees resist adherence to the imperative that so often accompanies moments of terror, 'every man for himself': the needs of individuals do not trump the collective desire to make content the family pet. Amidst violence, nurture persists. But then is violence, in turn, nurtured by the story? Given the 1915 publication date of Sinclair's journal, casting a group of refugees as exemplary survivors has propagandist implications.

Upon interpretation, small details scale up. Anthologies rarely include explicit interpretations: they are the beginnings of journeys that readers might embark upon themselves. Editors' introductions and afterwords act similarly to Sinclair's guide: they can point out details and ask questions. These will of course be motivated by particular concerns and interests. Entries in this volume have been included not always for what they tell us about the war, but for what they suggest about how writing mediates distance, displacement, conflict and loss. The organisation of the book is indicative of this, as is its title: the volume encourages consideration of the different ways in which writing accompanies the 'endeavour to balance', to coin the final lines of Amy Lowell's 'September. 1918', 'upon a broken world'. Titles and taxonomies can begin discussions even while they limit them. 'Broken world', expansive and macro-scale, draws out possible significances of Robert Graves's miniature story about the gunning down of 'a glass case full of artificial fruit and flowers'. Is the destruction of this relic of bourgeois living reflective of the impact of war on other 'artificial' things? Describing its effects in his war memoir *Now It Can Be Told* (1920), journalist Philip Gibbs wrote: 'They had been taught to believe that the whole object of life was to reach out to beauty and love […] Now the ideal had broken like a china vase dashed to hard ground.' Yet it is also the case that much was made, rather than 'broken', during wartime. This collection includes records of relationships forged in shared spaces (cultural encounters in homes, camps and train carriages), and, where physical proximity was not permitted, by writing (open letters which transcend national borders). It is also not the case that for all writers war was the only breaking point in their lives. One rationale of not organising this volume chronologically was to allow for the inclusion of memories that exceed the 1914-18 bracket. Events of military-strategic importance do not always correspond with moments that held most significance for individuals whose writing features here.

Readers of this collection are encouraged to make their own readings and patterns. Regardless of how the anthology is organised, there will always be alternative threads that can be drawn between entries. Parts of Edward Thomas's diary read like a birdwatcher's log; they might have been paired with Rosa Luxemburg's prison letters ('You can't think how much I had come to depend on the society of those little creatures', 2 August 1917). Listening to a soldier's story which blends brutality with birdsong, the holding of a blood-covered body with the hearing of a cuckoo, Ivor Gurney describes (in a letter included in this collection) his 'shame' at revelling in the artistic inspiration war provides. These examples in turn might have been paired with Sinclair's account. Does the logging of birds function similarly to her picking out of the little dog? Does it mark resistance: a wish to soar above the constraints of the immediate environment; to recognise that not everything can be circumscribed by the logic of military and state strategy? These questions are not intended to close the texts to alternative readings; there are other leads to be pursued. Birds also have, like the pilots of this volume, like the readers of this collection, the privilege of the panoramic. Sidney Rogerson's entry details how trench-life impacted upon the soldier's sense of perspective: 'he began to lose the wider view, and instead to see falconwise the minutest details around, details which will ever survive in his memory.' This anthology swoops between the bird's and (what veterans sometimes call) the worm's eye perspective. It combines letters and diaries unframed by hindsight with memories published and scribbled many years after the war. It has not sought to place these texts in a hierarchy; items have been chosen because in each case they have included details that have struck the anthologists.

Surveying the spectacle, Sinclair takes note of how circum-stances have flung together like with unlike: 'The rigidly righteous *bourgeoise* lies in the straw breast to breast with the harlot of the village slum, and her innocent daughter back to back with the parish drunkard.' Anthologies are similarly constitutive: making new allegiances and separating individuals and groups usually placed together. This anthology places accounts by professional writers alongside the memories of people whose names will not be found in biographical dictionaries. It encourages comparisons between the two. Both exhibit sensitivity to language, use form in interesting ways, and include arresting turns of phrase. The details that punctuate this volume, that interrupt the familiar, are not always things witnessed or experienced. They are often characteristics of the writing itself: whether Albert and Ernest Fletcher's bitter conclusion to their 1963 letter, 'rubbing our wounds', or Havildar Abdul Rahman's poignant simile for survivors: 'Those who have escaped so far are like the few grains left uncooked in a pot.' This is not to relegate the less unusual accounts to the 'dustheap': there is a case to be made for a duller anthology which reflects the grinding monotony of what was, for many, the typical experience of war. Yet, with writing, it is often the case that what at first seems familiar – Major E. W. J. Edgley's list of 'mud', 'rats', and 'the patience and endurance of the soldiers' – becomes less so upon closer inspection: 'mud' appears twice (oozing beyond the bounds of his numbered list), and, curiously, 'patience and endurance' are only noted 'in retrospect'.

Much of this volume is reliant on the work of other collectors: on what they chose to include and on the questions they asked of witnesses. There is still much work to be done establishing archives that give voice to colonial troops and civilians; there are letters, diaries and memories yet to be translated. We cannot create first-hand testimonies any more: there are no more First World War veterans to interview. And yet we can re-read the texts that we do have; and new stories are still coming to light, donated to museums or uploaded to websites. We can also make new selections from existing archives. These have often privileged the more visceral accounts: when compiling its half-centenary documentary series, the BBC asked for 'vivid' memories. Yet some of the most interesting replies actively resisted the wording of this call. The shortest answer received was: 'From August 1st 1915, to about April, 1916, nothing vivid happened. It was just hold on to what you have got' (cited in a drafted BBC newsletter entitled 'The Long and Short of It'). This concise contributor inspires consideration of the kinds of experience the search for vivid memories risks sidelining; more generally, it cautions collectors to think carefully about the questions they ask.

First World War writing encourages a peculiar kind of attentiveness from readers partly because of how much remains unsaid. Mrs S. E. Chessum is perhaps most eloquent when most laconic: 'we were 9 round the table, now. I am only one'. Like many writers included in this anthology, she adopted the role of the anthologist because she needed to speak of, and for, and perhaps to, those who could not tell their own story. In a letter from the front her son refers to the flower-seeds she had sent him: 'I have put them in. but do not suppose shall see them grow up. but some other sore head may be cheered.' Likewise, Mrs Chessum would never see her son 'grow up', but she transcribed her son's words, and donated many other stories about him to the Imperial War Museum. She sowed the seeds then; they spring up again now: the 'bunch of flowers' that the word 'anthology' derives from. This may seem too pretty an image for a war book. Yet unspeakable loss can be poignantly implied by attempts to cover, conceal and console. Mrs Chessum never turns the 'white spots' of her letters red, but flowers, birds and little dogs become striking against a background of mud, rats and bleeding bodies. This anthology is full of such strange juxtapositions: they can be found both between and within entries. If we are sensitive to 'undertones' – to borrow from the title of Edmund Blunden's 1928 war memoir – they are also created in the process of reading First World War memories.

Hope Wolf, 2014

BIBLIOGRAPHY

EPIGRAPH

Amy Lowell, 'September. 1918', in *Pictures of the Floating World* by Amy Lowell (Boston and New York: Houghton Mifflin Company, 1919), p. 244-5

DISTANT HAMMERS

H. J. Ewels to Millie (Mrs Harry Ewels), 29 May 1917, 'Censored Postcards, Western Front, 1917', Imperial War Museum, Documents, Misc. 124, Item 1937

D. H. Lawrence to Lady Ottoline Morrell, March 1915, in *The Letters of D. H. Lawrence*, ed. by Aldous Huxley (London: William Heinemann, 1932), pp. 222-3

Norman Demuth, quoted in Max Arthur, *Forgotten Voices of the Great War* (London: Ebury, 2002), p. 19

E. Sylvia Pankhurst, *The Home Front: A Mirror to Life in England During the World War* (London: Hutchinson, 1932), pp. 114-8

W. F. Tapp to Professor Stanley Weintraub, 12 October 1979, 'Reminiscences of Armistice Day (11 November 1918)', Imperial War Museum, Documents, Misc. 109, Item 1701, File 2, '11 Nov. in British Isles, Children – School'

Hermia Mills to Professor Stanley Weintraub, 10 October 1979,
    'Reminiscences of Armistice Day (11 November 1918)',
    Imperial War Museum, ibid.

Alex J. Booth to Professor Stanley Weintraub, undated,
    'Reminiscences of Armistice Day (11 November 1918)',
    Imperial War Museum, Documents, Misc. 109, Item 1701,
    File 3, 'Armistice in Remote Places and at Sea'

Muriel Dayrell-Browning to her mother, 4 September 1916,
    'Private Papers of Mrs M. Dayrell-Browning', Imperial War
    Museum, Documents, 92/49/1

John Frederick Macdonald, *Two Towns – One City: Paris – London*
    (London: Grant Richards, 1917), pp. 1739

Mrs M. Hall, quoted in Max Arthur, *Forgotten Voices*, pp. 67-8

Katharine Jex-Blake, 'Girton College, Cambridge: War Work,
    1914-1919', in *The Girton Review*, Jubilee number 1920,
    Girton College Archive, GCRF 2/1/1/10

A. F. E. Sanders, War Work Index Cards, Girton College Archive,
    GCAC 2/1/3/4

Mrs Howard Priestman, ibid.

Helen E. Macklin, ibid.

Muriel E. Jackson, ibid.

May S. Gratton, ibid.

Gertrude Exton, ibid.

Joan Denny, ibid.

F. E. Ashwell Cooke, ibid.

L. E. Blyth, ibid.

M. R. G. Bell, ibid.

Janet Case, ibid.

Mrs Ayrton, ibid.

Edith Helen Pratt, ibid.

J. H. Stephen, ibid.

Mrs Prichard to Anon., 18 June 1915, 'The First World War letters and papers of Mrs G. S. Prichard relating to RMS *Lusitania*', Imperial War Museum, Documents, PP/MCR/C43

Lilian Pye to Mrs Prichard, 26 November 1915, ibid.

Grace H. French to Mrs Prichard, 10 September 1915, ibid.

Olive North to Mrs Prichard, 11 September 1915, ibid.

Sergeant E. Cooper, quoted in Lyn Macdonald, *1914–1918: Voices and Images of the Great War* (London: Penguin, 1988), pp. 235-236, 234

Helen Thomas, *World Without End* (London: William Heinemann, 1931), pp. 181-194

Vera Brittain, *Testament of Youth: An Autobiographical Study of the Years 1900–1925* (London: Gollancz, 1933), pp. 251-4

Virginia Woolf, 'Heard on the Downs: The Genesis of Myth', in *The Essays of Virginia Woolf*, ed. by Andrew McNeillie, Vol. 2: 1912–1918 (London: The Hogarth Press, 1987), 40-2, pp. 40-1, initially published in *The Times*, 15 August 1916

Vincent Brown and 'Little Raymond' to Harry Brown, 'Postcard Damaged by Shrapnel, 1918', Imperial War Museum, Documents, Misc. 3346

MIND AND MATTER

Joseph Shaddick, 'Poppy, Framed', © Imperial War Museum, EPH 9960

Rudolf Binding, *A Fatalist at War*, transl. by Ian F. D. Morrow (Boston and New York: Houghton and Mifflin, 1929), pp. 59-63

Bert Bailey, quoted in Lyn Macdonald, *1914–1918*, pp.110-111

Frank Cocker, letters home, June 12 1915, July 1 1915, August 17 [1915], August 26 1915, January 6 1916, January 12 1916, 'Private Papers of Lieutenant F. Cocker MC', Imperial War Museum, Documents, 82/11/1

Jack Dorgan, quoted in Max Arthur, *Forgotten Voices*, p. 81-2

Ivor Gurney to Catherine Abercrombie, June 1916, and to Marion Scott, 21 June 1916, in *Ivor Gurney, Collected Letters*, ed. by R. K. R. Thornton (Manchester: Mid Northumberland Arts Group & Carcanet Press, 1991), pp. 91-2; 100-102

Ernest Swinton, quoted in *Death's Men: Soldiers of the Great War*, edited by Denis Winter (London: Penguin, 1988) pp. 159-160

Edward Thomas, 'War Diary, 1917', in Edward Thomas, *The Collected Poems and War Diary, 1917*, ed. by R. George Thomas (London: Faber and Faber, 2004), pp. 158, 164, 171-2

Paul Klee, *The Diaries of Paul Klee, 1898–1918*, ed. by Felix Klee (Berkeley and Los Angeles: University of California Press, 1964), pp. 348, 350, 380-1, 387-8

Horace Pippin, 'Letter, circa 1943', Archives of American Art, Smithsonian Institution, 'Horace Pippin Notebooks and Letters', Box 1, Folder 5

Stephen Graham, *The Challenge of the Dead* (London: Cassell, 1921), pp. 119-21

Martin Hieber, letter sent on 4 December 1916, in *German Students' War Letters*, transl. and arranged from the original edition of Philipp Witkop by A. F. Wedd (London: Methuen, 1929), pp. 346-8

Sidney Rogerson, *Twelve Days*, with a foreword by B. H. Liddell Hart (London, Arthur Barker, 1933), pp. 12-15

A Sikh in Palestine, 'Letters from Indian Army Troops', created by D. C. Phillott, 1918, Cambridge University Library, Department of Manuscripts and University Archives, MS Add.6170

Guy Chapman, *A Passionate Prodigality* (London: Ivor Nicholson, 1933), pp. 144-146

Stuart Cloete, *A Victorian Son: an Autobiography 1897-1922*
(London: Collins, 1972), pp. 236-7, 244, 245, 248

Joe Murray, quoted in Max Arthur, *Forgotten Voices*, p. 119

S. W. Brown to BBC, 2 August 1963, Imperial War Museum,
Documents, BBC Great War Series Correspondence Files,
Bro-Bry

A. F. Hibbert to BBC, 12 July 1963, Imperial War Museum, ibid.,
Hib-Hit

E. W. J. Edgley to BBC, 17 September 1963, Imperial War
Museum, ibid., Ead-Eic

Tom Adlam, quoted in Max Arthur, *Forgotten Voices*, p. 180-4

Ford Madox Ford to Joseph Conrad, 6 September 1916, in
Letters of Ford Madox Ford, ed. by Richard M. Ludwig
(New Jersey, Princeton University Press, 1965), pp. 73-4

Ronald Skirth, *The Reluctant Tommy*, ed. by Duncan Barrett
(London: Macmillan, 2010), pp. 94-7

Frederick W. Noyes, *Stretcher Bearers...at the Double!* (Toronto:
Hunter Rose Company, 1937), pp. 112-116

Ellen N. La Motte, 'Introduction' and 'Heroes' in *The Backwash of
War: The Human Wreckage of the Battlefield as Witnessed by an
American Hospital Nurse* (London: G. P. Putnam's Sons, 1919),
pp. v-vi, 3-13

Sarah MacNaughtan, *My War Experiences in Two Continents*
(London: John Murray: 1919), pp. 1-2, 5-7

Leslie Holden, *A Little Graffic Experience of a Coolgardie Boy*,
6 December 1916, pp. 24-7, 'Private Papers of L. Holden',
Imperial War Museum, Documents, 07/08/1

May Sinclair, *A Journal of Impressions in Belgium* (London:
Hutchinson, 1915), pp. 60-69

Robert Graves, *Goodbye to All That: An Autobiography* (London:
Jonathan Cape, 1929), pp. 157-9

Havildar Abdul Rahman to Naik Rajwali Khan, 20 May 1915,
Military Department Censor of Indian Mails, 1914-15, India
Office Records, British Library, IOR/L/MIL/5/825/3

Anon., 'Diary of an unknown Royal Army Medical Corps Orderly,
Western Front, 1916', Imperial War Museum, Documents, Misc.
105, Item no. 1663

W. G. Seymour, photograph taken in 1917, sent with letter to Tony
Essex, 6 August 1963, Imperial War Museum, Documents, BBC
Great War Series Correspondence Files, Sca-Sex

BETWEEN BORDERS

Anon. to Rosenberg Esquire, 'White Feather Postcard, August
1915', Imperial War Museum, Documents, Misc. 2984

W. H. Riddell to BBC, 19 May 1964, Imperial War Museum,
Documents, BBC Great War Series Correspondence Files,
Ric-Rix

Vernon Lee, 'Bach's Christmas Music in England and in Germany',
in *Jus Suffragii, Monthly Organ of the International Woman*

Suffrage Alliance, Vol. 9., No. 4, 1 January 1915 [Reissued in
International Woman Suffrage: Jus Suffragii, 1913-1920, ed. by
Sybil Oldfield, Vol. 2 (London: New York, Routledge, 2003),
p. 36]

John Reed, *The War in Eastern Europe* (London: Eveleigh Nash
Company, 1916), pp. 18-22, 249-250

Eleanor Barton, anecdote reported in Anon., 'Protest Against
War: International Meeting of Women in London, August 4',
Jus Suffragii, Vol. 8, No. 3, 1 September 1914 [Reissued in
International Woman Suffrage: Jus Suffragii, 1913-1920, ed. by
Sybil Oldfield, Vol. 1 (London: New York, Routledge, 2003),
pp. 208-9]

Emily Hobhouse et al., 'Open Christmas Letter to the Women
of Germany and Austria', *Jus Suffragii*, Vol. 9., No. 4, 1 January
1915 [Reissued in *International Woman Suffrage: Jus Suffragii,
1913-1920*, ed. by Sybil Oldfield, Vol. 2 (London: New York,
Routledge, 2003), pp. 46-7]

Lida Gustava Heymann et al., 'Open Letter in Reply to the Open
Christmas Letter from Englishwomen to German and Austrian
Women', *Jus Suffragii*, Vol. 9., No. 6, 1 March 1915. ibid., p. 67

Maude Onions, *A Woman at War: Being Experiences of an Army
Signaller in France 1917–1919* (London: C. W. Daniel Company,
1929), pp. 52-3

Stefan Westmann, quoted in Max Arthur, *Forgotten Voices*,
pp. 70-1

E. M. Forster, 'Reconstruction in the Marne and the Meuse' in
   Albergo Empedocle and other writings by E. M. Forster, ed. by
   George H. Thomson (New York: Liveright, 1971), pp. 263-268.
   Initially published in *Westminster Gazette,* 30 August 1915

Edith Wharton, 'Preface' in *The Book of the Homeless* (New York:
   Charles Scribner's Sons, 1916), pp. xix-xx

Sher Bahadur Khan to Raja Gul Nawaz Khan, 9 January 1916,
   Military Department Censor of Indian Mails, 1915-16, India
   Office Records, British Library, IOR/L/MIL/5/826/1

Ernst Toller, *I Was a German: An Autobiography*, transl. by Edward
   Crankshaw (London: John Lane, The Bodley Head, 1934),
   pp. 78-9, 119-122

Rosa Luxemburg, *Letters from Prison,* transl. by Eden & Cedar
   Paul (Berlin: Young International, 1923), pp. 48-9, 51, 54-5, 58

Edward Williamson Mason, *Made Free in Prison* (London: George
   Allen & Unwin, 1918), pp. 191-2

Anon., *Lager-Echo*, Knockaloe, No. 9, 26 September 1917, in
   A. L. Vischer, *Barbed Wire Disease: A Psychological Study of
   the Prisoner of War,* transl. by S. A. Kinnier Wilson (London:
   John Bale, 1919), p. 30

Anon., *Lager-Echo*, Knockaloe, No. 7, 18 August 1917, in
   A. L. Vischer, *Barbed Wire Disease: A Psychological Study of
   the Prisoner of War,* transl. by S. A. Kinnier Wilson (London:
   John Bale, 1919), pp. 31-2

G. H. M, 'Ruhleben Camp Journal Story', Imperial War Museum, Documents, Misc. 121, Item 1866. The article can be found in *The Ruhleben Camp Magazine*, No. 5, Christmas 1916, pp. 44-5

T. E. Lawrence, *Seven Pillars of Wisdom: a triumph* (London: Jonathan Cape, 1935), pp. 30-2

W. E. B. Du Bois, 'Close Ranks', in *The Crisis*, Vol. 16, July 1918, p. 111

W. E. B. Du Bois, 'Returning Soldiers', in *The Crisis*, Vol. 18, May 1919, pp. 13-14

Marina Yurlova, *Cossack Girl* (London: Cassell, 1934), pp. 44-6

Isabelle Rimbaud, *In the Whirlpool of War*, transl. by Archibald Williams (London: T. Fisher Unwin, 1918), pp. 5-6, 103-5, 125-7

X. to Mme L. G., 1 May 1916, in *The Deportation of Women and Girls from Lille* (London: Hodder and Stoughton, 1916), p. 22

R. to Madame B., undated, ibid., p. 26

M. Albert Camille L—, undated, ibid., p. 60

Mary Britnieva, *One Woman's Story* (London: Arthur Barker, 1934), pp. 45-8

Albert E. Peto, 'Field Service Postcard Bearing the Word "Peace" in Place of a Signature, First World War', Imperial War Museum, Documents, Misc. 2900

WHITE SPOTS

R. E. Roller to 'Uncle Arthur', 21 December 1918, 'Belgian
Railway Tickets, Pre-First World War', Imperial War Museum,
Documents, Misc. 359, Box 10

Henry Williamson to Gordon Watkins, 18 July 1963, Imperial War
Museum, Documents, BBC Great War Series Correspondence
Files, Wib-Wil

Henry Williamson to Gordon Watkins, 16 October 1963, ibid.

Kurt Tucholsky, 'The White Spots' (1919), in *Germany? Germany!
The Kurt Tucholsky Reader* ed. by Harry Zohn (Manchester:
Carcanet, 1990), pp. 56-7

A. A. Long to his wife, 3 March 1919, 'Private Papers of
A. A. Long', Imperial War Museum, Documents, 06/30/1

C. Bruce Taberner to BBC, 15 October 1963, Imperial War
Museum, Documents, BBC Great War Series Correspondence
Files, Tab-Tho

G. C. Clench to BBC, 8 August 1963, Imperial War Museum,
ibid., Cla-Cyl (includes G.C. Clench, 'Blown Up – With a
Thousand Men Aboard', published in *Daily Herald*,
8 November 1933)

National War Museum, 24 July 1917, Bond of Sacrifice
(listed under 'Memorial for the Fallen'), Imperial War Museum,
EN1/PHO/013)

Keeper of Photographs, 1 August 1918, ibid., EN1/1/PHO/21

Harry Quibell, 13 March 1919, ibid., EN1/1/PHO/27

Mrs Bodman, undated, ibid., EN1/1/PHO/14

M. F. Somers-Smith, 31 May 1918, ibid., EN1/1/PHO/26

Ethel Murphy, 8 March 1919, ibid., EN1/1/PHO/27

Mrs S. E. Chessum, Imperial War Museum, NAM.C. Bond of
Sacrifice, A-D, BOS 34

Charles Royston Jones and Charles and Amelia Jones, Notebook,
'Private Papers of C. R. Jones', Imperial War Museum,
Documents, 05/09/1

R. E. Roller to 'Uncle Arthur', 21 December 1918, 'Belgian
Railway Tickets, Pre-First World War', Imperial War Museum,
Documents, Misc. 359, Box 10

Anon. (for William Hatchell Boyd), Imperial War Museum,
NAM.C., Bond of Sacrifice, BOS 21

Charles Madge and Tom Harrisson, *Britain by Mass-Observation*
(London: Penguin, 1939), pp. 200-202

Miss M. Cooke, diary, 11 November 1937, 'Private Papers of Miss
M. Cooke', Imperial War Museum, Documents 09/59/1

E. Croxon, Day Survey 046, 11 November 1937, Mass Observation
Archive (accessed through Mass Observation Online)

Albert and Ernest Fletcher to BBC, 9 September 1963,
Imperial War Museum, Documents, BBC Great War Series
Correspondence Files, Fac-Fly

Tony Essex to Siegfried Sassoon, 22 October 1963, BBC Written
  Archives Centre, T32/1, 148/1, The Great War, Corres. & Memos

Siegfried Sassoon to Tony Essex, 24 October 1963, ibid.

Tony Essex to Siegfried Sassoon, 8 November 1963, ibid.

Tony Essex to Siegfried Sassoon, 16 December 1963, ibid.

Tony Essex to Siegfried Sassoon, 23 January 1964, ibid.

Siegfried Sassoon to Tony Essex, 24 January 1964, ibid.

Tony Essex to Siegfried Sassoon, 30 January 1964, ibid.

Arthur Mee, *Enchanted Land: Half-a-Million Miles in the King's
  England* (London: Hodder and Stoughton, 1936), pp. 158-162

Ronald Blythe, *Akenfield: Portrait of an English Village* (London:
  Penguin, 1969), pp. 31-2, 36, 38-42, 44

Tom Sams, three postcards, 'Private Papers of J. Sams', Imperial
  War Museum, Documents, 02/55/1

AFTERWORD

Virginia Woolf, *A Writer's Diary*, ed. by Leonard Woolf (London:
  Hogarth Press, 1953), p. 7

Rosa Luxemburg, *Letters from Prison, with a portrait and facsimile*,
  transl. by Eden & Cedar Paul (Berlin: Young International,
  1923), p. 44

Philip Gibbs, *Now It Can be Told* (New York and London: Harper
  and Brothers, 1920), p. 131

Anon, 'The Long and Short of It', BBC 2 newsletter posted 2. 1.
64, BBC Written Archives Centre, 'The Great War: Publicity.',
R44/907/1

Edmund Blunden, *Undertones of War* (London: Cobden-
Sanderson, 1928)

ANTHOLOGIES, BOOKS AND OTHER RESOURCES THAT HAVE BEEN HELPFUL IN MAKING THIS VOLUME INCLUDE:

Allyson Booth, *Postcards from the Trenches: Negotiating the Space
between Modernism and the First World War* (New York; Oxford:
Oxford University Press, 1996)

Guy Chapman ed., *Vain Glory: A Miscellany of the Great War,
1914-18* (London: Cassell, 1937)

Peter Brock ed., *'These Strange Criminals': An Anthology of Prison
Memoirs by Conscientious Objectors from the Great War to the
Cold War* (Toronto: Toronto University Press, 2004)

John Glover and Jon Silkin eds, *The Penguin Book of First World
War Prose* (London: Penguin, 1990)

Santanu Das, *Touch and Intimacy in First World War
Literature* (Cambridge: Cambridge University Press, 2005)

Margaret R. Higonnet ed., *Lines of Fire: Women Writers of World
War I* (New York: Penguin/Plume, 1999)

Brian MacArthur ed., *For King and Country: Voices from the First
World War* (London: Little Brown, 2008)

Joyce Marlow ed., *The Virago Book of Women and the Great War, 1914-18* (London: Virago, 1998)

David Omissi ed., *Indian Voices of the Great War: Soldiers' Letters, 1914-18* (London: Macmillan, 1999)

Max Saunders ed., *War Prose, Ford Madox Ford* (Carcanet: Manchester, 1999)

Angela Smith, ed., *Women's Writing of the First World War: An Anthology* (Manchester: Manchester University Press, 2000)

Ross J. Wilson, *Landscapes of the Western Front: materiality during the Great War* (London: Routledge, 2012)

Patrick Wright, *Iron Curtain: from Stage to Cold War* (Oxford: Oxford University Press, 2007)

Oxford Dictionary of National Biography (online)

A NOTE FROM
THE EDITORS

The editors of this volume would like to thank all who have donated to archives the letters, diaries and memories that have been included in this volume. We are also grateful to archivists and librarians at the Imperial War Museum, Girton College, BBC Written Archives Centre, Mass-Observation Archive, Cambridge University Library and British Library for their generous assistance in making this volume.

Corrections to texts from archives have been avoided where possible. Editorial interventions, indicated by square brackets, have been made at points for the sake of clarity; small silent corrections have been added only occasionally. Where letters are transcribed, full addresses of the sender (where available, and unless publicly known) are not given: just the village, town or area.

The editors and publisher would like to thank the following for permission to reproduce material:

Letter from a Sikh in Palestine reprinted with thanks to the Syndics of Cambridge University Library.

Tom Adlam, quoted in *Forgotten Voices of the Great War* by Max Arthur reprinted by permission of The Random House Group Ltd.

INDEX OF CONTRIBUTORS

(in alphabetical order)

BIRDSONG

SEBASTIAN FAULKS

THE NOVEL OF THE FIRST WORLD WAR
NOW WITH A NEW INTRODUCTION FROM THE AUTHOR

'Magnificent – deeply moving'
SUNDAY TIMES

'Amazing... I have read it and re-read it and can think of no
other novel for many, many years that has so moved me or
stimulated in me so much reflection on the human spirit'
DAILY MAIL

'An overpowering and beautiful novel... Ambitious,
outrageous, poignant, sleep-disturbing'
SIMON SCHAMA, *NEW YORKER*

VINTAGE BOOKS